Sermons On The Second Readings

Series I

Cycle B

Frederick R. Harm
Paul E. Robinson
Glenn W. McDonald
Harold C. Warlick, Jr.

CSS Publishing Company, Lima, Ohio

Copyright © 2002 by
CSS Publishing Company, Inc.
Lima, Ohio

Scripture quotations unless marked otherwise are from the *New Revised Standard Version of the Bible*, copyright 1989 by the Division of Christian Education of the National Council of the Churches of Christ in the USA. Used by permission.

Scripture quotations marked (NIV) are from the *Holy Bible, New International Version*. Copyright © 1973, 1978, 1984 International Bible Society. Used by permission of Zondervan Bible Publishers. All rights reserved.

Scripture quotations marked (RSV) are from the *Revised Standard Version of the Bible*, copyrighted 1946, 1952 ©, 1971, 1973, by the Division of Christian Education of the National Council of the Churches of Christ in the USA. Used by permission.

Scripture quotations marked (NCV) are from *The Youth Bible, New Century Version* copyright © 1991 by Word Publishing, Dallas, Texas 75039. Used by permission.

Scripture quotations marked (CEV) are from the *Contemporary English Version of the Holy Bible*. Copyright © The American Bible Society 1995. Used by permission.

Scripture quotations marked (KJV) are from the *King James Version of the Bible*, in the public domain.

Library of Congress Cataloging-in-Publication Data

Sermons on the second readings : Series I, Cycle B / Frederick R. Harm ... [et al.].
Includes bibliographical references.
    p. cm.
  ISBN 0-7880-1901-5 (pbk. : alk. paper)
  1. Bible. N.T. Acts—Sermons. 2. Bible. N.T. Epistles—Sermons. 3. Bible. N.T. Revelation—Sermons. 4. Sermons, American—21st century. 5. Church year sermons. I. Harm, Frederick R., 1933-
  BS2617.8 .S47 2002
  252'.6—dc21   2002004243

For more information about CSS Publishing Company resources, visit our website at www.csspub.com or e-mail us at custserv@csspub.com or call (800) 241-4056.

ISBN 0-7880-1901-5   PRINTED IN U.S.A.

Table Of Contents

Sermons For Sundays
In Lent And Easter
by Paul E. Robinson

**Sermons For Sundays
After Pentecost (First Third)
by Glenn W. McDonald**

Sermons For Sundays
After Pentecost (Middle Third)
by Harold C. Warlick, Jr.

Sermons For Sundays
After Pentecost (Last Third)
by Harold C. Warlick, Jr.

Sermons On The Second Readings

For Sundays In
Advent, Christmas,
And Epiphany

Frederick R. Harm

For Marjorie,

"How do I love thee? Let me count the ways."

Preface

Without question one of the patron saints of preachers is the Apostle Paul. If you are like me, you empathize when you hear him say, "I was with you in weakness and much fear and trembling" (1 Corinthians 2:3). Who among us has not experienced it? Fear? Lots of it! Trembling? How often those notes shook as we turned the pages, perhaps praying that we hadn't put page four before page two! What a task! But what a blessed one! Somehow in his wisdom the Lord of this vast universe has chosen to bring knowledge of himself and of his plan for man's redemption through the medium of words, Words in a Book, words from the lips of trembling servants like you — and me. "Behold, I bring you tidings of great joy," was the Angel's message at the Advent of the Savior. And we aspire to echo the same message with similar decisiveness — and joy!

The seasons of Advent and Epiphany lie before us, the seasons of adventure and revelation. What a challenge they present as we approach them year after year. The sermons in this collection include some prepared in the hectic rush of a growing parish; others were shaped in the serenity of a recent retirement. As you read them, you may find things you've discovered before, in some you may encounter thoughts that will stimulate further research; but in all it is hoped you will meet insights that will provide help as another Advent Adventure comes into view.

It is my prayer that as you proclaim the timeless message of "The Word made Flesh," some who hear you will experience something akin to what Simone Weil described in *Waiting on God*. She wrote, "At that moment Christ himself came down and took possession of me." She was reciting George Herbert's poem "Love" at the time. "I only felt, in the midst of my suffering, the presence of a love like that which one can read in the smile of a beloved face."

Blessed prospect! May your ministry convey it to many this year.

Frederick R. Harm
Ash Wednesday, 2001

Acknowledgments

Sincerest thanks to the following publishers for permission to quote from their publications.

Harper and Brothers, New York for permission to quote from:
Masterpieces of Religious Verse edited by James Dalton Morrison, copyright 1948;
The Power of His Name by Robert E. Luccock, copyright 1960;

Harcourt, Brace and Company, New York:
The Complete Poems and Plays of T. S. Eliot, copyright 1952;

Henry Holt and Company, New York:
The Collected Poems of Walter de la Mare, copyright 1920.

I would be terribly remiss if I did not express my gratitude for the writings of Halford E. Luccock and his son Robert E. Luccock. Anyone who knows and has been enriched by their grasp on the essentials of our faith will find in these pages evidence of the profound influence these servants of our Lord have had on this writer. Their writings continue to be a treasure-trove of things old and new!

Introduction

The reach of God through spoken Word into needy hearts is accomplished by the voice of the preacher. The proclamation of the Gospel that Jesus Christ died for our sins and rose again is the way God restores life to a dying world. The Reverend Frederick Harm has answered the call to preach and teach for almost forty years. His abiding faith and trust in Jesus Christ is the well from which he draws these refreshing and sustaining messages of God's grace for human sin. You will find the words of a compassionate pastor's heart shining through these pages. In my 27 years of ministry I have admired Pastor Harm's depth of wisdom and scholarship as both college and seminary professor and now valued pastor in our state.

Enclosed are sermons that are a treasure trove of literary quotes and illustrations that display a wondrous connectedness to the scriptural texts. The sermons are best appreciated by one who enjoys and knows the world of literature: novels, plays, poetry, and essays. Reading these sermons in my opinion is like reading a good novel. In a good novel, I learn and gain insights into people, places, and issues. My mind is sent soaring to ponder a truth. The time spent is elevating to the mind and spirit. A less than average novel may tell a story but drag one through the gutters of life in the process. The carefully crafted style of writing in these sermons is reminiscent of an era when the handwritten word in correspondence would paint a precious picture for friends and loved ones. This is a skill to be preserved in our visually dominated era.

The foremost treasure enclosed herein is the consistent proclamation of Law and Gospel. Often touching on the lives of heroes of the faith in God's plan of salvation in the Bible, a connection is made with the brokenness of their lives and ours. Recognizing the fallen world in which we live, the hearer is pointed to the Cross and the Open Tomb. Sermons lifting up sanctification in living are always rooted in a God Who loved us first, a Savior Who died for us and the Holy Spirit Who brings forth the good works we were created to do.

May our gracious God use you to touch the hearts and lives of many through the proclamation of the Word of God.

William R. Klettke
President
The New Jersey District of the
Lutheran Church Missouri Synod

Waiting For Godot?

As we embark on another Advent Adventure we pause to remind ourselves that this sacred season holds a twofold emphasis. Not only do we journey towards Christ's nativity but also we project our thoughts towards his second advent when the final curtain will be lowered on the world as we now know it. This twofold emphasis is underscored in Saint Paul's greeting to his friends in today's text.

In Samuel Beckett's tragicomedy, *Waiting for Godot*, we are introduced to Vladimir and Estragon who are waiting for the arrival of the mysterious Godot, who continually sends word that he will appear but who never does. They encounter Lucky and Posso, they discuss their misery and their lot in life, they even consider suicide, and yet they wait. Often perceived as being tramps, Vladimir and Estragon are a pair of human beings who do not know why they were put on the earth: they make the tenuous assumption that there must be some point to their existence, and they look to Godot for enlightenment. Unfortunately their waiting is futile, Godot never arrives, and we are left with the uncomfortable feeling that perhaps MacBeth was correct in his assessment, "Life is a tale told by an idiot, full of sound and fury, signifying nothing."

The Christian faith exposes the folly of such morbid pessimism when it joyfully declares that the God who made this world of ours will come, because he has come to us in Christ and in the interim our waiting is not an exercise in futility.

The first Sunday in this Advent season introduces us to the God who was, who is, and who is to come, and challenges us to

19

consider his astonishing provision for a life that is fulfilling and replete with meaning. No more hopeless waiting for Godot!

Our God is the God who will not let us off! Without question God deals with us in grace. "Grace to you and peace" (v. 3) "I give thanks ... because of the grace of God that has been given you in Christ Jesus" (v. 4).

But always remember that although grace is free, it is not cheap. It comes to us because Another loved us enough to travel to a cross to bring us back to the circle of God's love. How calamitous, how appalling our need must have been! In the Old Testament lesson for today, God will not let us off: God makes us face the unvarnished fact of our downright sinfulness and the emptiness of our lives before his grace reached us. Isaiah's picture is not a pretty one. He says: "Our deeds are like a filthy cloth." One Hebrew scholar suggests that the word *filthy* connotes a cloth "putrefied by the excretions of a leper's sores." Not a very complimentary evaluation of man, even the best among us, but an authentic one since the Evaluator is God himself. Small wonder, then, that John Newton wrote: "Amazing grace how sweet the sound, that saved a wretch like me." But it is amazing grace, and because it is, our text tells us that we will be "blameless on the day of our Lord Jesus Christ." Blameless. Does the word lay hold on us? The word, as W. E. Vine points out, "implies not merely acquittal, but the absence of even a charge or accusation against us." That, dear Christian, is good news. That is amazing, astonishing, astounding grace: love without limit! What kind of response on our part can begin to carry with it the measure of gratitude that rises to the surface when we stand before such unspeakable affection? Perhaps all of us put it best when we sing: "Were the whole realm of nature mine, it were a tribute far too small; love so amazing, so divine, demands my soul, my life, my all."

Our God is also the God who will not let us down! He is the one who has "enriched us in him [Christ] ... in knowledge of every kind." Knowledge: it is an elusive word, but it is a biblical word, another word of grace. An Arabic aphorism observes:

20

He that knows not and knows not that he knows not, is a fool. Shun him.

He that knows not and knows that he knows not, is simple. Teach him.

He that knows and knows not that he knows is asleep. Waken him.

He that knows and knows that he knows is wise. Follow him.

Surely Christians, "enriched by Christ in knowledge of every kind," are numbered among those who know, and who are convinced that what they do know contains the answer to life's most bewildering questions. What convictions do Christians hold?

They know assuredly that God will never let them down; therefore, all things that come to them in life will work together for good and will be used by God to contribute to their personal enrichment. They are aware that Christ has "never promised them a rose garden." They are not immune from the heartaches, trials, and adversities that are part of the human situation. But they are also convinced that whatever comes to them approaches on a mission designed to be used as an opportunity for growth and advancement in the faith. With God's help they have learned the profound lesson E. Stanley Jones so often taught that "when life throws a dagger one can grasp it by the blade and be cut or maimed by it, or one can grasp it by the handle and use it." The Christ-enriched person knows that every experience of life is an occasion to prove Christ's faithfulness. Each event is usable. The Eternal Architect never makes a mistake! He merits our unconditional trust. He will never let us down.

Because they know God will never let them down, Christians are convinced that none of them — not the least among them — need ever fear that he or she is living a life without purpose.

Unfortunately this happy conviction is not shared by those who have dismissed the claim of Christ upon their lives. Someone has suggested an imaginary conversation between inhabitants of Mars and residents of earth. After communication has been established, the Martians describe themselves as "beings inhabiting a planet which is the home of creatures who cannot agree what they are, or

21

where they came from, or where they are going, but they are on their way." In response, earth flashes back its message — "Same here." This imaginary conversation raises the biggest questions of human experience: What are we? Where did we come from? Where are we going? When these questions are not honestly faced, all of life becomes trivial and meaningless, and rushes toward disaster both for individuals and for society.

The Christian faith offers convincing answers to these foundational inquries. The enriched Christian sees in one small, yet classic, event in the life of Christ, persuasive answers to these issues. In Saint John, chapter 13, we have the record of Jesus washing his disciple's feet: "Jesus ... knowing that he had come from God and was going to God, rose from supper, laid aside his garments, and girded himself with a towel."

There it is — the splendor of *knowing*! Knowing that he came from God, and that his destiny was God, Jesus could bow and assume the lowliest duties of service to men. Here we find the Christian response to life's profoundest questions. Dear Christian friends, who are we? We are children of the Eternal Father; we came from him. What is our destiny? We will one day return to him who made us: the One who will never let us down.

Not only is our Advent Lord the One who will not let us off and who will never let us down, but also **he is the One who will never let us go!**

Our text reminds us: "He will also strengthen us to the end." Indeed his love will never let us go. Please, dear Christian, lay hold on this promise; keep it ever before you. Let it sustain you when difficult hours assault you. There comes to all of us the day when we must face the end. It may be the end of a relationship that we felt contained the answer to our dreams. Or the end of a job or profession we thought would last indefinitely. Or perhaps the end of vibrant health, or the most final experience: the end of life itself. At such a time, where do we go, what do we do? As one has put it: "What do we do when there is nothing left to do?" At this juncture Christ's promise becomes more than words — it becomes our most dependable source of strength. "He will strengthen us to the end."

Does our faith sometimes waver? Of course it does, frail vessels that we are. But so did the ancient Joseph waver in his confidence when he found himself down in that pit where his jealous brothers imprisoned him before they sold him into Egyptian slavery. Do you think he saw much of God's hand down in that dreadful pit? Do you suppose he could see himself actually on his way to the office of Prime Minister of the Egyptian Empire? Of course not. It was much later that he was able to put the right construction on his seemingly impossible situation.

Do you think that George Matheson, stricken by blindness, and his fiancee turning away and walking out of his life because of his handicap, could see the marvelous handiwork of an overruling God in that terrible darkness into which he was plunged? Later, in spite of his limitations, he rose to become the most honored preacher of his generation. Do you fancy for a moment that he could foresee the end effect of those priceless lines that were to be wrung from the anguish of his soul?

> *O Love that wilt not let me go, I rest my weary soul in*
> *thee:*
> *I give thee back the life I owe, That in thine ocean depths*
> *its flow*
> *May richer, fuller be.*
>
> *O Joy that seekest me through pain, I cannot close my*
> *heart to thee;*
> *I trace the rainbow through the rain, and feel the prom-*
> *ise is not vain,*
> *That morn shall tearless be.*
>
> *O cross that liftest up my head, I dare not ask to fly*
> *from thee;*
> *I lay in dust, life's glory dead, and from the ground*
> *there blossoms red*
> *Life that shall endless be.*

With this lingering confidence we begin another Advent Season. Be certain, fellow traveler, you and I are not futilely "waiting for Godot." Our present and future lie safely in the hands of our Advent Lord, who never lets us off, never lets us down, and will never let us go! Indeed, "he will strengthen us to the end" — yes, from this moment to the end ... and all the way between!

With A Bang Or A Whimper?

Back in 1925, T. S. Eliot wrote the poem, "The Hollow Men." It is an indictment of a whole generation of people whose lives are empty because they seem to believe nothing. They have been only a "paralyzed force, gesture without motion." They have accomplished nothing: they are the product of the dry intellectuality of modern life. Eliot describes them this way.

> *We are the hollow men*
> *We are the stuffed men*
> *Leaning together*
> *Headpiece filled with straw*

They are not "lost violent souls" but only hollow men. The last lines of the poem describe the way in which, for them and for so many of our own desiccated generation, the end of life comes:

> *This is the way the world ends*
> *This is the way the world ends*
> *This is the way the world ends*
> *Not with a bang but a whimper.*[1]

Today's challenging text anticipates God's plan for the end of our world, as we know it. It will be interesting to discover if T. S. Eliot's view correlates with the portrait Holy Scripture paints of the conclusion of this world's history. Will it end with a bang or a whimper?

Modern scientists are unanimous in their assumption that our world will one day cease to exist. Just how this will happen is an open question. Many opinions are being voiced in the scientific community. In our look at Saint Peter's "pre-scientific" explanation of this event, we wonder what we'll find. Surely one who lived before the "Copernican revolution," and almost 2,000 years before the advent of atomic and hydrogen explosives, could know nothing of the basic structure of the universe and its potential for almost unlimited power if those elements were somehow released. Or could he? Perhaps today's message will shed some light.

Think with me. First of all, how it all began.

Surely if something must end it must also have had a beginning. For Peter's understanding of this origin we look back at verse 4 of our chapter where he explains: "All things continue as they were at the beginning of creation." Please note his words: not development, not eternal existence, but creation: "In the beginning God created the heavens and the earth" (Genesis 1:1 NIV).

Without entering the realm of scientific investigation, what are the biblical affirmations respecting the origin of the universe?

The first certainly is this: The world with its harmony and orderliness and rationality and all the teeming life that crowds our planet came into existence through the creative activity of an Almighty God.

Secondly: The goal and crown of the divine activity is focused on man; man made in the image of his Creator, and endowed with the capacity of holding fellowship with his Maker. These affirmations have nothing to do with the manner, that is, with the "how" of creative action. Such things are the prerogative of science. Religion concerns itself with providing answers to the questions: "Whence?" "Whither?" "Why?" These are the fields of inquiry with which the Bible is concerned. John Dryden, who lived in the seventeenth century, voiced it well when he wrote:

> *This is a piece too fair*
> *To be the child of chance and not of care*
> *No atoms casually together hurl'd*
> *Could e'er produce so beautiful a world.*[2]

To paraphrase a word of Christ to those who look out upon this unutterably profound universe, "He that has eyes to see, let him see; and he that has ears to hear, let him hear." Elizabeth Barrett Browning laid the options before us as clearly as possible in her "Aurora Leigh":

> *Earth's crammed with heaven,*
> *And every common bush afire with God;*
> *But only he who sees, takes off his shoes,*
> *The rest sit round it and pluck blackberries ...*[3]

The Christian heart — and mind — is content in assenting to Peter's understanding of the earth's origin: "In the beginning God."

Then Peter moves on to discuss the end of all things: "But the day of the Lord will come like a thief, and then the heavens will pass away with a loud noise, and the elements will be dissolved with fire, and the earth and everything that is done on it will be disclosed" (v. 10).

Here we must tread softly. Peter discribes this event using apocalyptic terms, terms familiar to his original readers but somewhat perplexing to us. We sometimes use the phrase, "It's the end of the world," and, when we do, our minds coincide with Peter's. Whether Peter's words are accurate (for he does use some interesting ones!) history will determine; this morning we only have time to outline them briefly. And here they are.

This event is *certain*, Peter says. All of sacred scripture and human experience either predicts it or senses the ultimate reasonableness of it. Man cannot continue to defy all the moral principles inherent in the universe without a day of accounting arriving at last. That is certain! It will be *sudden*. Peter writes: "The day of the Lord will come as a thief in the night" — a thief doesn't announce his arrival at our homes. He comes suddenly. It will be *solemn* — can anything be more solemn than these words: "The heavens shall pass away with a great noise ... the elements shall melt with fervent heat ... the earth and all the works therein shall be burnt up"? To us who live in the atomic age, some of these statements sound strangely familiar; they sound as though they might have been

27

written in the year 2003 rather than almost 2,000 years ago. An unknown college student tried to describe a cataclysm like this, when she wrote:

> *When you hear the sound and see the flash*
> *Don't duck under the nearest table,*
> *'Cause there won't be any table;*
> *Don't pull the tablecloth over you,*
> *'Cause there won't be any tablecloth;*
> *Don't throw yourself flat on the floor,*
> *'Cause there won't be any floor;*
> *And don't, under any circumstances, try to leave the*
> *   city,*
> *'Cause there won't be any city left to leave.*
> *Simply pause for a moment to adjust your shroud*
> *And make your way leisurely to the nearest cloud.*

These words were written with tongue in cheek, surely. But they do give us pause. Perhaps you are wondering, "Why would pastor choose a text like this for his sermon when all of us are happily anticipating the arrival of another joyous Christmas celebration?" I'll tell you why. I've chosen it for the same reason Peter wrote the words centuries ago: not to intimidate those who read or hear his words but to urge upon them a quality of life that ought to characterize sincere Christians whether they look forward to a blessed Advent season or anticipate the end of the world! However, it is rather interesting to note that when we read the Latin version of this Epistle, each time it speaks of the "coming" of the Day of the Lord, it always uses the word "Adventus" to translate our word "come" or "coming." So, you see, Saint Peter is not far removed from the blessed season in which we find ourselves!

Finally, what is the type of life that should be expressed by those who look forward to the things Saint Peter describes? Verses 11 and 14 make it clear.

A key word in these verses is "strive." It means "to be zealous, to be eager." What is it that we are to be zealous about? Peter does not hesitate to tell us: "Lead lives of holiness and godliness ... be found by him at peace without spot or blemish." What a garland of

Advent graces to carry with us during these sacred days! What an amiable influence my life and yours would be if these graces were in evidence as we travel toward another Christmas celebration. Think of them, they are five in number. The first two describe qualities directed outward, toward those around us; the last three describe personal attributes, those experienced inwardly.

Those features directed toward others are holiness and godliness, both of which are plural nouns suggesting a multiplicity of action. In other words, the Christian's life exhibits not one but many holy and god-like behavior patterns.

The personal attributes, peace, spotlessness, and an unblemished mind-set or disposition, complete the garland. In effect, Peter is telling us the world is enriched and our personal lives are enhanced as these qualities become part of our Advent experience.

It is said that on one occasion a young student rushed up to Ralph Waldo Emerson saying, "Mr. Emerson, Mr. Emerson, the world is going to end tomorrow." To which Emerson responded, "All right, I can do without it!" All well and good, he and we can do without it, because the Lord Christ, through his life, death, and resurrection, has assured us that by trusting him we will one day experience a life with God that beggars description, a life that causes this world to fade into insignificance! Nevertheless, though we can do without the world, the world, whether it knows it or not, cannot do without us and the message of hope our faith embraces. We warmly offer this hope to all who sense the emptiness of life without it. Professor Rudolph H. Harm, from Concordia Seminary, St. Louis, often told his students, "The Christian faith takes a person out of this world and puts a person into it." This was not only a striking arrangement of words, but it is completely true. Our Christian faith does take us out of this world. It takes us out of time into eternity, into the mind of God. It is a tragedy to be "earthbound," to have no power in life which lifts us out of our darkness, sorrow, and night into the wonderful joy of the light of God in the face of Jesus Christ. But our Christian faith also "puts us into the world" in a new and deeper manner. When we live in the strength of our Advent hope we do not draw away from the world with its great need, but, fortified by communion with the living Lord who is "out of this world," we go into life to minister to its need in Christ's name. What a splendid halo this wonderful privilege drapes over this year's journey toward another Christmas celebration. May each of us embrace it with joy!

Returning to the question with which we began — "Will it end with a bang or a whimper?" Dear friends, after listening to Peter, it really doesn't matter, does it? Amen.

---

1. *The Complete Poems and Plays of T. S. Eliot* (New York: Harcourt, Brace and Company Inc., 1952), p. 344.

2. John Dryden, "Design" quoted in *Masterpieces of Religious Verse* (New York: Harper and Row, Publishers, 1948), p. 9.

3. Elizabeth Barrett Browning, "Aurora Leigh," *ibid.*

The Roads Less Traveled

A lecturer was talking about what he called "the most dangerous road in the world." Most people in the audience began to think of a journey into the African jungle, or facing shipwreck going through the Straits of Magellan. The lecturer explained: "More and more books are being sold about escaping prison with a toothpick or journeying up the Amazon on stilts. But the most dangerous journey is the journey of our everyday living. It is dangerous because it ends, for all of us, in death!" Not a very pleasant way to put it, but it does make one think.

The journey I have in mind this morning doesn't end in death, it ends in wholeness, in completeness, in maturity. Saint Paul describes it in our text: "The God of peace sanctify you completely." The word "completely" means "through and through" or "reaching that end for which it was made." Saint Paul is portraying for us the Christian's Advent journey that ends in a state of maturity and wholeness, a state in which he or she senses that life, at last, has meaning and purpose, life "adds up."

Unfortunately this sense of purpose is not grasped by everyone. Ernie Pyle, the much loved army reporter during World War II, once wrote to a friend: "There is no sense to the struggle, but there is no choice but to struggle. It seems to me that living is futile, and death the final indignity." He then concluded with, "I wish you would shine any of your light in my direction. God knows I've run out of light." I don't know what response came from his friend, but I feel confident that Saint Paul would have offered some enriching counsel to Ernie, or to any others who share Ernie's sense of futility. Perhaps part of it might have been the threefold prescription for wholeness we find in verse 16 of our text: "Rejoice always, pray without ceasing, give thanks in all circumstances." I prefer to call these "roads to fulfillment," but I note with some sadness that for many in our enlightened generation they have become "the roads less traveled." I urge you to ponder them this morning, then consider donning your walking shoes and starting the journey. I promise you, it will be worth the effort.

First, we consider the road of rejoicing. "Rejoice always," Saint Paul says. This is radiant counsel. There are two sources from which our joys may come. They may come from the outer occurrences of our lives which are pleasant and gratifying or from our inner fellowship with Christ. We live only a little while in this world before we discover that if we are depending on outer experiences to keep us happy, we are headed for a lot of disillusionment and wretchedness. The Christian answer to the rise and fall of outer circumstances is faith in Christ and the confidence his Word inspires as we face any situation.

In some congregations the organist is also the choir director. As the choir sings its anthem, we see the organist playing and directing simultaneously. At such times, you will see her raise her right hand to give the choir direction. Yet the organ music does not stop. Her other hand keeps the music flowing. So it is with the joy-side of the Christian's life; when the hand of our outward circumstances is lifted from the keyboard, the hand of our fellowship with Christ plays on. There is a gladness that nothing can shatter. A gladness that says: "I have the answer to anything that may come to me. My answer is Christ. I know that in his presence (right here in the world) there is fullness of joy and at his right hand there are pleasures ever more."

But we must not confuse this quality with mere boisterous hilarity. As Seneca once suggested, "True joy is a serene and sober motion, and they are miserably in error who take laughing for rejoicing." Poet John Keble put it so well in a poem he wrote for "St. Matthew's Day" back in 1789:

There are in this loud, stunning tide
Of human care and crime,
With whom the melodies abide
Of the everlasting chime;
Who carry music in their heart
Through dusty lane and wrangling mart,
Plying their daily task with busier feet
Because their secret souls some holy strain repeat.[1]

These are words worth noting not only on Saint Matthew's Day but also each day as we walk the road of joyfulness.

We move on to explore another "road less traveled," a basic or foundational route, a road so basic that perhaps all other routes flow from it. Saint Paul states it very simply; it is the road of prayer. He writes, "Pray without ceasing."

General Ulysses S. Grant and General O. O. Howard both came out of the Civil War covered with glory. For Howard, who was a devout Christian, the end of the war meant passing into quiet retirement. For Grant, on the other hand, it meant going on to the White House. Later, when Grant lay dying of cancer at Mount McGregor, General Howard went to call on him. He recalled for his old chief some of the battles and campaigns of the war, as old soldiers have a way of doing. Grant listened for a time, and then, his pale face full of a new and more obvious seriousness, he said, "Howard, tell me what you know about prayer." Grant, with death staring him in the face, was more interested in prayer than in soldierly reminiscences of battles long past.

In H. G. Wells' novel, *Ann Veronica*, the heroine cries out at a crisis in her life when things had piled up in overwhelming amount, "O God, how I wish I had been taught to pray!" There is a great lack of resources for facing life when one has not been taught to pray. You, fellow Christian, have been taught to pray. How we need to thank God for those who taught us. But, please remember that if we do not keep up the practice of prayer, all the lessons we have had will soon drop from us. Is it any wonder Saint Paul exhorts us, "Pray without ceasing"?

Earlier I suggested that prayer was perhaps the foundational quality in the Christian journey out of which the other important pursuits flow. Why do I say that? Perhaps it is because of a statement I read some time ago in a church bulletin. It comes from the preaching of Harry Emerson Fosdick. His assertion was first a rebuke then a stimulus to recognize the absolute necessity of maintaining a faithful prayer life. Listen as he speaks to each of us:

> *Prayer is the soul of religion — and failure there is not a superficial lack for the supply of which the spiritual life can leisurely wait. Failure in prayer is the loss of religion itself in its inward and dynamic aspect of fellowship with the Eternal God. Only a theoretical deity is left to any person who has ceased to commune with God, and a theoretical deity saves no person from sin and disheartenment and fills no life with a sense of divine commission. Such vital consequences require a living God who actually deals with men.*

Can you understand why I see prayer as the foundational factor in our life as Christian people?

What a pity that so often so many wait until some sharp crisis confronts them before they take seriously this matter of prayer! Prayer in crisis has its value, but prayer in constancy has its greater value. It is certainly of this that Saint Paul is speaking when he urges his fellow Christians, "Pray without ceasing."

Do the words "without ceasing" puzzle you? Surely Saint Paul isn't suggesting the continual utterance of audible prayers. Nor is there the faintest suggestion that he was thinking of a particular posture that must be struck and held in prayer. Rather the apostle's meaning would appear to be: "Don't let the practice of prayer die out in your life. Even as the breathing of your body is the atmosphere where the vital oxygen is forever at hand, so let the intake and outgo of your soul be in the atmosphere of God's nourishing presence." I wish we had time to discuss some of the secrets, benefits, and gratification of prayer, but possibly one familiar poem by the renowned scholar Richard Trench will sum it up better than an abundance of words:

Lord, what a change within us one short hour
Spent in Thy presence will prevail to make!
What heavy burdens from our bosoms take,
What parched grounds refresh as with a shower!
We kneel, and all around us seems to lower;
We rise, and all, the distant and the near,
Stands forth in sunny outline brave and clear;
We kneel, how weak! We rise, how full of power!
Why, therefore, should we do ourselves this wrong,
Or others, that we are not always strong,
That we are ever overborne with care,
That we should ever weak or heartless be,
Anxious or troubled, when with us is prayer,
And joy and strength and courage are with Thee![2]

May each of us gladly travel the road of prayer continuously.

And finally, as we journey toward Christian maturity, we approach another "road less traveled." Saint Paul describes it for us, "Give thanks in all circumstances." How difficult it is for us at times to set our feet on this thoroughfare, ungrateful children of God that we often are. Shakespeare has King Lear tell us, "How sharper than a serpent's tooth it is to have a thankless child."

You perhaps recall the story of Charlie and Jim who met on the street one morning. Charlie said: "Well, hello, Jim. How's my best friend today?" Jim simply continued on his way, not bothering to respond. So Charlie pleaded: "Jim, aren't you even going to speak to me, your best friend? Jim, how can you be so cold to me after all I've done for you? Jim, two years ago when you were broke and in the hospital for three months, who paid all the doctor's bills and the hospital bills as well?" Jim finally said, "You did, Charlie." "That's right, Jim, and a year ago, when you were laid off, who got you a job at his company?" Jim mumbled "You did." "And six months ago while at the beach you were drowning, who was it that risked his life, swam into the surf, and rescued you?" Jim answered, "Yes, yes, you did, Charlie — but tell me, Charlie, what have you done for me lately?"

We smile at this absurd story of ingratitude, but doesn't it sound strangely familiar? Perhaps the way we treat our loving Lord rather frequently?

Do you find it difficult to find things for which to be grateful? Do this, get out a pencil and piece of note paper. Set down the "benefits" that are yours. You have lost some money: be thankful you haven't lost your integrity. You have lost your hearing: be thankful you haven't lost your reason. You have lost your husband or wife: be thankful you didn't lose him or her by desertion or unfaithfulness. Your child is in the hospital: be thankful he isn't in a prison or reformatory. Never mind if, to start with, you don't feel the gushing of gratitude. Thankfulness is one of the disciplines of the Christian journey; it grows as we grow.

When a day arrives in which you find it difficult to "put on a happy face," recall the words of a poet who, looking out on God's wonderful world, felt that he owed a bill he could never repay:

> *Five thousand breathless dawns all new;*
> *Five thousand flowers fresh in dew;*
> *Five thousand sunsets wrapped in gold;*
> *One million snowflakes served ice-cold;*
> *Five quiet friends; one baby's love;*
> *One white mad sea with clouds above;*
> *One hundred music-haunted dreams.*
> *Of moon-drenched roads and hurrying streams;*
> *Of prophesying winds, and trees;*
> *Of silent stars and browsing bees;*
> *One June night in a fragrant wood;*
> *One heart that loved and understood;*
> *I wondered when I waked at day,*
> *How — how in God's name — I could ever pay!*[3]

If that doesn't "stab your spirit broad awake," as Robert Louis Stevenson once said, then take another thoughtful look at the cross on our altar, a reminder of the Prince of Glory who loved you enough to give his life on that cross to bring you back to the favor of God, and then join Saint Paul in saying: "Thanks be to God for his indescribable gift" (2 Corinthians 9:15).

The Advent Journey toward maturity is in urgent need of travelers. The trip, at times, may be somewhat lonesome. There will be many tempting divergences along the way. But at the end you'll discover that someone else has traveled this way before you. We will celebrate his birthday on the twenty-fifth day of this month! Amen.

---

1. John Keble, "St. Matthew's Day," quoted in *Masterpieces of Religious Verse*, p. 658.

2. Richard C. Trench, "Prayer," *ibid.*, p. 409.

3. Author unknown.

Ah, Sweet Mystery Of Life

An early movie version of Victor Herbert's romantic operetta *Naughty Marietta* has the young and dashing Nelson Eddy sing to an enraptured Jeanette MacDonald:

> *Ah, Sweet Mystery of Life, at last I've found you.*
> *Ah, at last I've found the secret of it all*
> *... Yes, 'tis love and love alone*
> *The world is seeking....*

This charming song expresses what the Christian has known to be true all along. It is love — and love alone — that unlocks the mysteries of life. Not the transient and sometimes trashy love of the modern novel but the eternal love of the Advent Christ who wrote the real meaning of love, not in words but in the greatest of deeds, the giving of himself on a cross in order to secure human-kind's profoundest need — the need for forgiveness.

At the conclusion of this epistle to the Romans, the grandest of all Paul's letters, theology turns to doxology as he speaks of the mystery of God's gracious action toward each of us in Christ, our Lord. May these words speak deeply to us today.

To begin with, we note the **Mystery Explained**. Saint Paul frequently used the word "mystery" in his letters to the early churches. To the Corinthians he wrote of the mystery of the wisdom of God revealed at the Cross (1 Corinthians 2:7); to the same church he spoke of the mystery of that generation of believers who, at the second coming of Christ, will never have to endure the experience of physical death (1 Corinthians 15:51); to the Ephesian church he wrote of the mystery of God's inclusion of the Gentiles in the Gospel of his grace (Ephesians 3:3-6). In each instance, however, he is speaking not so much of that which cannot be understood (our usual perception of the word "mystery"), but rather that which has been clearly revealed and is easily grasped by the Christian mind.

So in our text when Paul speaks of the "proclamation of Jesus Christ according to the revelation of the mystery hidden for long ages past, but now revealed" (Romans 16:25 NIV), he is accentuating the wonderful fact that the gracious plan of God, though misunderstood for centuries, finds its complete and unmistakable fulfillment in the saving life and death of Christ, the world's Redeemer.

In Christ all the pieces of life's puzzle fit together and find their meaning. When he came to our world, eternity merged with time. His coming was the catalyst of human history. Toward that single event, all prior history had traveled; from that event, all subsequent history has surged on. Remove Christ's coming and all becomes chaos, a confusion; retain his coming and all becomes cosmos, a composite charged with meaning and purpose.

Chesterton put it eloquently when he described his experience of reading the gospel story for the first time: "On the first reading you feel that it turns everything upside down, but the second time you read it you discover that it turns everything right side up. The first time you read it you feel that it is impossible; the second time, you feel that nothing else is possible."

Be certain of this, the mystery of life is resolved forever through Christ, our Advent Lord!

And then we encounter the **Mystery Applied**. As we journey toward Bethlehem this year, perhaps some of us find ourselves still enshrouded in unfathomable mystery. Perhaps a loved one has been suddenly taken from us, perhaps our business has failed, a marriage has gone sour, or a friend has betrayed us, and we move toward the holiday season with a heavy heart. Our text has something to say to this need as well. "Now to him who is able to establish you by my gospel and the proclamation of Jesus Christ."

40

This is what God is saying here. "If I have answered the need of the entire world through Christ, your Lord, do you think that I will be unable to meet your smaller need through the same means?" The suffering we endure always serves a greater and more meaningful purpose. No one really knows what his faith means to him until that faith has been tried in the furnace of affliction. There is something doubly precious about a faith which has come through difficulty, disappointment, and loss and which emerges burning more brightly than it did before. God promises to establish or sustain us in just such time of testing.

Permit me to make this simple suggestion. You have grappled with your problem with every resource at your disposal. Having done so, it is time to place it into the hands of God. Leave it to the love and power of One who has promised that he "will never leave us nor forsake us" (Hebrews 13:5) saying: "Lord, I have thought and I cannot find the reason and the way. I cannot grasp thy purpose, but with my whole heart I trust thee. May thy will be done." An unknown poet expressed it eloquently:

> *Whose eye foresaw this way? — not mine!*
> *Whose hand marked out this day? — not mine!*
> *A clearer eye than mine — 'twas thine.*
> *A wiser hand than mine — 'twas thine.*
> *Then let my hand be still — in thine!*
> *And let me find my will — in thine!*[1]

And finally we note the **Mystery Shared**. In his "The Inn Album," Robert Browning penned the familiar phrase: "A secret's safe 'twixt you, me, and the gate-post!" Some secrets are meant to be kept shrouded in mysterious silence, but the one of which our text speaks is to be shouted from the roof tops! Paul writes, "So that all nations might believe and obey him" (Romans 16:26 NIV). WiIlliam Barclay has put it this way: "Here is our privilege and duty. The Christian privilege is to appropriate the good news for ourselves; the Christian duty is to transmit the good news to others." Dr. Moffatt translates Proverbs 13:17, "A careless messenger is a calamity." This is a heart-searching statement. In the light of our responsibility for sharing the Good News, this description is something we cannot readily escape, at least not without being inordinately complacent. For every messenger who takes his mission seriously, these words contain a terribly solemn indictment: "A careless messenger is a calamity!" Who can doubt its far reaching truth, as he looks over the centuries since the days following the resurrection, when men went from Jerusalem with the message of Jesus? The great calamities of history are to be laid at the door of careless messengers.

The classic story of the calamity of a careless messenger is that of the clerk in the British Ministry in London during the American Revolution who, instead of writing to Sir William Howe the instructions for his cooperation with Burgoyne, felt them unimportant and placed them in one of the pigeonholes on his desk. The major calamity of the whole war, from the standpoint of Great Britain, was the carelessness of a forgetful clerk. Our mission of sharing Christ's message of love is no less vital. We must not fail him!

Perhaps you recall hearing the familiar story of how Jesus, after his death and resurrection, ascended to the heavenly realm still bearing the marks of his suffering. An angel commented, "You must have suffered terribly for men down there." "I did," Jesus responded. "Do they all know what you did for them?" asked the angel. "Well," said Jesus, "I asked Peter and James and John to make it their primary business to tell others, and the others still others, until the last person in the remotest part of the earth has heard what I have done." The angel looked doubtful, for he knew what poor creatures men were. "Yes," he said, "but what if Peter, James, and John forget? What if they grow weary of telling? What if, on into the twenty-first century, men fail to share the story of your love for them? What then? What are your alternate plans?" And back came the response of Jesus. "I haven't made alternate plans. I'm counting on them." Christ has done his part. His life, death, and resurrection have provided the gospel for us. He is counting on us to share it with men and women everywhere. He has no alternate plan. The well-known hymn reminds us:

Let none hear you idly saying
There is nothing I can do
While the multitudes are dying
And the Master calls for you.
Take the task he gives you gladly;
Let his work your pleasure be.
Answer quickly while he calls you,
Here am I. Send me, send me!

Ah, sweet mystery of life at last we've found you. At last we've found the secret of it all! And that secret is found in Christ, alone. May we trust him and share his gracious message of salvation — always!

---

1. I believe this is from the pen of John Oxenham but I cannot locate it in any of my books. I have it on a file card without any source attached.

Bedlam Or Bethlehem?

I wonder if you have ever realized how the word "bedlam" entered our language? Here's how it came about. St. Mary of Bethlehem was founded as a hospital in England in 1247. Two centuries later it was restructured as an institution for the hopelessly insane. The noise and confusion of the hospital became widely known throughout the country. The cockney accent, over the years, contracted Bethlehem into Bed'lam. So "bedlam," which means "a place, scene, or state of uproar or confusion" is simply a contracted form of the peaceful word "Bethlehem," which Phillips Brooks described in his beloved carol, "O little town of Bethlehem, how still we see thee lie."

If there were no more here than the corruption of a word, we would be unconcerned. In many ways we do make bedlam out of Bethlehem. The Christmas season itself has become, not a time of quiet thought and meditation and spiritual joy, but one of worldly greed and noise. The frantic pushing through malls in last minute Christmas gift buying, the carousing on Christmas Eve, the inordinate eating and drinking during the season — these are hardly in harmony with the message of Christmas. Have we not, too often, made bedlam out of Bethlehem? Perhaps it is time that we include ourselves in the little child's recitation of the Lord's Prayer when she said innocently, "Forgive us our Christmases, as we forgive those who have Christmased against us."

But we are not here today to bemoan the mistakes of the past. This Christmas offers us a clean slate, a renewed offer for a new beginning, a challenging opportunity to refocus our attention on the reason for the season, an opportunity to transform bedlam into Bethlehem! Our scripture lesson offers us the *ABC*'s of such a renewal; let's think about them for a few moments.

First, the *A*. We remove bedlam from Bethlehem when we remember what *appeared* at the first Christmas event. Our text tells us, "For the grace of God has appeared, bringing salvation to all." "Grace" is well defined as "love imparting itself, and producing its own image and likeness." It is important to recognize that in this context grace is serving a twofold function. It not only expresses a quality of mercy in God's dealing with us, but it also identifies the Person through whom this mercy comes to us. Using the familiar figure of speech, personification, it indicates that the Christ of Christmas is the one who personifies God's grace and who also accomplishes what that grace intends to provide, which is "salvation for all." And the word "salvation" is also important to consider. It most certainly implies salvation from sin and its misery; verse 14 makes that clear, "Who gave himself for us that he might redeem us from all iniquity."

Calvary's cross is the ever-present reality, even at the manger scene! But salvation also implies "wholeness," a wholeness that includes our relationship with others as well as our affinity with God through Christ, our Lord. This emphasis is often either forgotten or unnoticed.

A deeply suggestive touch has been given to the Christmas portrayal by a certain artist. He shows the shepherds on the hillside looking up into the heavens from which they hear the angelic chorus singing, "Glory to God in the highest, and on earth peace, good will toward men." But at the shepherds' feet is one of their dogs. The dog is alert, poised, but he is not looking into the heavens with the shepherds. His head is turned in another direction. The dog is aware that something unusual is happening, but he does not know what it is. He is missing the message heard by his masters, the shepherds. In depicting the difference between the dog and the shepherds, the artist was true to the Gospels' portrayals of the original Christmas story, for in them there are profound differences of observation! The Wise Men saw a star which others did not notice, not even the shepherds. The shepherds heard a song to which the

Wise Men were deaf. And neither the star nor the song disturbed the dining and slumber of the guests at the Inn. Mary, the mother, pondered thoughts too deep for even the Wise Men and the shepherds to comprehend. What varying degrees of meaning Bethlehem held for those first beholders! And then there was the dog. He, too, went along with the shepherds. He looked on in a prosaic way. He was in Bethlehem, but the meaning of Bethlehem was not in him. Today's text urges us to behold the reason for the season, the reason behind the mere tapestry of Christmas. He, the Lord of heaven, appeared to provide salvation and wholeness for all who have eyes to see. Surely there is no bedlam in this understanding of Bethlehem.

We move on to the second of our *ABC*'s. We remove bedlam from Bethlehem when we perceive the *behavior* the Christmas message urges upon us. Verse 12 makes it clear, "Training us to renounce impiety and worldly passions, and in this present age live lives that are self-controlled, upright, and godly." Dear Christian friend, welcome to the University of Advent Behavior! Each of us matriculated in this august institution on the day of our baptism into Christ. The courses continue throughout life — and perhaps beyond! But what a blessed learning experience lies before us. The training concerns itself with all the important areas of life: our relation to ourselves, to others, and to God. Let's consider them.

"Live a life that is self-controlled." So important, yet so difficult at times. I've often turned to Proverbs 16:32 when reflecting on the matter of self-control. It reads, "Better is he who controls his own spirit, than he who takes a city." One's mind recalls, sadly, the experience of Alexander the Great, who, at the age of 29 had conquered the entire known world. Then, it is said, he wept because there were no more worlds to conquer. Four years later he was dead, the victim of fever brought on by intemperate living. He had conquered the world but had never conquered Alexander! An old song, "I'm sitting on top of the world," has been sung by many people who were not "on top of the world." The world was on top of them. A New York newspaper recorded the fact that on New Year's Eve a man was taken to a police station, drunk and disorderly, singing this song at the top of his voice. It was not very convincing. We are really on top of the world when we have mastered the art of self-control, when we are on top of those forces which might draw us down: our appetites, our greed, our hatreds, our anxieties, our fears. It is Christ whose power and love make us masters of ourselves — and our circumstances. In reality it is Christ-control not self-control, but more of that later.

Then, there is our relation to others, "Live a life that is upright." To be upright in all our relationships is to be honorable — to be sincere — to be devoid of sham. "Sham," according to Webster, is "an imitation that is meant to deceive." It is like two thin layers of veneer over inexpensive wood to make a table or a wall appear better than it is. Sham is harmless when it is confined to furniture, but when it appears in people it is deadly. Appearance may be deceptive for a time, but as Nathaniel Hawthorne noted in the *Scarlet Letter*, "No man, for a considerable period, can wear one face to himself, and another to the multitude, without finally getting bewildered as to which may be true." Sooner or later the mask slips and the inner reality shows through.

Children are remarkably discerning, seeing beneath the surface of our appearance. One lad, sitting on his father's knee remarked, "Daddy, when I'm a man I want to be just like you." Then suddenly realizing his father was not exactly handsome, the youngster added with childish candor. "Inside, Daddy, not outside." The father smiled knowingly, he had received a sublime compliment. The Christ of Christmas sees through the outside to the inside of us and our shams fall away. He wants us to express uprightness in all our relationships, the outward and the inward person as one.

The third aspect of our Advent behavior involves our relationship with God, "Live a life that is godly." Me, godly? It sounds as though we are being asked for the impossible. But is it really so far beyond the reach of possibility, for you, for me? Surely we are not to view godliness as Don Quixote's impossible dream! Recall Browning's advice: "Ah, but a man's reach should exceed his grasp. Or what's a heaven for?"

Perhaps it will be helpful to view the word "godly" as meaning "Godliness" or "Christ-likeness." Here we can see the Christ of Christmas giving himself to us in such a way as to produce a measure of his likeness in our lives which so often exhibit quite different qualities, qualities for which we plead forgiveness every day. Christ-likeness — can you think of a greater pursuit for this Christmas season or any season, for that matter?

Recall Nathaniel Hawthorne's wonderful short story, "The Great Stone Face." In it the young Ernest is taken by his mother to the edge of their New England village where she points to the face of a man nature has chiseled into the mountainside some distance away. When Ernest begins to see the likeness, his mother tells him the old, old legend that some day a native son of the valley will return home to lead his village to the greatest happiness it has ever known. This person's face will be the very image of the Great Stone Face. Ernest grows from childhood into boyhood, boyhood into manhood, manhood into old age, breathlessly awaiting the coming of his hero. Mr. Gather — Copper — and — Scatter — Gold comes first, then General Blood — and — Thunder, the epaulettes of his rank dazzling on his shoulders; then Old Stony Phiz, the grizzled statesman, and finally the gentle poet. But always there is disappointment, until one day, late in his life, the villagers look about them, and lo and behold, they make a startling discovery! It is Ernest himself who looks like the Great Stone Face! He had lived so long in the presence of his ideal that he had at last become like his ideal. In similar fashion, whoever thinks long enough in terms of Christ, acts long enough in terms of Christ, lives long enough in terms of Christ will in the end become like Christ. Our text again, "Live lives that are self-controlled, upright and godly — or Christ-like." Noble behavior attributes, indeed. May the Divine Artist paint them boldly on the canvass of your life and mine.

In the third, and final, of our *ABC*'s we remove bedlam from Bethlehem when we realize who is *coming* one day to usher in the final act in the Eternal Christmas Pageant. Verse 13 tells us, "While we wait for the blessed hope and the manifestation of the glory of our great God and Savior, Jesus Christ." Be certain of this, dear Christian friend, the Christ of Christmas who came once as a babe to be our deliverer will one day come as King of kings and Lord of lords. The future belongs to him!

E. Stanley Jones loved to tell of his visit to the Mosque of Saint Sophia in Constantinople. The Mosque is a transformed Christian church. It was one of the most beautiful churches in the world. All the Christian inscriptions and symbols had been painted out and Moslem inscriptions and symbols put in their places. As Jones and his wife stood under the great dome, they could see that the figure of the ascending Christ with outstretched hands in blessing, which had been painted out, was coming back through the wearing off of the covering paint. Jones turned to his wife and said: "He is coming back. You cannot blot him out. Through the secretion and daubs of the centuries he is coming back again. He shall yet reign. The future belongs to him." It does, never forget it!

Now as we conclude another Advent journey, we see that Bethlehem can never become bedlam when we remember the grace of God that appeared on that sacred day, the behavior that event urges upon us, and the triumphant final coming of the King of kings and Lord of lords. "Even so, come Lord Jesus!" Amen.

The Story Behind The Glory

Welcome to the Sunday after Christmas! Tell me, has the glory begun to fade?

A pastor recently described his shopping experience at one of the busy malls. He watched a small boy put his hand hopefully on an inexpensive Christ-child on a counter. "What is this?" he asked his mother, who had him by the hand. "C'mon," the hurried woman answered, "you don't want that." She dragged him grimly away, her mind dark with gift thoughts, following a star of her own devising.

Strange, isn't it, the way the story behind the glory gets lost in the Christmas rush? It is something of a paradox, but a day that should be holy with thoughts and dreams of the highest becomes cluttered with the irritations and frustrations that come with shopping. Maybe the hurried mother was right, and we don't want Christ. And yet, maybe we are tired and irritable because we have lost sight of the story behind the glory of Christmas. The fact that God came into human life to share it, enrich it, and save it is the story that flows from Bethlehem. The "news of a great joy" remind us that we are loved by an everlasting love even when we are unlovable, forgiven when we are unforgivable, and accepted when we are unacceptable. This is the Story behind the Glory! Let's think about it for a few moments on this Sunday after Christmas.

As our text conveys the Christmas message, we will see that the glory grows as the story unfolds.

First of all, it is a **Mystery Story**. "When the fullness of time had come, God sent his Son, born of a woman" (v. 4).

51

Agatha Christie or John Grisham couldn't match this story for sheer excitement! Think of it, Almighty God invading human life in the person of his Son. Next Sunday's Gospel will say it in another way: "The Word became flesh and lived among us, and we have seen his glory, the glory as of a father's only son, full of grace and truth" (John 1:14). Only a crass blindness could fail to see that such a truth as that presented in the sentence, "The Word became flesh," is over-poweringly dramatic in itself and utterly revolutionary in its consequences. "If this is dull," exclaimed Dorothy Sayers, "then what, in heaven's name, is worthy to be called exciting?" And to put it even more precisely, Ms. Sayers continued, "From the beginning of time until now, this is the only thing that has ever REALLY happened. When you understand this, you will understand all prophecies, and all history."

Think of it, fellow Christian, here is the mystery that unlocks the meaning of all history. And what is history but his-story, the story of the God who became man on that first Christmas day. Recall his words, "Whoever has seen me has seen the Father" (John 14:9). And, wonder of wonders, he is the one who "walks with us, and talks with and tells us we are his own." He is not just a fact of history but an ever-present factor in the living of these lives of ours. As Lord Tennyson put it, "Speak to him, thou, for he hears, and Spirit to Spirit can meet; closer is he than breathing, nearer than hands and feet." Perhaps it was thoughts like these that inspired Harry Farrington to write:

> *I know not how that Bethlehem's babe*
> *Could in the Godhead be*
> *I only know the Manger-Child*
> *Has brought God's Life to me.*

> *I know not how that Calvary's cross*
> *A world from sin could free*
> *I only know its matchless love*
> *Has brought God's love to me.*

I know not how that Joseph's tomb
Could solve death's mystery
I only know a living Christ
Our immortality.

Our text moves on to show us that this is also an **Adventure Story** — "God sent His Son ... to redeem those who were under the law" (vv. 4, 5).

In the comic strip, *Hi and Lois*, the next door neighbor and his wife are seated in the living room. She speaks up, "Thirsty, get away from that TV set. You watched golf yesterday afternoon, tennis last night, and now baseball. Get out and see the real world," to which Thirsty responds, "I don't like the real world!" And, sometimes that's true of us. We don't like the real world. But, of course, the remedy is not to retreat into fantasy or entertainment. The remedy is to get to work to change the real world into a better world.

The story behind the glory of Christmas is the record of God's plan for transforming a world that had lost its way into what it was meant to be: his world. Our text tells us that the mission of God's Son was a redemptive one. "To redeem those who were under the law." This entire human race was in bondage to the law, because the law of God, the law written into the very fabric of the universe, stood over it in judgment.

Follow me for a moment. There is a mystery of evil in our world. Those evils from which we suffer are in the main the fruit of man's sin. It is man's inhumanity to man that has made countless thousands to mourn. The wars, cruelties, and wrongs which form such a grievous part of the burden of humanity are the outcome of human lust and passion. This is a world, I am sad to admit, which is in rebellion against God. The depth and intensity of that spirit of evil is made manifest at the Cross. Here is the true measure of evil and the final judgment upon it. If the question were asked, "What sort of a world is this and how does it stand in relation to God?" the truest answer is that it is a world that could not tolerate in its presence the Christ of Christmas, the blessed Son of God Almighty. When he came, full of grace and truth, he got a scant welcome. When he spoke as no other ever spoke, there were

53

few who responded to him. When he went about doing good, ever willing to help and to save, the opposition to him grew more and more bitter until at last they cried out, "Away with him, crucify him." It is a world that has fully earned and brought upon itself the just judgment of God.

Martin Luther once said, "If I were almighty God, and the world treated my son as it treated God's Son, I'd knock the world to pieces."

But here is the crowning mystery of the story behind the glory of the Christmas event. He tells us, "My thoughts are not your thoughts and my ways are not your ways" (Isaiah 55:8). There is no desire in him to retaliate, or in any way act as man would act under similar provocation. On the contrary, the cross of Calvary, which is the supreme evidence of human wickedness, proves to be at the same time the crowning revelation of God's redeeming grace. It was all in his loving purpose; it was the price he was willing to pay. Since humankind's need was so desperate and the world could be redeemed in no other way: "God sent his Son ... to redeem those who were under the law." Yes, this is the story behind the glory of what we celebrated so few days ago. I wonder if the hymn writer thought of each of us when he penned these words:

> *What language can I borrow, to thank thee, dearest*
> *friend*
> *For this thy dying sorrow, thy pity without end*
> *Oh, make me thine forever, and should I fainting be*
> *Lord, let me never, never, outlive my love for thee.*

What an Adventure Story!

In our third look at the "story behind the glory," we discover that it is a **Love Story**. "So that we might receive adoption as children. And because you are children, God has sent the Spirit of his Son into our hearts, crying, 'Abba! Father!' "(vv. 7, 8). Everybody loves a love story!

Can you conceive of anything more loving than the experience of adoption? Here is a child, orphaned or unwanted, because of some tragic event beyond his control. A childless couple, anxious to pour their love into a needy child, learn about him, see him, fall in love with him, and choose to make him part of their family with all the rights of one born to them naturally. He is adopted! In a similar sense, our text tells us, every Christian has passed through this experience. Orphaned because of our sin, separated from the God who made us, we later became the objects of a love that would not let us go. So great was that love that it entered our world, lived our life, died our death, then conquered death for us on that first Easter morning. Having done all this, the Eternal God, through the gift of his Son, bestows on us the blessing of reconciliation: adoption into his family, with all the rights and privileges of an heir. No wonder the scripture has us responding joyfully: "Abba, Father, now, dear God, we belong to you!"

When did all this take place? At the moment of our baptism into Christ, or at the time, in later life, when we realized the emptiness of life without God and turned in faith to the lover of our souls, saying, "If you have loved me that much, I will trust you, and gladly commit the direction of my whole life to you!" Call it what you will, this is the defining moment, the moment of adoption, or reconciliation, or conversion. Our wandering is over, the prodigal has come home. Isn't that what Phillips Brooks had in mind when he wrote in his carol: "O Holy Child of Bethlehem, Descend to us, we pray. Cast out our sin, and enter in, be born in us today."

Blessed Love Story!

Having looked at the "story behind the Glory," is there perhaps one thing more we need to consider? As Paul Harvey often puts it, "Now for the rest of the story." What, dear friend, is the rest of the story? I think we get our clue from the action of the Wise Men. They came to the Child, they worshiped, they sensed a measure of the story behind the glory, and responded by presenting gifts of gold, frankincense, and myrrh. In essence they presented all that their lives represented. That, dear friends, is the "rest of the story."

A person of color was applying for membership in a Southern church. When questioned about his willingness to support the congregation with his time, talent, and treasure, he frankly said, "Brethren, I'se all I'se got." In sober truth that is all any of us possess, but if we give it, we give all else, as well. We will leave this fellowship this morning and return to a terribly needy world. What a blessing we will communicate if the "rest of the story" radiates from our lives.

Do you recall how the story of the Wise Men ends? Matthew tells us, "They departed into their own country another way" (Matthew 2:12). Of course he is saying that they took another route homeward, but doesn't it also tell us that they, themselves, went back "another way," different persons, changed by what they had seen and heard? No person can visit this Christ and return home the same person he was before that encounter. He/she must return "another way." May it be true of each of us today.

Once there was a man, according to an old story, who was so filled with despondency that he decided to commit suicide. He started on a long walk to a bridge that was to be his jumping off place. But he promised himself that if he met one smiling, happy, friendly face on the way he would turn back. Oddly, the story ends without answering the question whether the mission ended in suicide. The story, however, poses a question. If that man had met you, would he have turned back?

"I'se all I'se got" to offer this tired world. We can give the laughter and joy of those who have caught some hint of Bethlehem's meaning. We can give hope and confidence because we have beheld the love of God flooding down the ages from the Manger-child who will never let us go.

An unknown poet summed it up for us:

> Wise men, indeed, to know a newborn star
> Would be the herald of a King! Wise men,
> To watch in readiness and travel far
> To seek a light beyond their fellow's ken!
> At star-bathed stable to rejoice, and when
> They saw the Babe, to kneel and humbly lay
> Their riches gifts of gold, of myrrh; and then
> To travel back, dream-told, another way.

Ah, rare and wondrous wisdom, in our day
To read God's portents and to find his key!
Sweet manger baby, to thy gentle sway
We yield all pride, all knowledge, gifts for thee.
We worship in the radiance of thy Face,
And rise, a different way of life to trace.

This is the "rest of the story." Amen.

A New Look For The New Year

Just a few days ago we greeted loved ones and friends with a cheery, "Happy New Year." And we sincerely hoped it would be a year of joy and happiness for all. A New Year's card put it beautifully: "I am the New Year — all that I have I give with love unspoken. All that I ask — you keep the faith unbroken!"

Newspapers and magazines covered the fascinating story of Admiral Richard Byrd's second trip to the South Pole. The 180th meridian is an imaginary but important marker. It is the International Date Line. When a traveler crosses it, he either adds a day or subtracts a day, depending on his direction. Admiral Byrd spoke of his experience of flying southward to the pole: "All the time we continued flying as closely as possible along the 180th meridian. Even without wind drift — for which adequate correction can be made — it is obvious that no navigator can fly exactly along a mathematical straight line. Consequently, we were zigzagging constantly from today into tomorrow, and back again into yesterday."

At this season of the year our minds are crowded with recollections of the past year, some cheering and some sobering. But before long we find our minds occupied with anticipations of the coming year, some hopeful and some fearful. At this time the past and the future wrestle for dominance in our thinking. During this season there is a strange mingling of memory and hope. None of us are strangers to this experience.

As we begin to reflect on this morning's text, we see it bidding each of us to wear a "New Look for the New Year." And as we probe more closely, we find that this newness is the result of three important looks that are being urged upon us: the backward look, the inward look, and the upward look. Let's think about them for a few moments and see if they do not, in fact, open up fresh opportunities for newness in the New Year.

First, we note the **Backward Look**: "In him [Christ] we have redemption through his blood" (v. 7).

As we glance backward we are confronted immediately with a lonely cross erected on a hill centuries ago. Calvary is the solemn place at which man's redemption was accomplished. The New Testament Word "redemption" refers to the act of ransoming a person who is a prisoner of war or a slave. Whenever it is used, the word describes the delivering or setting free of a person from a situation from which he was powerless to liberate himself, or from a penalty or debt which he could never have paid. This backward look reminds us that our Savior has delivered us from a situation from which we could never have delivered ourselves. And this has always been so. Every honest person is conscious of his own inadequacy and sin. Seneca, the Roman philosopher who tutored Nero, wrote prolifically. His writings are replete with a feeling of sheer helpless frustration. He said of himself that he was a *homo nontolerabilis*, "an intolerable man." He said, despairingly, that men love their vices and hate them at the same time. In an oft-quoted statement, he said that mankind needed a hand reaching down from heaven to lift them up. It is exactly that need that Jesus Christ has fulfilled. In his life, death, and resurrection a power is released that can liberate humankind from its helpless slavery to those things which attract and disgust them at one and the same time. To put it in simplest terms, Jesus Christ can still make bad men good. Dear people, that is redemption! As we remember this, and embrace it by faith, we begin to experience newness.

Our second look is the **Look Inward**: "the forgiveness of our trespasses according to the riches of his grace" (v. 7).

Having seen the redeeming love of God expressed at the cross, we look within and see that forgiveness is ours, forgiveness even for things we thought unforgivable. Recall some of God's promises. "Though your sins be as scarlet they shall be as wool, though they be red like crimson, they shall be as white as snow" (Isaiah

1:18). "As far as the east is from the west, so far he removes our transgressions from us" (Psalm 103:12). That, dear people, is forgiveness; and that assurance begets newness.

Other biblical words are used to express this same newness. Propitiation is one. Justification is another. Someone has defined justification or justified: "just — as — if — I'd — never — sinned." That takes care of your sins and mine, yes, even the worst of them. C. B. Macartney tells of a cemetery on Long Island located behind a quaint colonial church. Many headstones bear the name of the deceased, dates of birth and death, and occasionally an expression of Christian hope. One headstone stands out from the others. It bears no name, no date of birth or death. The stone is unembellished by the sculptor's art. There is no epitaph, no fulsome eulogy. Just one word is inscribed upon it — "Forgiven." But that is sufficient. The greatest thing that can be said of any person, or written upon his grave, is that simple, yet all inclusive word, forgiven. Embrace that forgiveness as your own and be certain that Christ purchased it for you personally, with no strings attached!

One of the happy results that emerge from the assurance of forgiveness is the fact that now it becomes quite natural for us to express this forgiveness to others as well. It is a concomitant of our newness. Later in this epistle, Saint Paul reminds us that we most resemble the God we worship when we extend forgiveness to those who have wronged us. He writes, "And, be kind to one another, tenderhearted, forgiving one another, as God in Christ has forgiven you. Therefore be imitators of God, as beloved children" (Ephesians 5:1). Be certain of this, there is nothing in his terribly needy world that bears the gracious impress of the Son of God so surely as forgiveness. James Hilton, in *Time and Time Again*, demonstrates wholesome insight when he says, "If you forgive people enough you belong to them, and they to you, whether or not either person knows or likes it — squatter's rights of the heart." Almost 200 years ago, Francis Quarles also stated it with Christ-honoring clarity: "Hath any one wronged Thee? — Seek revenge as a Christian — slight it, and the work is begun: forgive and it is finished. He is below himself that is not above injury."

Let's take John Oxenham's advice to heart:

> *Love ever gives*
> *Forgives — outlives,*
> *And ever stands*
> *With open hands.*
> *And, while it lives,*
> *It gives.*
> *For this is love's prerogative,*
> *To give — forgive — and give.*[1]

We turn now to the final direction our text suggests: the **Upward Look**. "To the praise of God's glorious grace that he freely bestowed on us in the Beloved" (v. 6). The words we underscore here are "God's glorious grace" and "in the Beloved." All that has come to us in the past, all that we have in the present, all that we ever hope to have in the future are gifts of grace from our loving Father through the merits of his Son, Jesus Christ. That is why, whenever we hear the blessed Words of Absolution, our eyes drift heavenward in gratitude for so great a love.

Greg Albrecht tells his favorite story of how vital Jesus is to the lives of his people. A wealthy Englishman loved fine art and shared that love with his son. Together they gathered a priceless collection that became known to many collectors throughout the world as one of the finest. As World War II began in Europe, the son was one of the first to join the armed forces to serve his country. The son had only been gone a few months when the father received a telegram notifying him that his son had been killed in battle while rescuing a fellow soldier. The father started a long period of grief and pain, mourning the loss of his son. One cold day in the midst of winter he answered his front door to be greeted by a young soldier who was carrying a package. The young man explained that he was the one the rich man's son had rescued, and that earlier he had painted a portrait of his comrade. The young soldier apologized, as he knew he was an unskilled artist, but he thought the father might like the portrait. They talked all afternoon, and after the soldier left, the father sat for a long time admiring the painting of his son. It would never be considered a masterpiece, but it did capture his son's character. The old man decided to hang the painting of his son over the fireplace, moving several priceless pieces of art to make room.

After a few years the old man became ill and eventually died. His will called for all his works of art to auctioned. News of the auction caused art collectors around the world to make travel plans for London to be present for this once-in-a-lifetime auction. When the auction started, priceless pieces of art filled the room and the stage, but the first painting to be offered for sale was the simple portrait of the old man's son. The auctioneer asked for an opening bid. The room of experts and collectors was silent. Everyone could tell that this painting had little or no value. Someone in the back of the room yelled, "Who cares about that worthless thing? It's just a picture of the old man's son. Let's forget about it and move on to the treasures of his collection." The auctioneer responded, "No, we have to sell this one first." After a long silence, a trusted long-time household servant of the old man who was attending the auction out of respect to the family he had loved and served said, "All I have is ten pounds. I'll offer that. I knew the young man, and I would like to have the painting." No one else offered another bid, and the auctioneer's gavel came crashing down. The painting was sold to the household servant for ten pounds (about $18).

Anticipation filled the room, as everyone looked forward to the real business of bidding for the art treasures from the estate. But the auctioneer's gavel came down once again, and to the amazement of everyone the auctioneer declared that the auction was over. Stunned disbelief filled the room. One person yelled, "What do you mean it's over? We have come from all over the world. We didn't come to bid for a second-rate portrait. What about all these priceless treasures?"

The auctioneer explained, "It's really very simple. According to the will of the father, whoever takes the son — takes all."

It's a lesson we can take to heart and live by. If we have Christ, we have everything. Without him, we have nothing. When we have him, our priority in life is to worship him, celebrate him, and obey him in everything we do, and share him and his message with the world.

63

Dear friends, on this first Sunday in January, as we have been reminded of God's gracious provisions for newness, permit me to ask each of us, including myself: "How about a New You for the New Year?" Amen.

---

1. *Selected Poems of John Oxenham,* edited by Charles L. Wallis (New York: Harper and Brothers, 1948), p. 84.

What Goes On When He Comes In?

As we grapple with the meaning of our first text for today, Acts chapter 19, how appropriate is the oft-used phrase, "We only get one chance to make a first impression." Unquestionably the disciples of John the Baptist, whom Paul met early in his visit to Ephesus, seemed to lack some evidence of God's Spirit in their lives. Their "first impression" was spiritually deficient! Christian scholars throughout the centuries have sought to determine what Paul sensed in these disciples that caused him to question the fullness of their faith. No consensus appears to have been reached. Perhaps we, who live so many years after the event, can profit from the "wisdom" of Yogi Berra. Before an all-star game in the 1960s, the American League strategists were debating how to pitch to Stan "the Man" Musial, the great National League hitter. Should you pitch to him high and inside or low and away? Could you sneak a hard fast one by him or fool him with a big slow curve? Yogi Berra, who was to be the catcher, listened for awhile then ended the discussion with a single sentence: "The trouble with you guys is that you are trying to figure out in fifteen minutes what nobody has figured out in fifteen years!"

That is substantially the situation we could find ourselves in this morning. We could spend twenty minutes trying to find out what nobody has really figured out in twenty centuries. I hope we will use our time more profitably. We are going to look at Paul's second letter to Timothy as he simply, and precisely, explains what factors are present when one possesses — and is possessed by — the Holy Spirit.

To begin with, Paul makes mention of the laying on of hands: "The gift of God which is in you through the laying on of my hands" (v. 6). What is the "gift of God"? Or better, who is the gift of God? Surely Paul is making reference to the Holy Spirit who comes to make his abode in our lives the moment our beloved pastor traces the sign of the cross on our forehead and breast and speaks those precious words, "I baptize you in the Name of the Father, and of the Son, and of the Holy Spirit." At the moment he "lays his hands" on us, we enter "the land of beginning again" where all things have become new.

Paul moves on to urge us to "stir up," or rekindle, this precious gift each of us possesses. We recall an answer that was given by a waitress in a New York restaurant. It was during World War II, a time of shortages imposed by the war. Sugar was one of the rationed commodities. A customer who had already gotten his share called out loudly for more sugar. The waitress' answer was a classic in brevity and wisdom, "Stir up what you've got!" Saint Paul is offering the same advice to Timothy and to you and me, "If you are longing for a more satisfying Christian experience, stir up what you've got. All that you need to live the life Christ meant you to live is already yours — a gift of his amazing grace." Remember it! Rekindle it! This gift actually includes a trinity of provisions, "You have received the Spirit of power and love and a focused mind." There you have it! What goes on when he comes in? Power, love, and a focused mind, the Spirit's gifts for a well rounded and satisfying Christian experience. Let's consider these gifts for a few moments.

Let's talk about **power**. Much is said these days about power. We hear about atomic power, military power, the balance of power, economic power, white power, people power, power structures — the list is almost endless.

The power the Spirit provides is not the ability to move mountains of earth or manipulate masses of people; it is rather the provision of a strength that makes us adequate for any possible experience that life may bring. Dr. William Barclay of Scotland often observed that the really important thing the pagan world saw in the first century Christians was that they possessed strength or power that enabled them to cope with and mend the human situation. They saw in them strength that they themselves did not possess — and they wanted it — and *needed* it!

It will always be true that those outside the Christian family will have no use for a faith that is obviously ineffective. Almost a century ago the atheistic philosopher, Friedrich Wilhelm Nietzche, issued the challenge: "Show me that you are redeemed and I will believe in your redeemer." The most effective witness of all is a life that clearly possesses "a strength that can cope with the human situation with all its problems, all its tragedy, and all its pain." This is *exactly* the power the Spirit provides. It is power to break the shackles of a misspent past. It is power to set us right with our creator and our fellow humans. It is power to cleanse us in the deepest recesses of our nature where no psychiatrist's couch can be effective. It is, to repeat Barclay's words, power to cope with the human situation in all its problems, in all its tragedy, and in all its pain.

Paul goes on to speak about **love**. "Religion," said Robert Hastings, "is not an eight-letter word, but a four-letter word. And that word is L-O-V-E." And that four-letter word is exactly what the Holy Spirit provides. In Romans 5:5, Saint Paul reminds us, "God's love is poured into our hearts through the Holy Spirit who has been given us." How desperately our world needs to see that love expressed, in all its sincerity, in every area of our lives!

David Augsburger has related the story of a young man proposing to the girl he has been dating. "I love you, darling," he said. "I'm not wealthy, and I don't have a sharp Mercedes convertible and a luxury yacht like Jerome Green, but I do love you!"

The girl thought for a moment, "I love you, too" she said, "but tell me a little more about Jerome Green."

Beyond all argument, the term "love" is one of the most misused words in our language. Someone has called it "a semantic swamp." Its use ranges all the way from out and out lust to the highest form of unselfish care we are capable of. But real love, New Testament love, the love the Holy Spirit provides, is no soft, sentimental thing. It enlists the total personality. As Jesus expressed it, love involves the whole heart, soul, and mind. And love's importance is seen even in the most basic of human experiences.

When Burt Bacharach wrote the popular song, "What the world needs now, is love, sweet love," he may not have realized it, but he was expressing more than a vague wish for a more harmonious world; he was actually stating a biological fact! For love is necessary from the first moment of our lives until the last. Let me explain.

Love's real significance can be clearly seen when we consider a disease from which almost one-third of the children of our nation died early in the twentieth century. It happened during the very first year of the child's life. Anthropologist Ashley Montague called the disease "morasmus," from the Greek word meaning "wasting away." It was discovered that babies in the best homes and hospitals were most often its victims, babies who were apparently receiving the best and most careful physical attention, while babies in the poorest homes, with a good mother, despite the lack of hygenic physical conditions, often overcame the physical handicaps and flourished. What was lacking in the sterilized environment? Simply this: Mother love!

So you see, dear friend, you and I were born with a need for love. Without it in one way or another, we waste away. What comfort comes when we discover that at the heart of our universe there is not emptiness or meaninglessness but love, the very thing for which we were made, the very thing for which we yearn at the center of our humanness. Listen as the scripture describes the nature of the One who created and sustains all that exists: "Love is of God ... For *God is love*" (1 John 4:8). His defining essence, the attribute that coordinates all that he is and all the he does, is Love, the very quality that meets the essential need of each of us. But *never* forget that the clearest evidence of that love is seen at the cross. There God is saying to every person: "I love you! Yes, I love you *that* much!" It is as personal and intimate as that. It does not mean that God will love you if you are good and worthy of his love. It means that God loves you just as you are — even if you are in despair of yourself, even if you have forfeited the love of those nearest and dearest to you. Such is God's love for you. Never, never forget it!

And when that love is "poured into our hearts by the Holy Spirit" and we surrender to it, some amazing things begin to happen. We begin to realize that love is the only power that is able to save this world of ours. We've tried other means only to be disillusioned time and time again because every other method has been applied externally. Only Love — God's love seen in Christ — reaches the heart of the matter: the soul of man. And when we express that love in all our relationships we discover happily that we are part of the answer to the world's problems, no longer part of the problem.

Remember that lovely scene in Charles Dickens' book, *A Tale of Two Cities*, when the brave hero Sidney Carton was taking the place of another man and was on his way to the guillotine? Beside him on the horse-drawn cart was a little girl, little more than a child. In prison his strong, calm face had impressed her. On the way to the execution she said, "If I may ride with you, will you let me hold your hand? I am not afraid, but I am very small, and it will give me courage." They rode together, her hand in his. Fear left her eyes and soul. She looked up into his face and said, "I think you were sent to me from heaven." Love does that. As we live and walk in love we celebrate the truth of 1 Corinthians 13:8, "Love *never fails!*" Never!

A final ingredient of the Spirit's presence is mentioned in our text: "a **focused** or **balanced mind**."

Several years ago someone described the city of Los Angeles as sixty suburbs in search of a city. Apart from the work of the Holy Spirit, this aptly describes the lives of countless persons we know. Sixty — or perhaps a hundred or more — interests in search of a person, a center or focal point that would give life significance and direction. Here is where the Holy Spirit provides balance for the Christian. The Spirit always focuses our attention on the Living Christ, encouraging us to identify ourselves with him. And who is this Jesus Christ? I submit to you that he, and he alone, is the center of gravity for all human life.

An observatory telescope weights 40,000 pounds, yet its vast weight can be moved about by the pressure of one's little finger. How is this possible? Because that mass of glass and steel is poised on its center of gravity, that spot where all 40,000 pounds are in perfect balance. Dear friend, Jesus is the center of gravity for the burdened life of humankind. In him the impossible becomes possible. Because of him life, at last, has meaning and purpose. And the Holy Spirit enables each of us to embark on the adventure of proving to a watching world that Christ is indeed the answer — the only answer! Remember the bumper sticker that read: "Christ is the answer?" Some wiseacre put on his bumper: "But what is the question?" I'll tell you the question, the question that haunts every thinking person: Who am I? Why am I here? And where am I going? No one — but no one — holds the answer except Jesus Christ! Later in the Epiphany season we will explore these questions in depth.

No wonder an unknown poet wrote of Christ:

> *I tried the broken cisterns, Lord,*
> *But all their waters failed,*
> *Even as I stooped to drink, they fled,*
> *And mocked me as I wailed.*
>
> *For pleasures lost I sadly mourned,*
> *But never wept for thee,*
> *Till Grace my sightless eyes received,*
> *Thy loveliness to see.*
>
> *Now none but Christ can satisfy*
> *No other one for me.*
> *'Tis life and love and lasting joy,*
> *Lord Jesus, found in thee!*

What goes on when he comes in? He gives us a power for adequate living, a love that transforms all of life, and a balanced mind focused on the Lord of all life, Jesus Christ, our Lord.

"Thanks be unto God for his unspeakable gift." Amen!

Don't Fence Me In!

Goodspeed translates our text: "I may do anything I please but not everything I do is good for me. I may do anything I please but I am not going to let anything master me." So Saint Paul is saying, "I am free and yet I am not free; I rejoice in my freedom, and yet I recognize that there are limits to my freedom." With these inspired insights we come face to face with one of the most critical issues in our world — and in your life and mine. How do we interpret and how do we exercise our freedom? This is an issue that concerns every sincere Christian. More than that, it is, in some of its aspects, an issue that confronts every American.

For a few moments let's consider the *problems* that exist at the very heart of our freedom — or freedoms. How absolute are they?

It doesn't take long for us to discover that our political freedoms are much easier to shout about than they are to define or maintain. Take freedom of speech, for example. Is it absolute — with no strings attached whatsoever? No! If it were, there would be no laws governing libel and slander. If it is not absolute, where does the government draw the line? Or, take the issue of freedom as it appears in connection with our personal living. An increasing number of Americans have espoused the notion that no one has the right to put any restraints on their liberties. "Don't fence me in" is their catchword. "It's my life, isn't it; if it feels good, I'll do it." Some time ago, a teacher, writing in one of our education magazines, spoke of the rejection of discipline, the vandalism and general disorderliness of the students in her large suburban high school. She quoted one of the seniors as saying, "This is a public school; I can do what I please in it." You say, "What that boy needs is a good whipping." Perhaps so, but don't be too sure about it. Long before he adopted such an idea, he needed the help and guidance of some older folks who knew the meaning of life. Instead of getting such help, he probably came under the influence of the sort of persons who write some of our modern novels and plays. The advice offered by one of these writers is: "Let a man give rein to his impulses as they come." It is that kind of heresy that has helped produce the moral anarchy we see about us so frequently. Dr. Paul Scherer somewhere remarked that one of the definitions of freedom in his dictionary was, "The state of being without physical — or moral — control." Scherer continued: "If that is what freedom is, we ought to get down on our knees right now and pray God fervently for someone to come along and take it away!" Precisely! We don't get far in this business of personal living before we discover that our liberties must have some controls set about them or life — both for ourselves and others — goes to pieces.

That's enough about *problems,* let's search out some inspired *solutions.* I believe we find them in our text for this morning. Listen as Saint Paul speaks: "I may do anything I please, but not everything I do is good for me." The New Revised Standard Version has this last clause read: "But not all things are beneficial." This puts us on the track of thought that I want to suggest. The Greek word translated "beneficial" means "fitting, profitable, appropriate, helpful." This points us to the first solution to the problem of our freedom, the Christian understanding of how our faith controls — and enriches — our freedom. When we arrive at decisions, we travel a route that makes us consider the result of that action not only on ourselves but also on others who journey with us. Few of us ever discover how very much our personal influence impacts the lives of those among whom we spend our moments.

A young missionary returned from India very disappointed. His work, he felt, had accomplished so little in the five years he had labored there. He began to assess his life and the future that lay before him. In the midst of this he received a letter from India which said: "When you left us, it seemed as though the flags were lowered, and the music stopped." It goes without saying that the young missionary, E. Stanley Jones, returned to India and provided thirty years of fruitful service to Christ and the people of that needy nation. We cannot measure influence. We can weigh sugar but we cannot measure sweetness. We can register heat, but the beam of light that creates it can fall upon the most delicate scale and not move it at all. So with our influence, it cannot be measured, but its impact on others could change a life, and, in some extraordinary cases, may change the world!

A certain Miss Murphy taught third grade in a parochial school in Massachusetts. She had taught her class the Psalm 23 and asked them to recite it for her. As the little voices chorused out the words, she detected a false sound. She heard the children one by one to find out what and where the trouble was. She found it when little Jack, concluded the Psalm by saying, "Surely good Miss Murphy will follow me all the days of my life." The correct rendering is, of course, "goodness and mercy shall follow me." But was he wrong? Perhaps Good Miss Murphy did follow Jack (John F. Kennedy) all the days of his life! "I may do anything I please, but not everything is helpful to others." The awesome power of influence!

Saint Paul moves on to share his *second solution* to his problem of freedom: "I may do anything I please, but I am not going to let anything master me." The principle involved is simply this: the Christian recognizes that his freedom must be restricted for the sake of his own personal well being. When Paul writes, "I am not going to let anything master me," he is reminding each of us that too much freedom — or freedom wrongly exercised — is a boomerang. It turns on the indulgent person and enslaves him. Freedom without limits leads to the loss of freedom. In Upton Sinclair's words: "The oldest form of slavery is self-indulgence."

A soldier, having returned from Vietnam, asked to speak with his pastor. During the visit there were guilt feelings that needed to be talked out and laid at the feet of the forgiving Christ. There were patterns of conduct, formed during the war, that only God could reshape into a worthy design for living. At one point in the conversation the young man described the immoral indulgences which he and other servicemen practiced when they came to certain cities where they found easy access to loose women. It was with no air of bravado or "macho-ism" but rather with a sense of shame and disgust that the young man confessed: "We took what we wanted until we didn't want what we took." Free? Oh, yes, they were frightfully free. Free to make a joke out of the moral law! But it was not long until that moral law turned on them and mastered them with self-loathing, frustration, and guilt. How eternally right was Jesus: "Verily, Verily, I tell you, everyone who continues to commit sin becomes the slave of sin" (John 8:34).

So the Spirit of God is saying to each of us, through the pen of Saint Paul: be aware of the limits to your freedom. Be self-regarding enough to watch your own spiritual health. No license that will ultimately enslave you is worthy of the name freedom. Be certain of this; it is true.

My final word can be spoken briefly. Freedom! Yes, freedom within Christ-honoring limits! We've looked at the *problem* of freedom. We've considered Christ-like *principles* that limit our freedom. In closing, let's ponder the *price* of our freedom. Here it is in verses 19 and 20 of our chapter: "Do you not know that your body is a temple of the Holy Spirit within you, which you have from God, and that you are not your own? For you were bought with a price; therefore glorify God in your body."

There are two prices, as a matter of fact. One has been paid and need never be paid again: "You were bought with a price." Jesus Christ, by his self-giving for us and by bearing the cost of our redemption from sin at Calvary's cross, has won the right to possess us for himself and his kingdom forever. The cross has put a mark upon every one of us. That mark declares: *You belong to God.* You may not admit it. You may resist the thought. But you cannot alter the fact: *you belong to God!*

You perhaps remember the story of the twice-owned boat? A lad fashioned a crude sailboat out of scraps of lumber his dad had left on his worktable. Attaching fishline to his boat, he took it to a nearby lake and, holding the line, pushed the boat from the shore. It sailed beautifully, but somehow the line was severed and the boat sailed out on the lake beyond the boy's sight. He was heartbroken. Some days later he discovered his little boat in the window of a local pawnshop. Entering he learned that he would have to pay a certain price to regain the cherished boat. He raised the money, purchased the boat, and held it close to his heart as he walked home. Adoringly he patted the boat and said: "Little boat, I love you. I love you because you have been mine twice. First, because I made you, and second, because I bought you."

In a similar manner God speaks to each of us saying, "I love you because you are mine twice. First because I made you and second because I bought you at the price of my own life, surrendered at the cross. You belong to me!" Yes, dear friend, we do.

The other price is the one *we* must pay. It can be seen negatively in the words, "You are not your own," and positively in the words, "Therefore glorify God in your body." It is the price of self-surrender. It is the price of recognizing that freedom is not an end in itself, but a means to an end. And the end is the human soul voluntarily yielding itself to the control of the infinitely loving Savior. It is the price of handing over our independence in order to find our true liberty in dependence upon the God and Father of our Lord Jesus Christ.

Something like this must have been in George Matheson's mind when he wrote:

> *Make me a captive, Lord.*
> *And then I shall be free;*
> *Force me to render up my sword*
> *And I shall conqueror be.*
>
> *I sink in life's alarms*
> *When by myself I stand;*
> *Imprison me with thine arms,*
> *And strong shall be my hand.*
>
> *My will is not my own*
> *Till thou has made it thine;*
> *If it would reach a monarch's throne*
> *It must its crown resign:*

It only stands unbent
Amid the clashing strife,
When on thy bosom it has leant
And found in thee its life.

Permit me to alter our theme for today with a quiet prayer: "Lord, please fence me in with your love, for then I will be truly free!" *This is the freedom that frees! Amen.*

Everybody Loves A Parade!

This is the season for parades. Not long ago we watched the Rose Bowl parade on television; on Thanksgiving Day, Macys of New York entertained us with its Turkey Day extravaganza. Our text for today calls attention to another, and more sobering, parade: the parade of life, the pageant of this world. "For the present form of this world is passing away" (v. 31). The words "passing away" are a translation of a Greek word meaning "to lead by." It suggests the picture of a parade of soldiers being led past a reviewing stand. Look at them! Notice the evidence of their manly strength and skill. But then, in a moment, they are gone, out of sight. "So it is with this world," says our text, "there it is — but watch — soon it will be gone. How foolish it is to put all of your time and energies into something so transitory, so temporary."

Dear friend, do you realize that, at this moment, you are not the same person who entered this church this morning? Ever so imperceptibly you have changed physically into someone quite different. This pulpit, solid as it appears, is not the same pulpit you observed when you entered this sanctuary. It has diminished ever so slightly and if we were to see it one hundred years or more from now it would be nothing more than a handful of dust. And you and I, and the whole world, move inexorably toward the same finale. This is the message of our text.

At the cathedral in Milan there are three large doorways. Over each is a splendid arch, and on each is an inscription. On the left is carved a wreath of roses with the inscription: "All that which pleases is but for a moment." Over the arch to the right is sculpted a cross

77

accompanied by these words: "All that which troubles is but for a moment." But over the great central entrance to the cathedral is this inscription: "That only is important which is eternal." What wisdom to take with us in the early days of this New Year! "All that pleases is but for a moment; all that which troubles is but for a moment; that only is important which is eternal."

Take another look at our text for this morning, "The present form of this world is passing away." This suggests at least three things to me during this Epiphany season.

To begin with this season is a good time to consider the serious implications of living. Dear people, this pageant of life in which we find ourselves is the real thing!

Those of you who participated in high school and college plays, musicals, or operettas remember how the rehearsals went. Things moved slowly at first; not many took the matter very seriously. Lots of fun and horseplay was engaged in by most. Then, as the opening date drew near, the rehearsals took on a more serious tone. Finally the day arrived. This was it! The audience was there, the play had to go on. This was the real thing!

So we need to be reminded that life for us — every moment of it — is the real thing. This is not just a dress rehearsal. This is it! And this is the only life we will have, there is no "second time around." God grant that each of us may look at life with sobriety. Life is real! God is real! Death is real!

I'm a sports fan, and I'll never forget reading an article in one of our sports magazines narrating the life and times of Max Baer. Some of you may recall that Max Baer was a heavyweight boxer in the 1930s. His name was familiar to all who lived in that era. Max fought Max Schmelling from Germany, Primo Canerra of Italy, and the great Joe Louis. For a short time he was heavyweight champion of the world. Quite an achievement! After retiring from the ring, he had a series of heart attacks and lived his life apart from the spotlight. On the day that he died, he was sitting on the side of his bed when he was suddenly gripped with severe chest pains. He put his hand to his heart and said to his wife, "My God, this is it!" In a moment he was gone. How quickly life comes and goes.

Yes, dear people, this is it. This is your life, your only life. Who knows what a day will bring with it? May each of us live life under this sanctifying influence: "Only that is important which is eternal."

Secondly, this season is an appropriate time to discriminate between what is essential and that which is merely the scenery, the secondary things in life, the folderol, if you please. Some years ago someone coined a phrase that expresses clearly what I have in mind. The phrase is "majoring on minors." It aptly describes the person who spends a major share of his time on minor issues and leaves undone those things that are essential.

Clyde W. Widdmeyer was a very successful wholesale grocer. He wrote his own epitaph before his death and had it chiseled on his tombstone. Here it is: Born 1884, a human being; died 19__, a wholesale grocer. When asked what it meant, Mr. Widdmeyer said, "I was so busy selling groceries that I never had time to get married and have a family. Here was a whole area of my life crowded out by my business. I was so busy selling that I never had time to do any traveling, even though I had the money to do so. I was so busy selling that I never had time for community service, religion, social or political activity. I was successful, men said. I became a well-known and wealthy wholesaler. But I was so busy making a living that I never found time to live." He was majoring on minors, an addiction toward which too many of us are inclined. This season, so close to the New Year, is saying to us, "Major on majors, minor on minors. Discriminate. Distinguish between the vital and the trivial, the important and the inconsequential." Our Savior showed us the way when he laid down his life for each of us. We were not trivial; we were essential to the purposes of God. As one has put it, "We were so important to him that he was willing to go to hell for us, rather than to go to heaven without us." So he traveled, without hesitation, toward a cross on a hill outside Jerusalem. Because of this we are all his debtors!

A final thought comes to mind. Not long ago many of us made New Year resolutions. May I suggest just one more? Here it is: resolve to become involved — genuinely involved — in the things that really matter!

Someone came to Horace Traubel and asked, "What can I do, just me?" Traubel answered, "What can I do? I can talk when others are silent. I can say, 'Persons,' when others say, 'Money.' I can stay up when others are asleep. I can keep working when others have stopped to play. I can give life big meanings when others give life small meanings. I can say, 'Love,' when others say, 'Hate.' I can say, 'Every man,' when others say, 'One man.' I can give myself to the Lord of life when others refuse to do so. Will you join me?" For the record, many did join him, and life has been enriched because of them. Perhaps some of us can resolve today to join their company.

A pastor friend has an interesting custom, one he has followed throughout his ministry. On the Sunday closest to the New Year he includes a small pocket calendar in the church bulletin. At the close of the service he says, "Soon our Lord will give us the gift of another year. It contains twelve months, 52 weeks, 365 days, 8,760 hours. What are you going to do with them?" Something to think about isn't it? We have used a small fraction of the year 2003 already, most of it still lies before us. What will we do with it? Perhaps it's not too late to reflect on two New Year poems that have often challenged the hearts of God's people.

O year that is going, take with you
Some evil that dwells in my heart.
Let selfishness, doubt,
With the old year go out,
With joy I would see them depart.

O year that is going, take with you
Impatience and willfulness, pride;
The sharp word that slips
From these too hasty lips
I would cast, with the old year, aside.

O year that is coming, bring with you
Some virtue of which I have need;
More patience to bear
And more kindness to share,
And more love that is true love, indeed.

80

And a final one in the form of a prayer:

O Lord, I pray, that from this day
I may not swerve
By foot or hand, from Thy command
Not to be served, but to serve.

This, too, I pray, that from this day
No love of ease
Nor pride prevent, my good intent
Not to be pleased, but to please.

And if I may, I'd have this day
Strength from above
To set my heart — in heavenly art
Not to be loved — but to love![1]

Somehow these words remind me of that central arch over the entrance to the cathedral at Milan and the timeless words carved above it: "Only that is important which is eternal." I will carry these words with me throughout this year. My life may never be quite the same again. Will you keep me company? Amen.

---

1. Both of the New Year poems were quoted in a New Year newsletter from Holy Cross Lutheran Church, St. Charles, Missouri, in 1987. The source is not available.

Epiphany 4
Ordinary Time 4
1 Corinthians 8:1-13

Who Can Ask For Anything More?

Those who have read Charles Dickens' famous story, *Oliver Twist*, will recall that little Oliver, still hungry after receiving the thin gruel doled out to him in the orphanage, was always saying, "More, please." Whether we are entitled to more or not, we human beings are very much like Oliver. We are always saying, one way or another, "We want more." Who was it that first said, "Enough is always a little more than a man has"? Philosophers and sages of long ago were sure that happiness does not lie in acquiring many "things" but in taming our desires. An ancient Greek thinker named Epicurus said of a friend, "If you want to make Pythocles happy, do not add to his possessions, rather, take away from his desires."

Surely the happy ones are those who sing along with the shepherd boy in John Bunyan's song in *Pilgrim's Progress*: "I am content with what I have, Little be it or much, And, Lord, contentment still I crave, because Thou lovest such."

After pondering over the words of our text for today, three things began to emerge. Reflecting on them, it became clear that those who perceive these concepts, and are possessed by them, are among those who can sincerely say, "Who can ask for anything more?"

The first thing that emerges from our text is this: we have a Father who provides for us. "For us there is one God, the Father, from whom are all things and for whom we exist" (v. 6).

It was Jesus who experienced, and reveled in, this Father-Son relationship, and he tells us that we can know God in the same way. He assures us that at the heart of this universe is One whom we, too, may call Father, One who calls us son/daughter. We marvel, do we not, that so many we know feel they cannot lay hold on this transforming relationship? For some, Walter de la Mare's "The Listeners" is a vivid description,

> *"Is there anybody there?" Said the Traveler,*
> *Knocking on the moonlit door;*
> *And he smote upon the door a second time;*
> *"Is anybody there?" he said,*
> *But no one descended to the Traveler*
> *Where he stood perplexed and still.*[1]

Whatever the poet may have intended by these lines, surely this much we can say: it expresses a hunger in numerous lives for the assurance that a Father's heart beats in their behalf somewhere, but somehow they have not found him. Perhaps, only perhaps, they have been knocking at the wrong door.

An old story is told of a man who was asked if he found shade while crossing the desert. He said he had found shade but was not able to get into it. When asked why he could not, he replied, "Have you ever tried to sit down in your own shadow?" A life without a Father-God is like nothing more than trying to sit down in our own shadow. Under burning sun, traveling across parched wasteland which affords no oasis against either heat or thirst, some do try to take refuge in the shadow of themselves. But a person overcome by guilt, appalled by his own insufficiency, alarmed at life's demands, finds in his shadow no refuge. Then comes the Savior offering, in his Father, a strength not our own, to lead us to a sanctuary above ourselves. "He who dwells in the shelter of the Most High (Father), who abides in the Shadow of the Almighty, will say to the Lord, 'My refuge and my fortress is my God, in whom I trust.' " Dear people, there is a strength in the sheltering love of a Father who loves his children, a strength these children take with them even when they go forth to cross the sands of life's fiercest trials and dissonant testings.

The sum of what we've been saying is seen in a story told in the terrible days of the blitz in London during World War II. A father, holding his son by the hand, ran from a building that had been struck by a bomb. In the yard was a shell hole, and seeking shelter, the father jumped in, then held up his hands for his son to follow. But the small boy, hearing his father's plea for him to jump, cried out, "I can't see you." The father, however, could see his son outlined against the night sky, standing hesitant and anxious, and he replied, "But I can see you. Jump!" In similar fashion the faith that enables us to face all of life — and death as well — with dignity and confidence is not that we can see, but that we are seen by our Father; not that we know, but that we are known; not that we understand, but that we are understood, and that all of life, and every event within it, is part of our Father's gift. Nothing can separate us from his love. Such a faith gives dimension and dignity to your life and mine. "Who can ask for anything more?" But there is more!

Not only do we have a Father to provide for us, but also we possess a Friend who loves and walks with us. "For us there is one Lord, Jesus Christ, through whom all things are, and through whom we exist" (v. 6).

John Newton's most familiar hymn is "Amazing Grace." Another of his hymns, though less familiar, is one of my favorites.

> One there is above all others,
> Well deserves the name of Friend;
> His is love beyond a brother's,
> Faultless, free and knows no end;
> They who once his kindness prove,
> Find it ever-lasting love.
>
> Which of all our friends to save us,
> Could or would have shed his blood?
> But this Savior died to have us
> Reconciled in him to God;
> This was boundless love indeed
> Jesus is a Friend in need.

Recall our Lord's words, "No one has greater love than this, to lay down one's life for one's friends. You are my friends ..." (John

15:13, 14). Tie these words in tandem with "What a Friend we have in Jesus. All our sin and grief to bear," and "He walks with me and he talks with me and he tells me I am his own." Then we begin to see what our text is seeking to tell us. We do have a Friend who loves us, who walks beside us; but first this Friend walked the painful path of the Via Dolorosa, the path that ended at Calvary's Cross. There, this Friend gave his life to bring each of us back to the circle of the Father's love. Yes, he is a Friend indeed!

And what does this divine friendship imply? Perhaps the most precious implication is that it provides each of us with a divine identity. In Christ, everybody is somebody. He knows your name! One little fellow aged six, one night said a new prayer he had just learned. "Our Father who art in New Haven, how do you know my name?"

Without realizing it, this child asked doubt's most stubborn question. How does our divine Friend know our name? With all of New Haven to look after, that question seems not entirely out of order. Then add to that, the measure of our insignificance is not only New Haven, but also the whole world! But if God, in Christ, is our Friend, he does know our names. Everybody is somebody! The humblest life takes on a divine identity. Christ is present at every birth, at every baptism. Christ shares the loneliest life with every person who may sit in darkness. Life means something when Christ shares it. On the birth certificate signed at Bethlehem was your name along with that of Jesus, son of Joseph of Nazareth!

Doesn't this add a new dimension to your Friend's word, "And remember I am with you always, to the end of the age" (Matthew 28:20) and "I will never let go of you or desert you" (Hebrews 13:5 Goodspeed)?

I offer a final incident that sums up the central truth of the unfailing presence of our Divine Friend. It comes to us from Pastor John Short of Toronto. A young man was observed to enter a Roman Catholic church at lunch time and to kneel before the altar for a few moments and then to depart. That went on for quite some time. The priest's curiosity was stirred. One day he stopped the young man and asked him why he did it and why his devotions were so brief. The lad explained that he had to come during his lunch hour, and that he only had time for a very brief prayer before he reported back for duty. "What do you say?" asked the priest. "I say, 'Jesus, it's Jimmie,' " replied the lad. The priest was deeply moved. Some time later that same priest stood in a bedroom and, as the incident was reported, a "greater" than the priest was present. Jimmie hadn't many more days to spend in this world. The priest said he was certain as he stood there he heard a Voice saying, "Jimmie, it's Jesus." The unfailing, inescapable presence of Christ, our Friend! Who can ask for anything more? And yet there is more!

To the Father who provides for us and the Friend who loves and walks with us, our text adds a final gift: we have a brother and sister who need us. "Wherefore, if meat make my brother to offend, I will eat no flesh while the world standeth, lest I make my brother to offend" (v. 13 KJV). Without entering a discussion of meats offered to idols, we draw one clear conclusion from our text: each of us exerts an influence on other believers for good or for ill. They need us; they are God's gift to us. Our faithfulness to them is crucial. We must never lose sight of this.

Dr. William Barclay tells the story of Egerton Young, who first preached the gospel to the Indians in Saskatchewan. He found that the truth of the Fatherhood of God fascinated men and women who had hitherto seen God only in the thunder and lightning and the blast of the storm. An old chief said to Egerton, "Did I hear you say to God, 'Our Father'?" "You did," said Young. "God is your Father?" "Yes." "And," went on the chief, "is he also my Father?" "He certainly is," said Young. Suddenly the chief's face lit up with a new radiance. His hand reached out. "Then, you and I are brothers," he said, like a man making a dazzling discovery. To really discover that we are brother or sister to every other person is a dazzling discovery for anyone to make. But this is what our text asks of us.

As time permits, look about you this morning. Behold! These are your brothers; these are your sisters. Do you have a Father who provides for you? What need of your sister or brother can *you* provide? Do you have a Friend who walks beside you? Which one, close by you, needs a friend to stand with him/her in the storm? Can you conceive of the transformation that might occur in this congregation if each of us, including the one who speaks, were touched with the greatness of our need for one another? May the One who is both Friend and Brother of us all provide both inspiration and strength for us to demonstrate to all who observe us the same kind of compassion and brotherly affection that once prompted a pagan leader to say of the early Christians, "Behold how they love one another!"

Ralph Harlow expressed it beautifully when he wrote:

> *Who is so low that I am not his brother?*
> *Who is so high that I have no path to him?*
> *Who is so poor I may not feel his hunger?*
> *Who is so rich I may not pity him?*
>
> *Who is so hurt I may not know his heartache?*
> *Who sings for joy my heart may never share?*
> *Who in God's heaven has passed beyond my vision?*
> *Who in hell's depths where I may never fare?*
>
> *May none, then, call on me for understanding,*
> *May none, then, turn to me for help in pain,*
> *And drain alone his bitter cup of sorrow,*
> *Or find he knocks upon my heart in vain.*[2]

A final time I ask you, "Who can ask for anything more?" Amen.

---

1. *The Collected Poems of Walter de la Mare* (New York: Henry Holt and Co., 1920), p. 144.

2. Quoted in *Masterpieces of Religious Verse*, p. 465.

What Are You Going To Do With My World?

A friend tells of his son who asked for a globe of the world as one of his Christmas gifts last year. Of course his parents were pleased to purchase something so useful for their child. So many Christmas lists leave much to be desired! The boy thoroughly enjoyed his gift and kept it on a small table in his bedroom. One evening his parents were discussing the fact that so many of our clothing items are imported from foreign countries. The wife recalled that a recently purchased scarf had come from Sri Lanka. Neither of the parents could recall where Sri Lanka was located. The father, wanting to clear up the matter, went to the boy's room, picked up the globe and began to carry it out. As he was leaving he heard his son inquire, "Daddy, what are you going to do with my world?" The father explained briefly and continued on. In case you were wondering, they located Sri Lanka just off the southern coast of India. Later, when the father was alone, his son's words took on a more profound meaning, "Daddy, what are you going to do with my world?" Perhaps this is a question more of us parents ought to take to heart: what *are we going to do with our children's world?*

The New Testament describes the life of the writer of today's text; he was one who did something about his world. Acts chapter 17 records it for us. Paul and his friend Silas had come to Thessalonica, anxious to share the gospel with the people there. After a short time, one of the residents who was not pleased with what Paul was doing and saying complained to one of the local authorities, "These who have turned the world upside down have come to our city also." It was meant to vilify Paul and his companion, but it was actually a supreme compliment. Paul's message did turn lives upside down; to state it better, it turned lives right side up!

In our text for today, Paul explains his modus operandi for turning the world upside down. "I am made all things to all people, that I might by all means save some" (v. 22). The word "save" is the one I want to focus upon today. It has a much larger meaning in scripture than we usually assign to it. Our first thought is that it refers to our being freed from God's wrath; in other instances it refers to "wholeness" or restored health, as in the case of the woman mentioned in Matthew 9:20, where Jesus says, "Your faith has made you whole [saved you]." Our task today is to explore what Paul means by his word "save" and see how it relates to us in the year 2003.

To begin with, the word certainly suggests what we have been saved *from*. When we use the Word, we instinctively think of being saved from sin, or lostness, or punishment in a life to come. All of this is profoundly true. Sin is a reality. Life as we live it has eternal consequences. It would be folly to deny this; but we also need to be aware of what scripture means by the word "sin." Let's spend some time looking at that ugly word which we find so difficult, and sometimes infuriating, to understand: sin! What is it, this thing from which, we are told, Christ saves us? The Christian faith has always looked upon sin as something far more serious than a catalog of immoralities. You are cruel to your parents, you commit adultery, you steal money from the company where you work, you deliberately lie about something, you destroy your neighbor's property — these are sins. You are not to take them lightly. But our Christian faith is troubled by something more serious than these. It sees that humankind, made in the image of God, has willfully spoiled that image. So this is the essence of sin, that humankind, made in the image of God, has made itself into the kind of persons who can do the things we've just mentioned. And the list can go on and on. We have only to look at Jesus, the model man, to see the measure by which we have spoiled the image, the distance we have fallen from being the creatures God intended us to be. The closer we come to Christ, the more we understand the precious worth of a human soul with its capacity to respond to the love that is at the heart of all creation. And the more precious we discover life to be, the more terrible the fact of human sin becomes.

Robert Luccock offers an excellent analogy.[1] Suppose I hold a cup in my hand. At first glance it looks like any other cup — perhaps like one purchased at a local dollar store. If I were to drop it, the breakage would be unimportant. It would be just another broken cup. In other words, I do not take that cup very seriously. But suppose this cup were a piece of Limoges china, not easily replaced at any price. To anyone who knows and loves fine china, destroying that cup would be shocking. Why? Because of the value of what was broken. Now think of the souls of men and women like us in a way comparable to the way lovers of china would evaluate the Limoges cup in my hand. But now suppose *I deliberately smash the cup on the floor!* This is precisely what sin does. Not that I have broken the cup, but that I have broken the image of God in myself in the way that I broke the cup. This is what I mean by the terrible nature of what sin is and what sin does.

This breaking of the image of God disturbs us because through the love of Christ revealed at the cross, we know what a human soul is worth. Human souls are not manufactured and sold at some celestial Walmart! We were bought at a much greater price. Jesus Christ, born in Bethlehem, crucified under Pontius Pilate, and raised from the dead by the power of God can and does "save" us from the power of sin. Moreover, he offers us, in his Word and sacraments, the means by which every one of us may see that defaced image progressively restored to the usefulness and splendor it was meant to display. Dear people, never lose sight of the awesome power of the cross! There, as nowhere else, you behold not only Christ's matchless love but also your own personal worth in the sight of God. It has power to turn your world upside down!

But there is more than this to God's "saving" activity. Not only does God save us *from* something, God also saves us *for* something!

Once the saving grace of Christ enters the life of a person, he is a new person, life is turned upside down! That grace becomes in him, among other things, a loving concern for the needs of others. E. Stanley Jones tells how, when an epidemic swept though his district in India, he asked two Brahmin saints to leave their wayside meditations and join him in helping the diseased and dying. "We are holy men," they said, "we don't help anyone." Not so with one who is touched by the grace of Christ. He helps. He reaches out. He serves. He longs to share what he has found.

Return to our text again. In the short space of five sentences, Paul repeats four words no less than five times: "That I may win." These four words appear like a dominating theme of a great symphony. It is not only the dominating theme of the paragraph, it is the compelling theme, the high music of his whole life. No language is strong enough to describe it. He had found so much in Christ that he could not bear to have others live — and die — without it. Christ for him was life, pardon, peace, and power. Without Christ others did not really live, they merely existed. Historian H. G. Wells echoed the same conviction: "Until a man has found God, and has been found by him, he begins at no beginning and works to no end." Paul would have agreed, and we assent as well. Paul's passion was — and ours should be — "that by all means I may save some." Perhaps one or more may be saved from unbelief and eternal loss, but all will be saved *for* a life that has meaning and purpose, a life that has found the secret for facing life in the present and all that the future holds, as well! As one has put it, "We do not know what the future holds but we do know who holds the future."

> *I know not where the Islands lift, their fronded palms*
> *in air*
> *I only know I cannot drift beyond HIS love and care!*

And he is ours — and we are his! This truth the Christian finds too good to be kept for himself alone. It must be shared in one way or another.

What we are referring to is sometimes included in the term "evangelism." During the Epiphany season many congregations set aside a Sunday and designate it as Evangelism Sunday, Friendship Sunday, or Good News Sunday. This day provides members the opportunity for inviting unchurched neighbors and friends to visit their church. It is the hope and prayer of the congregation that Christ's love will so impress these guests that they will desire more. It also gives concerned members a taste of the joy that comes in sharing with another person the sense of fulfillment they have discovered in Christ. It is a thrilling moment when one person can take the hand of another and place it in the hand of God. The joy of reaching another is vividly put, in a medical setting, by psychiatrist Samuel Howe. He spent uncounted hours "fishing," so to speak, in the dark stream of blindness, deafness, and dumbness, hoping to bring a little girl, Laura Bridgman, to self-consciousness. He tells the story. "I worked patiently for three months without a 'nibble,' then there came a tug, and up came the soul of Laura Bridgman." "Up came the soul" — that's great fishing! A similar joy comes to those who reach out, in love, to bring a wandering friend to the lover of his soul. But what does one say in this happy encounter? How do we respond when an uncommitted friend asks, "What's so important about this thing called 'religion'?" Permit me to suggest a few sentences that we may use to provoke some interest and further discussion. "What is so important about religion? Quite frankly, Christ has changed my past, my present, and my future and he promises to do the same for each person who trusts him. Will you permit me to tell you why?"

Christ changes our *past*. That seems quite impossible at first, doesn't it? The past is a closed book. We have written what we have written. We wish we could change a few pages or even rip them out because they are not pleasant reading. All of us have what W. E. Orchard described as "those sad turned pages, which some chance wind of memory blows back again with shame." In a word, we are sinners. But God says to the human race: "Take my life. I give it to you. And hand your life over to me so I can carry your sin away." Here again we see the meaning of Christ's cross. There the matter was settled. There our past was cancelled out. There we stand forgiven.

Christ also changes our *present*. God says to each of us in effect, "Identify yourself with Christ, his life, death, and resurrection, and that will change everything." It will change your present circumstance because it will change you, make you a different person with a new mind and hence a new way of looking at life, new eyes that can see in all the old tasks and relationships hidden glimpses of loveliness and meaning. That brilliant soul Henry Thoreau once said: "How many a man has dated a new era in his life from the reading of a book." Indeed many have, but each Christian can affirm that he has dated a new era in his life when Christ was embraced as Savior and Friend.

Christ is also the One who changes our *future*. We said earlier, "But we know who holds the future." This becomes increasingly critical at that point in life when we sense that our time is running out. The past gets larger and the future gets smaller, like the sand in the top of an egg timer, until one day the last grain has dropped and none are left. What then of the future? At that point, the fact of Christ's victory over death becomes the most important fact in all human history. Here is the historical event of a man whose friends saw him after he was dead, because in him the power of death was impotent. It could not hold him. And he and he alone, says to us: "Because I live, you will live also" (John 14:18).

After World War II, during the Nuremberg war-crime trials, a witness appeared who had lived for a time in a Jewish cemetery in Poland. It was the only place where he and many others could hide after they had escaped from the gas chambers. During this time he wrote poetry, and in one poem described an unusual birth. In one of the graves, a young woman, assisted by an old gravedigger, gave birth to a baby. When the infant uttered his first cry, the old man prayed, "Great God, hast thou finally sent the Messiah to us? For who else than a Messiah can be born in a grave?" The old gravedigger spoke the truth in a larger sense than he realized. The Messiah, Christ, was born in a graveyard from which he came forth on Easter Day to fill the world with his presence and to assure an anxious world that death had been defeated forever! And if we are Christ's men and women, the grave is not the place of our death but the place of our birth. We don't die there; we are born there. Our future in eternity has begun.[2]

There you have it, dear people, our life, our sin, and our Savior. I wonder, can you begin to hear God asking, "What are you going to do with my world?" I can! Amen!

1. *The Power of His Name* (New York: Harper and Brothers, Publishers, 1960), p. 24.

2. For many of the final insights I am indebted to an unpublished message by A. Leonard Griffith; however the story of the Nuremberg Trial and the child born in a graveyard comes from a sermon by Paul Tillich, "Born in a Grave" found in his book *The Shaking of the Foundations.*

Congratulations, You've Made The Team!

Perhaps you remember, in high school or college, trying out for the varsity or junior varsity baseball, track, tennis, or football team. The competition was keen, you tried your level best, and finally the tryouts were concluded. A day or so later the bulletin board in the athletic department told the story. You stood there, and you read the list of those who made the team. Either your name was there or it was conspicuously absent. Joy or disappointment prevailed.

Saint Paul is speaking to each of us this morning and is saying without equivocation: "Congratulations, you've made the team; the race has already begun."

When did we make the team? In that defining moment when the sign of the cross was traced on our forehead and breast and our beloved pastor spoke the life-changing words: "I baptize you, in the Name of the Father and of the Son and of the Holy Spirit." At that gracious moment all that Christ accomplished for us in his life, death, and resurrection became ours. Camelot's "one brief shining moment" was nothing by comparison. Yes, you've made the team — and the race has begun.

Our first text, 1 Corinthians 9:24-27, is the bulletin board announcing we've made the team; our second text, Hebrews 12:1, 2, takes the next step and lays down training rules that guide us to the finish line. So let's begin, rulebook in hand. We mustn't let the team down!

Our first training rule tells us to *keep our memory alert*. "But what of ourselves? With all these witnesses to faith around us like a cloud ... let us run" (v. 1).

James Moffatt said that this section of scripture is one of the most moving passages of the New Testament, and in it we find a well-nigh-perfect summary of the Christian life. Here we see the Christian's inspiration as he enters life's race. We are asked to remember the cloud of witnesses who have run the race before us. These dear ones are witnesses in a two-fold sense, for they bear witness to their own faithfulness to Christ and they are now those who witness our performance. The Christian is like a runner in a crowded stadium. As he presses on, the crowd looks down, and the crowds who watch him are those who have already won the race. What an inspiration they are to each of us, and what a mark they have left on our lives. Emerson once wrote of Seneca, the Roman philosopher and statesman, "His thoughts are excellent if only he had the right to utter them." Words and life did not synchronize. Contrast this with Arthur Gossip who informs us that Principal John Cairns once wrote to his teacher, Sir William Hamilton, "I do not know what life or lives may lie before me. But this I know, that to the end of the last of them, I shall bear your salutary mark upon me." I'm quite certain it did. Perhaps this is also what Rudyard Kipling meant when he wrote of the inspiration he found whenever he thought of his mother.

> *If I were hanged on the highest hill,*
> *I know whose love would follow me still*
> *Mother o'mine, o mother o'mine!*
>
> *If I were drowned in the deepest sea,*
> *I know whose tears would come down to me*
> *Mother o'mine, o mother o'mine!*
>
> *If I were damned o'body and soul,*
> *I know whose prayers would make me whole,*
> *Mother o'mine, o mother o'mine!*[1]

How can we avoid the struggle for greatness when an audience like that is looking down on us, urging us on in the race? Indeed, we must *keep the memory alert.*

The second of our training rules reminds us to *keep the pace steady*: "And run with resolution the race in which we are entered" (v. 1).

Our pace is to be a measured one. It is to be with resolution, with patience or perseverance. Dr. William Barclay discusses the Greek word translated "resolution" and calls it "a manly virtue." He prefers to translate it "patience or endurance." It is not a patience that can sit down, bow its head, let things descend on it, and passively endure until the storm subsides. This patience does not follow the easy path. No Christian worth his salt, whatever his age, is to emulate the man who on his one-hundredth birthday was asked the secret of his longevity. "Just takin' the gifts of the Creator," he answered. "He made the night fer sleepin', the day fer restin'!" Nothing of the kind for the Christian athlete! His pace possesses a spirit that can accept life not simply with resignation, but with blazing hope. It is not a patience which grimly waits for the end, but the resolution that radiantly plans for the dawn.

The ancient saint Chrysostom called this patience or resolution the root of all that is good, the mother of piety, fruit that never withers, a fortress that is never taken, a harbor that knows no storms. Quite a word; quite a pace! George Matheson, who was stricken with blindness and disappointed in love, wrote a prayer in which he asks that he might accept the pace of life, which at times is troubling, "not with dumb resignation, but with holy joy; not only with the absence of murmur, but with a song of praise." Only a Christ-motivated "resolution" can enable a person to do that.

And isn't it also true that we soon discover that we not only have a *pace to keep* but also a pace-maker who *keeps us*! Christ himself is our companion in the race. His is a presence that is real, an influence that masters us and keeps us going. And as we travel patiently, we find in him a Friend to love, a cause to serve, a truth to believe in, and a loyalty to be true to. That is the pace that sustains us. Such is the life that wins.

The third training rule advises us to *keep our eyes on the goal*: "Keep our eyes fixed on Jesus, on whom faith depends from start to finish" (v. 2).

The King James version reads: "Looking unto Jesus, the Author and finisher of our faith."

Have you ever heard the word "archegos"? Does it sound like a foreign word for someone, or perhaps something, in the same family of words in which archangel or archbishop is found? Actually it is the English form of a fascinating Greek word. In the ancient world, many ships carried among their crews an exceptionally strong swimmer. If the ship were wrecked, this man would swim ashore, provided it was possible for a human swimmer to reach it. He would carry with him the end of a rope that he fastened to a solid object on shore. Then the others would follow the rope that guided them safely ashore. This man was called "archegos."

This honored name was given in the New Testament to Jesus. "Looking unto Jesus, the 'archegos' and perfector of our faith," says our text. Jesus was, to the early Christians, the strong swimmer who had crossed the tide from this world to the next, from earth to heaven, from things temporal to things eternal. It is through him and what he accomplished for us in his death and resurrection that we, too, may pass to safety.

A story is told of Arturo Toscanini and his rehearsal of the New York Philharmonic Orchestra. They were rehearsing Beethoven's Ninth Symphony. When the maestro judged that all were ready, he had them play the entire work without interruption. When the finale reached its stirring close, there was silence. "Who am I?" he asked. "Who is Toscanini? I am nobody. Beethoven — he is everything." In the realm of music, it is true. To the Christian, a similar question comes: Who am I? Who are you? We are nobody. Christ is everything!

And who is this Jesus Christ? He is our "archegos," the author of our faith, but he is much more. It is said that a man came to Whistler, the artist, and asked his help in hanging a new and beautiful painting. The man complained that he could not make the painting fit the room. Whistler, looking over the matter, said, "Sir, you're beginning at the wrong end. You can't make the painting fit the room. You will have to make the room fit the painting."

So when we carry into this modern world the picture of spiritual life that our Lord brought, we cannot make it fit the room. Put

100

it over against our private morals, our disintegrating family life, our economic systems, our international order, and it will not fit the room. We must change the room to fit the picture. That is serious business. Only Christ, our "archegos," the Master of life, can do it, one person at a time. When we keep our eyes on him, what we thought impossible is no longer so.

He is the difference! Just as he transformed and sustained the cloud of witnesses before us, he does the same for you and me as we travel toward the finish line.

But there is something more our text asks us to consider and keep ever before us. Not only is Christ the Author of our faith, he is also the finisher, the completer, of all that God has promised those who trust him.

Because of Christ we know how things will eventually work out. He and his truth will win in the end! As E. Stanley Jones put it so well, "The whole universe is on the side of Christ. Why? Because truth is stronger than falsehood, hope is stronger than fear, life is stronger than death, and Christ embodies them all."

Woodrow Wilson, past president of Princeton University, the twenty-eighth president of the United States, led his nation through the horrors of World War I. His shining achievement, his consuming passion, was to establish a League of Nations whose purpose was to see that another world war would never occur in his or any future generation. It is difficult to imagine Wilson's heartache when his own nation, the United States, voted against participation in his dream. On one occasion, when commenting on this disappointment, he said, "I would rather fail in a cause that will ultimately succeed, than succeed in a cause that will ultimately fail." In 1945, at San Francisco, Wilson's dream came true — the charter of the United Nations was signed by 51 nations. By the year 2000 their number had grown to 184.

In a way that far exceeds our wildest dreams, one day our Christ and his message of love will hold sway over the entire world. This is the confidence our scripture presents; this is the assurance every Christian affirms at his baptism: Love *never fails*: it has never and will never experience defeat in a moral universe!

In 1968 a church was being built in Honolulu. The architect asked the pastor to give him a text to be carved in the chancel over the altar. It was an interesting commission, for the architect said it must not contain more than eighteen letters. It was to present something of significance to people of many moods. The text must share the joy of Christmas, and be in harmony with the stern note of Good Friday. When Easter morning comes, it must still be true and luminous with the vision of eternity. Youth and middle-aged must understand its message of challenge and responsibility. When the old in age looked at the text, it should compel them to say, "Yes, that's so! I know, for life has proved it to me!" The inscription must have permanence in it, for the years may bring changes to a church that stands at the crossroads of the Orient and the Occident. And Christ's cross would be there where every eye would be drawn to it. There must be something ever old, ever new, eternal about it. So with these varying needs and the requirement of permanence in mind, the pastor chose the text: "Love never faileth." And there it stands, high above the altar, where all who lift their eyes may read.

Love never fails. The love Christ revealed at the cross is eternal. And beyond that, the love you have given, and continue to give, is eternal, for it is linked with the One who is love incarnate. The love you give to others is not lost. It will meet you again one day. The love you give to Christ is not lost. It binds you to him in bonds that nothing can break. Even beyond death, love goes on loving, for love never fails. There was something inherently appropriate about Dr. Charles Kingsley's request that three Latin words be engraved on the headstone which marked the place where he and his wife are now buried: "Amivimus, Amamus, Amibimus. We *have loved*, we *love*, we *shall love!*" Thank God this is true! So, dear people keep your eyes on the goal. The victory is assured because the Victor is yours! Congratulations, you've made the team! Amen.

---

1. Quoted in *Masterpieces of Religious Verse*, p. 339.

Epiphany 7
Ordinary Time 7
2 Corinthians 1:18-22

The Answer Waiting For A Question

A number of years ago some Christians placed bumper stickers on their vehicles stating, "Christ is the answer." After some time a wiseacre started displaying a sticker that read, "If Christ is the answer, what is the question?" Of course this made a hilarious impression on those who seem to have "three sneers for everything and three cheers for nothing."

As we consider our text for today we discover God telling us that "Christ *is* the answer"; he is the eternal "yes" to all the promises of God, and the final answer to all the questions man can propose. Verse 20 affirms, "For all the promises of God, he supplies the yes that confirms them."

What are the insistent questions that haunt the thinking person as he seeks to find his place in life and to discover his role in it. Rolla May has suggested that the critical questions are these: Who am I? Why am I here? And where am I going? It is the Christian's conviction that only Christ can answer them adequately. Let's think about them this morning.

The first question that confronts us is: "Can I know who I am?" To this our text responds, "Christ is the answer, for he is God's yes to all that confounds you." But the supreme problem that faces the person who lives apart from Christ rests right here. He doesn't know who he is.

In Arthur Miller's excellent play, *The Death of a Salesman,* the leading character is Willie Lohman, a philandering salesman. Willie has two sons. Biff, one of the sons, speaks up in a dramatic scene, saying, "All that I want is out there waiting for me the minute

103

I say I know who I am." After Willie has been discovered by his sons in an adulterous relationship, he becomes terribly depressed and finally takes his own life. The last scene finds the family gathered at Willie's grave. Again Biff speaks up and says concerning his father, "He had the wrong dreams — he never knew who he was!"

And this — I repeat — is the tragic situation in which the person who lives apart from Christ finds himself: he never really comes to know who he is. Not so with the Christian — he knows! Listen to Saint John as he writes in 1 John 3:1, "See what love the Father has given us that we should be called children of God and *that is what we are.*" In verse 2 of the same chapter, he says, "Beloved, we *are* God's children *now*." With all the confidence he can muster, the Christian says: "At the heart of this universe beats the heart of its Creator-God, and I am his child. I belong to him because he made me, and also because he bought me back at the cost of his own life." You may recall the story I told several weeks ago about the boy and his boat — he made it, then lost it, then bought it back again. In a similar manner, Christ stands and says to each of us today, "This is who you are — you are mine! Your wandering and wondering are over. You are mine because I made you and you are mine because I bought you back at the cost of my life on a cross.

Can I know who I am? The Christian answers, "Yes, I am his."

> *I heard the voice of Jesus say, "Come unto me and rest,*
> *Lay down, o weary one, lay down, thy head upon my*
> *   breast."*
> *I came to Jesus, as I was, weary and worn and sad;*
> *I found in him a resting-place, and he has made me*
> *   glad.*

And with his gift of gladness, he tells me who I am. I need never be puzzled again.

The second question we encounter asks, "Can I know why I am here?" And once more the One who is God's "Yes" assures us that we can.

About thirty years ago one of the popular Country Western hit songs was titled, "Please, Mr. Custer, I Don't Wanna Go." It was an amusing ballad and many found it delightful listening. The ballad told the story of a poor army soldier who had a premonition of impending doom and who wanted to be left at camp instead of going with the foolhardy General George Custer as he was about to start on that campaign that ended in his famous "last stand." Again and again we hear the soldier say, "Please, Mr. Custer, I don't wanna go." But, of course, he *has* to go! In time the Indians surround the regiment, arrows begin to fly wildly about, and many of his friends are being killed. In the midst of all this confusion, our poor private cries out pleadingly, "What am I doing here?" It was an amusing ballad; I'd love to hear it again, but it asks the question that haunts every person who seeks to live apart from Christ, "What *am* I doing here? Is there any rhyme, reason, or purpose in my living?" How tragic it must be to find oneself in a world like this and not to know why on earth we are here. How often we have heard people say words similar to those. Heard them expressed in the lives these persons were living, for lives speak more clearly than many are honest enough to admit. Recall Emerson's precept, "Your life speaks so loudly I cannot hear what you say." Look about you. Observe the unfaithful wife, the philandering husband, the dishonest businessman, the irresponsible worker in factory or office, the young person who feels that life is "just one big blast." What are their lives saying? They are asking, almost shouting, "What am I doing here?" Or to use Burt Bacharach's words, "What's it all about, Alfie?"

Into this distressing milieu of meaninglessness, nihilism, nothingness, and purposelessness comes the answer of Christ to every Christian man and woman: "For this cause were you born and for this cause you came into this world, to bear witness to the Truth." You are here to love the truth, to live the truth, to share the truth; to get your eyes off yourself and recognize that you are here to invest your life in the common good of the human race. You are here not to be part of the world's problems. God knows we have enough of them already. You are here to be part of the answer to life's miseries. And the Christ who lives within you *is* the answer! John Oxenham put it so well:

> *But once I pass this way, and then no more.*
> *But once, and then the silent door swings on its hinges,*
> *Opens, closes, and no more I pass this way.*
> *So while I may, I will assay*
> *Sweet comfort and delight to all I meet along the pil-*
>   *grim way.*
> *For no man passes twice the great highway*
> *That climbs through darkness up to light,*
> *Through night, to day!*[1]

A third, and final, question faces the thinking person: "Can I know where I am going?" And once again Christ answers decisively, "Yes!" And where is the Christian going? He's going home, home to his Father's house. Jesus said, "In my Father's house there are many dwelling places. If it were not so, would I have told you that I go to prepare a place for you? And if I go and prepare a place for you, I will come again and take you to myself, so that where I am you, there you may be also" (John 14:1-3). "In a little while the world will no longer see me, but you will see me; because I live [because I will conquer death for you!], you also will live" (John 14:19). Going home! Sounds old-fashioned, doesn't it? Otherworldly? Unrealistic? But the Christian gains his unruffled certainty from the Word of Christ. He said it. I believe it. That settles it! This is the Word of the Prince of Life who endured the worst that death could hurl at him and walked out of the tomb on Easter morning as death's *Victor* not its *Victim.* What confidence this inspires in all who look at life with eyes of faith.

The novel *The Road* tells of an ex-officer who in any crisis, when life seemed to be so twisted by evil, so mean and crushed by misfortune, that it looked as though it could not be retrieved, always recalled himself and others, and rallied them with the words, "Christ is risen, Christ is risen." This idea he kept repeating in desperate moments as a guarantee of recovery and victory. For Christ's resurrection is God's power for repair available to all broken lives and all hearts fearful and anxious about what lies ahead.

"Be not anxious," said Christ to his own. The thing that redeems those words from being mere hollow advice is this: the One who spoke them was the One who also said, "I am the resurrection and the Life." And he was the One who rose victorious over sin, death, and despair. Nothing less than this "blessed assurance" could cause John Donne to write his defiant challenge:

> *Death, be not proud, though some have called thee*
> *Mighty and dreadful, for thou art not so:*
> *For those whom thou think'st thou dost overthrow*
> *Die not, poor death; nor can'st thou kill me ...*
> *One short sleep past, we wake eternally,*
> *And death shall be no more: Death, thou shalt die!*[2]

Those of you who are familiar with the Boy Scout movement will perhaps recall the name Sir Robert Baden-Powell. Sir Robert served with distinction in the British army and was the founder of the Boy Scout movement in Great Britain. In 1908 he brought the movement to the United States. Because of his work among young people of both nations, he received countless honors. When Sir Robert died in 1941, Winston Churchill offered to have him buried with other notables in Westminster Abbey. His children declined this honor, saying that they felt their father would have preferred to be buried next to his wife. In a quiet cemetery he now rests, a small gravestone marking the spot. On the gravestone one can read simply his name, the dates of his birth and death, and, underneath, a small symbol understood by those who have been Scouts. The symbol is used by Scouts who break camp to inform their comrades where they have gone and where they might meet again. The symbol means simply, "I have gone home." The Christian knows exactly what Sir Robert meant, for that is his destination as well: he is going home, home to his father's house.

A pastor friend tells of standing in a quiet cemetery behind his first parish, in a small town in Illinois. With him there were two others, a heartbroken father and a funeral director holding a small white casket containing the remains of an infant boy. The little child, a firstborn, had died only a few hours after birth. The mother was still hospitalized, too weak to attend the short service. The pastor read Jesus' words: "In my Father's house are many dwelling places," along with other comforting passages from the New Testament that speak of our reunion with loved ones who have gone on before us. When the brief service ended, the young father put his arms around the pastor and said, "Pastor, if it were not for the words you have just read, I think I would lose my mind."

I beg you, dear people, every time you think of death and parting and the losing of those beloved faces of your loved ones, get down on your knees and thank God for Jesus Christ! For he has shown you death defeated and parting ended and you and your loved ones reunited in God's heaven — the Father's house.

> *O blessed hope! With this elate,*
> *Let not our hearts be desolate,*
> *But strong in faith, with patience wait,*
> *Until He comes!*

Christ, our Lord, the answer waiting for a question. He tells us who we are, why we are here, and where we are going!

Let's trust him, always. Amen.

---

1. "The Pilgrim Way," quoted in *Selected Poems of John Oxenham* (New York: Harper and Brothers, 1948), p. 47.

2. "Holy Sonnets," quoted in *Masterpieces of Religious Verse*, p. 617.

What A Resumé!

If you were to visit the Library of Congress and look up Jesus of Nazareth in the card catalog of authors, you will not find a single entry. Thousands of books have been written about Jesus, but he himself wrote no books, not even a pamphlet or tract. He was able to write, we know. When a woman accused of adultery was brought to him, Jesus "bent down and started to write on the ground with his finger" (John 8:5). Giovanni Papini suggested that he chose the sand on which to write "expressly that the wind might carry away the words." Our Lord wrote his words of truth on material more permanent than parchment or paper; he wrote his message on human hearts. This is what our text is saying to us this morning. Christ is still active in the life and ministry of his servants, writing as clearly as possible, what he has done and intends to do in the lives of his people, the Church. What a resumé that would be! Where can we find it?

What a challenge it has been to search one's memory and a Bible concordance to discover these parts of scripture that might provide the information needed for such a descriptive resumé. But I believe I found it — of all places — in a hymnal! Let me explain. Some of our Christian friends who follow a more detailed liturgical worship experience include a weekly "introit" as part of each service of worship. While thumbing through a hymnal containing the introits for the Epiphany season, I noted that Epiphany 2 provides an introit that uses Psalm 40 as its theme. As I read the introit, I mused, "Here it is; Psalm 40 presents one of the clearest and most complete resumés of Christian experience that one can find anywhere." Let me share the resumé with you this morning. I hope as we move along, the resumé will become more and more familiar. In fact, some, if not all of us, may be constrained to say: "That has been my experience! That closely resembles my resumé!" Listen as the scripture unfolds it.

To begin with, the psalm suggests that the Christian is one who has been *brought up*. "He brought me up also out of an horrible pit" (Psalm 40:1). The phrase "an horrible pit" in the Hebrew language means literally, "a pit of noise." How very well this describes a person before he has committed himself to Christ. He or she exists in the noise of spiritual death, of unbelief, of utter frustration and meaninglessness. Something akin to this is seen in Macbeth, who, after the death of his wife with whom he had treacherously murdered King Duncan, cries, "Out, out brief candle! Life's but a walking shadow, a poor player that struts and frets his hour on the stage and then is heard no more. Life is a tale told by an idiot, full of sound and fury — signifying *nothing!*" Omar Khayyam echoes the same litany of hopelessness when he says, "The sun is setting, the caravan is starting for the goal of *nothing!*"

Thank God we were *brought up* out of that pathetic "pit of noise" in the defining moment when those precious words were spoken over us, "I baptize you, in the Name of the Father and of the Son and of the Holy Spirit."

If you have attended a symphony orchestra concert, you will recall seeing the various members of the orchestra entering the stage before the concert began. They began to tune their instruments each in his or her own way. The noise, at times, was deafening, a cacophony of thirty or forty instruments sounding a different note all at the same time! Then, suddenly the maestro appeared and walked to the podium. He tapped his baton several times and there was complete silence. Then his hands moved and the music began. What a difference the presence of the maestro made!

> 'Twas battered and scarred and the auctioneer thought
> it scarcely worth his while
> To waste much time on the old violin, but he held it up
> with the bow.

"What am I bidden, good folks?" said he. "Who'll start
the bidding for me?
A dollar, a dollar, now two, only two. Two dollars and
who'll make it three?
Three dollars once, three dollars twice, going for three"
— but no!
From the room far back a grey-haired man came for-
ward and picked up the bow,
Then wiping the dust from the old violin and tightening
up all the strings,
He played a melody pure and sweet, as sweet as an
angel sings.
The music ceased and the auctioneer with a voice that
was quiet and low,
Said, "What am I bid for the old violin?" and held it up
with the bow.
"One thousand dollars and who'll make it two? Two
thousand and who'll make it three?
Three thousand once and Three thousand twice and
going and gone," said he.
The people cheered, but some of them cried, "We do
not quite understand
What changed it's worth?" The man replied, "The touch
of the master's hand."
And many a person with life out of tune, and battered
and torn with sin,
Is auctioned cheap to a thoughtless crowd, much like
the old violin.
A mess of pottage, another drink, a game — and he
travels on.
He's going once and going twice, he's going and al-
most gone!
But the Master comes. And the foolish crowd never can
quite understand
The worth of a soul and the change that's wrought, by
the touch of the Master's hand![1]

How wonderful it is that our lives have been touched by our
Lord's nail-pierced hand. He has brought us up out of a pit of

meaninglessness into the radiance of a life filled with purpose and meaning! What a resumé!

The resumé continues: not only has he brought us up, he has also *set us up.* "He set my feet upon a rock and established my goings" (v. 2). After he has brought us up, he doesn't leave us to find our way alone. My dear friend, this same Lord has a specific plan for your life, a plan that was prepared before you took your first breath. Listen to his Word as it speaks clearly about this awesome provision. "For we are his workmanship, created in Christ Jesus to do good works, which God *prepared in advance* for us to do" (Ephesians 2:10 NIV). Is this difficult for you to imagine? Me, insignificant me, a person for whom God has a special plan and purpose? Even before I was born? Hard to accept at times, isn't it? But listen. Perhaps today the winter winds will blow and snow will begin to fall and cover the earth. If you were to stand outside as the snow is falling you might catch a few flakes on your outstretched hand, but in a moment they would be reduced to simple drops of water. But if you were to go outside with a powerful microscope, allow ten or more flakes to fall on a cold glass slide, then view them under the microscope, you would discover something quite interesting. Every snowflake would have a pattern different from all the rest. Not one would be exactly like another. My dear fellow Christian, do you for one moment believe that the Almighty God who created the heavens, the earth, and everything that exists would have a unique plan for each snowflake that is here for a moment and gone the next and not have a plan for your life and mine, lives that Christ has redeemed at the cost of his own life? Preposterous!

But someone says, "What can one person like me do? I feel so inadequate, so insignificant at times." I'll tell you what you can do. You can live *one Christian life!* And as you do, the next step will be made crystal clear. God will see to it. Read and ponder the promise in Proverbs 3:5, 6. It is worthy of being memorized. "Trust in the Lord with all your heart, lean not unto your own understanding. In all your ways acknowledge him and he will direct your paths." That is his Word; it is meant for you!

Not only has he brought us up and set us up, but our resumé continues; he has also *tuned us up!* "He has put a new song into my mouth, even praise unto my God, many shall see it and trust in the Lord" (v. 3). This is the final entry in our resumé, as Dr. Guy King once expressed it, "Out of the mire into the choir!"

And what is the result of that new song? Many shall see it and trust in the Lord. Have you ever *seen* a song? I've heard many songs, so have you. But *seen* a song, that is something quite new. Well, dear ones, I *have* seen that new song! It is the expression of the presence and nearness of Jesus *seen* when one person who has great need is touched in love by another who is living the new baptized life in Christ. That's the new song, and you and I have seen it many times. An old Vacation Bible School chorus had us sing, "Let the beauty of Jesus be seen in me; all his wonderful passion and purity. Oh, Thou Spirit divine, cleanse this nature of mine. Let the beauty of Jesus be seen in me!" This is the *new song* — the song of the new life in Christ — seen and expressed in your life and mine.

Let me close with a story and two brief quotes.

In 1910, a medical school graduate was encouraged by his loved ones to begin a family practice in Queens, New York, a venture certain to bring him a measure of wealth and success. But somehow he felt that he was needed in a more meaningful medical practice. He approached his pastor and was directed to contact the mission board of the Evangelical Lutheran Church. There he was presented with the challenge of going to a mission field to establish a hospital and begin a missionary outreach in that land. He accepted the challenge, went abroad, and in about ten years had established a much needed hospital and, aided by other missionaries, began preaching and teaching ministries in about twenty villages in the area. One day while traveling to one of the villages he noticed a little boy sitting against a tree. He stopped his Model-T Ford and went over to check the child. It was obvious that the child was desperately ill. The child's family, who felt that he possessed an evil spirit and was a danger to the rest of the family, had probably abandoned him. The missionary took the boy back to the hospital and began to treat him. At first he thought he was going to lose the child, but finally he began to improve. When the boy was completely well, the doctor told him he was going to return him to his family, but before he did he wanted to tell him about someone very wonderful. He told him of the Lord Jesus, of his love, how he healed the sick and did all that he could to bring happiness into the lives of all he met. The doctor concluded by asking, "Wouldn't you like to know him and trust him?" The little fellow replied, "I do know him." "You do?" asked the doctor. "Yes," responded the boy, "I do know him; *you* are Jesus!" This faithful servant had so beautifully expressed the new song of the new life in Christ that the boy actually thought he was Jesus. I wonder what others think of us?

Now two brief quotes. The first is from Martin Luther. "Christ for every person and every person a Christ to his neighbor." Think about it for a few minutes. Christ is *for* you, dear friend. He was for you in your baptism; he was for you at the cross — as he gave his life to redeem you. He will be for you when you walk through the valley of the shadow of death. You will not walk alone! He is for you! But there is another side to the coin, "And every person a Christ to his neighbor."

Men, what are we to be to our wives and children? That swashbuckling macho-man who demands his way and will get it no matter what it costs? No, we are to be a Christ to these precious gifts of God. Wives, what are you to be to your husbands? What are you children to be to your beloved parents and brothers and sisters? You are to be a Christ to them. Something to think about, isn't it?

The final quote comes from Phillips Brooks, the author of "O Little Town Of Bethlehem." "Be such a person, live such a life, that if everyone were such as you and every life a life like yours, this world would be a paradise." Can you think of a more beautiful desire than this? Is it any wonder that some hymnals include the inspiring hymn that has us sing:

> O master let me walk with thee, in lowly paths of service free;
> Tell me thy secret, help me bear, the strain of toil the fret of care.
>
> Help me the slow of heart to move, by some clear winning word of love;

Teach me the wayward feet to stay, and guide them in
the homeward way.

In hope that sends a shining ray, far down the future's
broadening way;
In peace that only thou canst give, with thee, O Master,
let me live.[2]

He has brought us up, set us up, and tuned us up. What a resumé!
Dear Christian friend, this is your life! Amen.

---

1. Author unknown.

2. Washington Gladden.

**Transfiguration Of The Lord
(Last Sunday After Epiphany)
2 Corinthians 4:3-6**

The Face That Launched
A Thousand Lives

You will recall the ancient myth that lies behind our sermon theme for today. Helen, the wife of Sparta's king Menelaus, was acclaimed the most beautiful woman of Greece. The Greeks fought the Trojan War in order to get her back from Troy, where Paris, the son of King Priam, had taken her. In Christopher Marlowe's *Dr. Faustus*, the question is asked concerning Helen, "Was this the face that launched a thousand ships and burned the topless towers of Ilium?" Today's text speaks of a far greater face, a face that launched a thousand, perhaps ten thousand times ten thousand, lives into an experience that beggars description. It is, of course, the face of Christ, our Lord. Verse 5 describes it for us, "For the same God who said, out of darkness let light shine, has caused his light to shine within us to give the light of revelation — the revelation of the glory of God in the face of Jesus Christ." What would we not give for one look at the face of Jesus? No face in all history has evoked so much human interest. The physical contour of that face we cannot determine for certain, but its actual features mean little compared with the divine life that was expressed through it.

The Gospel writers have given us several pen portraits of Jesus' face which tell us more of him than any physical likeness can do. If it is true that the soul shines through the face, these portraits will be worth considering for these moments today.

The first portrait shows us Christ bearing a *divine* countenance. Our text explains that in the face of Jesus we also see the glory of Almighty God himself. In the Gospel lesson for today we find Jesus transfigured before his disciples. "And the appearance of his face

117

changed" (Luke 9:29). Matthew describes it: "And his face shone like the sun" (17:2). For those few dazzling moments, God's presence was not only felt, it was seen. What a moment! How we wish we were there! No wonder Peter wanted to remain on the mount.

A little girl, who was afraid to go to sleep in the dark, wanted her mother to stay with her. Her mother told her God would be with her, so she did not need to be afraid. "Yes, I know, Mama," the girl said, "but I want someone with a face." The message of our text, the message of Advent, Christmas, and Epiphany is just that. The gift of Christ to us is Emmanuel — "God with us." Jesus is "God with a face," a face turned toward us in love and good will.

Recall the remarkable answer Christ gave when Philip requested, "Lord, show us the Father, and we will be satisfied." Jesus responded, "Have I been with you all this time, Philip, and you still do not know me? Whoever has seen me has seen the Father" (John 14:8, 9). In essence he was saying, "If you want to see God, look at my face. All that you ever need to know about God, and all of life, you will find in me." Look again, Philip, look again!

In one of her poems, Elizabeth Browning describes how someone was pressed and baffled with hard questions until she could find no answer except this: "Look at my face and see." How does Christ answer our perplexed questions about ourselves, our companions along the way, and the meaning of this world and the mystery of the world to come? How does he make our doubts depart — those gloomy thoughts that rise up and haunt us in lonely sorrowful hours, when we wonder if any duty is certain and whether any sacrifice is worthwhile? Our Lord does not respond by giving us definitions or explanations. He simply confronts us with himself. He says, in effect, "Look at my face and see."

The other Browning, Elizabeth's beloved Robert, in his poem "Dramatis Personae," sets before us three speakers. King David speaks first and describes the glory of the Temple service, with the people singing repeatedly, "Rejoice in God, whose mercy endures forever." Renan, the French skeptic, speaks next. From his pensive point of view he describes the vanished figure of the God-man, the friend of man, and says, "We are orphans." Then Browning speaks and declares:

That one Face, far from vanished, rather grows,
Or decomposes but to recompose,
Become my universe that feels and knows.[1]

Who could put it more eloquently? Christ has become our universe. It is he who makes us feel and know and understand. While being interviewed in Hamburg, Germany, Helmut Thielike spoke of the Christian response to the grandeur of Jesus. "Once it happened. Once in the world's history it happened, that someone came forward with the claim that he was the Son of God, and with the assertion, 'I and the Father are one.' He proved the legitimacy of that claim through the depths to which he descended. A Son of God who defends his title with the argument that he is the brother of even the poorest and the guilty and takes their burden upon himself. This is a fact one can only note and shake one's head in unbelief — or one must worship and adore. I must worship." And so must we.

We find a second portrait in Saint Luke's Gospel, chapter 9. "As the time approached for him to be taken up to heaven, Jesus resolutely set out for Jerusalem" (Luke 9:51). Here we discover the *determined face.*

The time had come; he had a task to complete; it could only be done outside Jerusalem on a hill called Calvary. So the determined face of Jesus turned toward the City of Peace to accomplish on a Roman cross what no other had the right — or the ability — to achieve: forgiveness for the accumulated guilt of the human race. The old hymn put it well:

> *There was no other good enough, to pay the price of*
> *sin,*
> *He only could unlock the door of heav'n and let us in.*

Mark Twain wrote a short story bearing the interesting title, "The Terrible Catastrophe." Before he had finished, he had worked his characters into such a predicament that whatever any one of them did would destroy them all. Reflecting on his creation, he concluded by saying, "I have these characters in such a fix I cannot get them out. Anyone who thinks he can is welcome to try!" That may be an unusual literary device for ending a story, but it is not unfamiliar to anyone who takes a sober look at the human race, especially after watching the evening news. We have, by our stubborn willfulness, so marred the image of God in which we were created that only God himself can make things right. God's way is simple, but painful and costly: forgiveness, by way of a cross.

Eugene O'Neill expressed this truth in his play *Days Without End*. John Loving has been unfaithful to his wife Elsa, and the discovery of his infidelity has so shocked her that she lies close to death in a crisis of delirium. Seeing the result of his sin, John's cynical composure is shattered until he is distraught with remorse and shame. But he cannot forgive himself, and he cannot make it right with Elsa. Finally as the crisis approaches, a priest tells John to go to the church and pray there, asking God's forgiveness. This John wants to do, but he can't; if only God would show him that his love exists, then he would believe. But the priest tells him that he cannot bargain with God. Only by seeking God's grace at the foot of the cross will he find faith and love. At last John is able to find the presence of love coming through his prayer, as he says, "Ah, thou hast heard me at last. Thou hast not forsaken me! Thou hast always loved me! I am forgiven! I can forgive myself — through thee. I can believe! At last I see! I have always loved. O Lord of love, forgive thy blind fool! Thou art the Way, the Truth — the Resurrection and the Life, and he that believeth in thy love, his love shall never die."

For John and Elsa, only when love has had the final word could there be a new creation of their own love. But playwright O'Neill sees here a further aspect of the entire picture. This love must come from a source outside themselves. "The wages of sin is death, but the gift of God is eternal life through Jesus Christ, our Lord." Elsa's forgiveness was from God; John received it through the grace of Jesus Christ. And how does it come to us today? It comes to us as it came to John Loving and as it has greeted men and women across the Christian ages: through the cross. There, God himself faced the blank wall of sin, evil, and rejection, but spoke a final word of love and opened the way for forgiveness and a new life for all.

And wasn't that what Christian, in that old classic *Pilgrim's Progress*, also discovered? As he journeyed toward the Celestial City, he came to a place fenced on either side by a wall. Christian ran, but not without difficulty, because of the burden on his back. He came to a rise and there stood a cross and below it a sepulcher. Just as he came to the cross, the burden fell from his back and tumbled into the mouth of the sepulcher. With a grateful heart, Christian said, "He has given me rest by his sorrow, and life by his death." Then he went on his way singing:

> *How far did I come laden with my sin:*
> *Nothing could ease the grief I was in,*
> *Until I came here: what a place is this!*
> *Can this be the beginning of my bliss?*
> *Is this where the burden falls from my back?*
> *Can this be where the ropes of bondage crack?*
> *Bless'd cross! Bless'd sepulcher! Blessed rather be*
> *The Man who there was put to shame for me!*[2]

What would we do, where would we be, if it were not for the Face of the One who resolutely walked toward Jerusalem that day so long ago?

A final portrait emerges as we read the first chapter of John's Gospel. Here we discover the *discerning face*.

Reading the chapter we meet Andrew who is captured by Christ's vitality and message; he finds his brother Simon and brings him to Jesus. When Simon is face to face with him, Jesus says, "Thou art Simon, the son of Jona; thou shalt be Cephas," or Peter (John 1:42). Note the words, "thou *art*; thou *shalt be*." The discerning Christ sees each one as he is, but he also knows what each one shall become, what role each must fulfil in the purpose of God. This truth just as certainly applies to all who are gathered in this church today!

It was three years later, after the tragedy of Good Friday and the triumph of Easter, that Peter and the others began to see their task through the eyes of their discerning Lord. They were to be witnesses! Witnesses of what? Witnesses to the love of God revealed in Christ's passion. Witnesses to the fact that in God's sight everybody is somebody. Every life is important; not one is expendable. We were made for God and for each other, and we find our true selves and each other in the community of those who love him.

How our world-weary companions need to hear this message. Some things, we say, are too good to be true. These tidings are too good *not* to be true! But how difficult it is for some to believe us. Some will say, "There cannot be a God of love, because if there were, and he looked at this world, his heart would break." The Christian points to the cross and says, "*There* his heart *did* break." Another will say, "It is God who made the world. It is God who is responsible; it is he who should bear the load." Again we point to the cross and say, "*There*, yes *there*, he did bear the load. Believe it, he loved you *that much!*" What news! It is too good to be kept only for ourselves. It must be shouted from the rooftops! Is it any wonder when Dr. Karl Barth, perhaps the greatest theologian of the twentieth century, was asked, "Dr. Barth, what is the most profound thought that has ever entered your mind?" He responded without hesitation, "Jesus loves me this I know, for the Bible tells me so."

A pastor friend was greeting his congregation at the close of a morning service. One young woman, after shaking his hand, drew closer and said softly, "Please keep telling us how very much we mean to God; it has *changed my life!*" Yes, and it will keep changing the lives of any who will believe it, so we keep on sharing. Without question, it is the most important news our world has ever heard!

This is the message brought to us by the "face that launched a thousand lives." It is ours to hear, to believe, and to share with any who will lend a listening ear.

I can't think of any finer words with which to conclude our Epiphany season than those penned by Charles Wesley in 1772:

> Love divine, all love excelling, joy of heav'n to earth
> come down!
> Fix in us thy humble dwelling, all thy faithful mercies
> crown.

Jesus, thou art all compassion, pure unbounded love
thou art;
Visit us with thy salvation, enter every trembling heart.

Amen.

---

1. "Epilogue: Dramatis Personae," quoted in *Masterpieces of Religious Verse*, p. 135.

2. John Bunyan, *The Pilgrim's Progress* (New York: Rand, McNally and Company, 1923), p. 104.

Sermons On The Second Readings

For Sundays In
Lent And Easter

Paul E. Robinson

To my first grandson
Marc André Christophe Randy,
Whose young life and total dependence
On caring parents
(and grandparents)
Remind me of me
And my dependence on others
And on God's love and amazing grace
Revealed in Jesus Christ.

Foreword

Paul Robinson has written thought-provoking and action-provoking sermons covering the Lenten and Easter seasons. His warmhearted style is earthy in that it not only allows, but also encourages a realistic look at life. In the sermons we are invited to consider the meaning of God's self-revelation in Jesus and what that means in view of the pains and distresses of ordinary life. We are reminded that persons of all ages face dilemmas and fears and long for a Power and Presence that will keep them going.

As Mr. Robinson leads us to consider our encounter with the Divine, he lovingly takes us all (children, youth, members of young families, mid-lifers, and older persons) by the hand as we look at our lives and at God. His earthy images include grandfathers (he recently became one), playing ball, bird nests, spider webs, BASE jumping, space images (if one calls that earthy), relay races, and many more. His style is also heavenly in that he points us beyond ourselves and our personal resources to divine help from God who is revealed in Jesus.

Mr. Robinson's sermons are filled with illustrations and biblical interpretations which are easy to understand and apply. With touches of humor and gentle persuasion he leads us to look at the power of a great truth. As one might look at a truly great piece of architecture, he invites his readers and listeners to consider the truth and power of the Gospel by looking at it inside and outside from many different angles. The wonder of the invitation and exploration is that I feel he is holding my hand and the hands of young and old as we dare to take another look at our lives and the God who gave them.

This series of sermons begins with a challenge that during Lent we consider what "Job #1" is for us. The series ends with a challenge that we become "BASE jumpers," as we courageously take chances in living a God-directed life.

The Rev. James A. Lange
Pastor Emeritus
Trinity United Methodist Church
Grand Island, New York

Introduction

I have book shelves lined with books, read and unread. I have books and magazines lying in all sorts of places around the house and in my study at church. I have books sitting on the back seat of my car, on top of my computer desk, underneath my desk at church, in my brief case. I even have books that are lost, given one day to an eager reader or accidentally left on a stack of newspapers in an airport while buying a bottle of water for the journey.

To think that I am just one more person seeking to use the miracle of the invention of movable type (now movable bits and bytes) to communicate a message! I find myself wondering where this collection of thoughts and ideas and illustrations will end up someday. Perhaps, it will end up like a stack of shiny, new books I purchased two Pastor's Schools ago. They look like great books ... but I still haven't gotten around to reading them yet.

Or maybe this book will be used in years hence to lift upward a bit a slide projector at a family night program during Lent.

What I really hope is that these sermons, intended for a particular congregation at a particular time, might in fact give the reader an upward lift, either to cast new light on our treasured "old, old story," or to provide a hungry, hard-working preacher an illustration or reflection that nudges the sermon preparation along a bit, to feed his or her own flock in another setting,

My hope and prayer is that I have rightly divided the Word of Truth. If I have, then you will be blessed by the very Presence of Almighty God. If I have not, then you'd better leave what you have in your hands on a pile of newspapers somewhere, or just stick it under a slide projector.

However effective this collection of sermons may be in communicating God's amazing grace in Jesus Christ revealed in the tumultuous, agonizing, and exhilarating pre- and post-Easter scriptures, the effort to do so has surely had more impact on the writer than the words ever could have on the listener or reader. For that I am grateful.

Paul E. Robinson
Grand Island, New York
August, 2001

What It Takes To Do The Job

What is Job #1 in your life? We know what it is for Ford, right? At least they say it's Quality.

What is Job #1 in your life? That's not all that bad a question to be asking at the beginning of Lent.

Of course we get a lot of answers from our parents, from our teachers, from our politicians, and even from our pastors. Job #1 is being home on time, keeping your room clean, not talking back, doing your homework, getting an A, paying your bills, being successful, supporting the party, staying off drugs, knowing your Bible, loving your neighbor, keeping your nose and all other parts clean.

The list is long. Of course when you get inside the heads of individuals and move away from the oughts of authority figures to the real desires of a person, things change a bit, don't they? Job #1 for a child may be keeping her distance from that bossy Erin or finding a way to convince Mom and Dad to buy her that new Pokeman or Game Boy. Job #1 for a sixteen-year-old may be dressing right at school, not narking on a friend, or landing a boyfriend. Job #1 for an adult may be getting that advancement or surviving a boss or caring for an elderly parent or dealing with a troubled marriage or a chronically sick or retarded child.

What is Job #1 for you. For me? Lent, that time leading up to Easter, has always been a time of reflection and learning, a time to make some adjustments in our lives. Ah, but what kind of adjustments?

We're getting into the baseball season a bit. My son and I went to the pre-season doubleheader between the Blue Jays and the Indians last Saturday. It got the juices going again. In baseball, the word adjustment is used all the time. You hear the radio announcers talking about it and you hear the hitters and the pitchers talking about. "I need to make an adjustment in the way I release the ball." "He is working on adjusting the position of his elbow as he brings the bat around." You've heard it, right?

But imagine if my batting coach told me, "You know, Paul, you need to make an adjustment in your swing ..." but never told me what I need to adjust! The coach might come up to me game after game, angry with me for not making the needed adjustment, while I'm trying this and that and the other, not knowing what I'm doing wrong. How much more helpful if I had a skilled batting instructor who would be able to tell me, "Now, Paul, you need to keep your elbow higher and your stance a little more open ..." There, now I could try to do something constructive to improve my hitting.

I think we sometimes enter Lent with a general idea that there is probably something wrong with us and we probably should find out what it is and then try to change it — and we've got forty days to complete the job!

The scripture we're looking at this evening is in the middle of a letter Saint Paul, the first Christian missionary, wrote to a small, new, fledgling Christian house church he got started when he was there. The letter, the second letter to this church that has been saved, was meant to encourage and correct this group of Christians. He first of all explains why he was unable to come to visit them as soon as he had promised them he would. Then he instructs them about the importance of forgiving people within the church who have sinned, and then nails down as clearly as he could what his and their job was as followers of Jesus Christ, what their Job #1 was.

In chapter 5 he says clearly that the job of the Christian, the job given to all disciples of Jesus Christ, the job description that defines their task is this: to be representatives of Christ, doing what Christ did. And what is that? Was Christ known primarily for being moral and following all the rules? I don't think so. Not according to the religious folks. He broke the Sabbath, talked with women,

132

ate with blatant sinners, and rubbed elbows with dreaded lepers. No, he was crucified for breaking what would be known clearly as moral and religious laws.

So what was Job #1 for Jesus? He was always breaking down any barrier that had been erected by human beings or by the religious establishment which kept people from God or from one another. No, writes Saint Paul, his quill pen going as fast as he could on that rough scroll paper,

> *Anyone who belongs to Christ is a new person. The past is forgotten, and everything is new. God has done it all! He sent Christ to make peace between himself and us, and he has given us the work of making peace between himself and others.*
> — 2 Corinthians 5:17-18 (NCV)

Lest the Corinth church not get it, he says it again, in a different way:

> *What we mean is that God was in Christ, offering peace and forgiveness to the people of this world. And he has given us the work of sharing his message about peace. We were sent to speak for Christ, and God is begging you to listen to our message. We speak for Christ and sincerely ask you to make peace with God.*
> — 2 Corinthians 5:19-20 (NCV)

If our Job #1 in our walk with God is the work of sharing God's message of peace, of being "ambassadors for Christ," doing what he did then, here and now in our time, what then might that mean in the way we think about what adjustments need to be made in our lives this Lent?

Does this put a new perspective on our proud striving to drop a pound or two this Lent by limiting ourselves to only two helpings at dinner and dropping our chocolate intake to only two Hershey bars a day?

Does this even give us pause in our proud goal to read a chapter of the Bible a day, if the purpose is simply to know more about the Bible so we can have more ammunition for those arguments about the Bible at work?

Saint Paul goes on in the sixth chapter to say this: "We don't want anyone to find fault with our work, and so we try hard not to cause problems. But in everything and in every way we show that we truly are God's servants" (2 Corinthians 6:3-4a CEV).

What does that mean? What does it mean to be truly God's servants? Never to swear? To keep your room clean? Never to talk back to your parents or your teachers? To know lots of Bible verses by heart? Well, each of these could be important, if they were means to accomplish Job #1, which is helping to break down barriers between God and people and between people and people.

Saint Paul goes on in the succeeding verses to tell about all the trials and hassles he and his compatriots had gone through, and that how they dealt with those crises was vital in their effectiveness in being a valid, powerful witness to the kind of God they serve, the kind of God they had come to know in Jesus.

So, today, it might be that during Lent we might look at the way we deal with the major and minor crises in our lives. Does the way we handle them in front of our children and our spouse and our co-workers and our playmates at school and on the playground reflect a closeness with a God others might like finally to come to know? Or do our lives look just as up-tight and our responses to life's traumas just as hopeless and cynical as the next guy's? What might we need to change in our insides, in our relationship with God, that might have an impact on how we relate to the trials we face in the world? That could put a new spin on our Lenten journey, don't you think?

Just a couple of days ago my wife and I were touched by a story in *The Upper Room*. It was written by John W. Warner from Texas. The scripture sentence he took as his text was 1 Timothy 4:12: "Set an example for the believers in speech, in life, in love, in faith and in purity."

This is what he wrote:

> *When I was in high school, I had the only air pump on the block, so I pumped up all the basketballs in the*

neighborhood. One day, John, who was in grade school, brought me his basketball I pumped it up and handed it back to him. He tossed it up and down on his hand and gave me an inquisitive look.

"Scooter," he asked. "why do you spit on the needle?"

"It makes the needle go into the ball a little easier and keeps it from bending," I replied.

Then he said, "I always spit on the needle too, because you do it, but I always wondered why."

His response startled me! What else would he do simply because I did it?

We all have a person like John in our lives. Somebody, a friend, a family member, a person we don't even know is influenced by our example. If we live as an example to others by following the example of Jesus Christ, then those who imitate us will be led to the light of Christ.

Job #1. What is your Job #1? Oh, we know that we can't just try to put on a happy face to make a great witness for the Lord. People see through that. But if whatever we do this Lent to improve our health, our faith, our self esteem — whatever — is not just for ourselves alone, but also for the purpose of witnessing to the Gospel of Jesus Christ, if what we do this Lent has this double purpose, then perhaps it will also draw from us a double effort, and we and those who come in contact with us will be doubly blessed.

Too Good To Miss

C. S. Lewis, in his famous book *Mere Christianity,* tells the story of a school boy who was asked what he thought God was like. He replied that, as far as he could make out, God was "the sort of person who is always snooping round to see if anyone is enjoying himself and then trying to stop it!"

Those who see God as that kind of a deity would then most likely see Lent as one long God-filled forty days, when we are to make room in our hearts and our homes for this fun-bashing divine guest, who checks out every nook and cranny of our lives to be sure we aren't having any fun yet. Even if we don't go that far, though, the typical question, "So, what are you giving up for Lent?" doesn't make Lent sound like much fun! Funny, you rarely hear that question at Christmas time!

It is true that Lent (the word coming from the old Anglo-Saxon word "Lencten," meaning "spring") began as a time for self-examination, the number forty coming from Jesus' forty days of temptation in the wilderness. But originally, way back within a hundred years or so after Jesus' death and resurrection, it was very brief, including only a forty-hour period of fasting, then later a week long. But the Council of Nicaea in 325 A.D. assumed a forty-day Lenten observance including Sundays. Sometime in the seventh century, Ash Wednesday was established as the beginning of Lent and Sundays were eliminated in the counting of the forty-day period.

So what are we to make of Lent? Is it supposed to be a down-in-the-mouth period of excluding anything joyful from our lives, or is it something else?

The Reverend Dan Hoffman, pastor of a Lutheran church in Geneva, New York, wrote an article in his newsletter that speaks well, I believe, to the real meaning of Lent for us. In his article he said that rather than Lent being a time of denial, it should be seen as a wonderful time for "pampering and self-indulgence." But rather than pampering our every desire and whim, we "pamper our spirit and indulge our deep human need for love." Dan believes that Lent "is the time when we let the guilt come right up to the surface and pay close attention to how God has dealt with our sin and guilt in the cross of Christ." He concludes: "The discipline of Lent is an invitation to come out of ourselves and discover how God truly wants to pamper us with the gift of his own love for us in Jesus Christ." Good stuff, Dan!

God wants to care for us, our bodies and our souls. Contrast that with that boy's "snooping around God" quoted in C. S. Lewis' book.

Yes, of course it is possible for us to assume too easily God's love and forgiveness. Yes, of course it is a serious problem that many people simply do whatever they want and assume that either it doesn't matter or God will forgive them, so what's the big deal? It's that old thing called "cheap grace."

But I continue to believe that there is a deep dis-ease that is simmering in the belly of our culture which is driving our violence and our need for things and drugs and alcohol, and is causing our lack of willingness to work with commitment and hope through troubled relationships in companies, marriages, or institutions. The next toy, the next sexual encounter, the next fix, the next drink, the next bonus is what we need, we think.

In fact, I believe without a shadow of a doubt that these are all symptoms of a deep, deep suffering of the spirit, which comes from being cut off from our Creator. Our umbilical cord between God and us, through which the true nourishment of meaning and life is intended to flow, has been stepped on by sin and apathy and glitz and misguided thinking, and many do not know what's even happening to them.

In fact, what they are finding is the truth of a poster I saw once. Underneath a picture of a beautifully round earth was this caption: "Without God, it's a vicious circle." I believe that's true.

The New Testament book of 1 Peter was written in a similar time, a time when, while there was no out-and-out persecution by the Emperor, there was still plenty of abuse of Christians by society. The writer of 1 Peter was writing to the early church which was suffering simply by their commitment to Jesus Christ. The letter begins this way: "Peter, an apostle of Jesus Christ, to the exiles of the Dispersion in Pontus, Galatia, Cappadocia, Asia, and Bithynia ..." (1 Peter 1:1 RSV).

All of these localities are in Asia Minor, what is present day Turkey. His letter was sent to those Christians who were in exile, that is separated from the mother church in Palestine. The letter seems to be addressed to former Gentiles, non-Jews whose lives were being made tough by their former buddies who could not appreciate their newfound faith. Ring any bells?

This letter of 1 Peter is a letter for us, for our time. It is a letter of encouragement for people who are suffering for their faith, people who feel like exiles, people who are always having to be on the defensive regarding their commitment to Jesus Christ. And the job of being parents of youth who are growing up in a culture whose values are radically different from their families' can cause great stress in a home. Can any of us relate to that? Such a constant struggle can become truly burdensome over time and the author of this letter knew that.

So what did these folks need to hear? What do we need to hear today when we feel like exiles, aliens in our own land, where most of what we proclaim as faith is either mocked or tolerated or undercut in the society in which we live?

The writer of 1 Peter in the third chapter wrote this: "For Christ also died for sins once for all, the righteous for the unrighteous, that he might bring us to God, being put to death in the flesh but made alive in the spirit ..." (1 Peter 3:18).

Peter reminds his readers that the core of the Gospel they live by proclaims the simple truth that Jesus Christ died for their sins so that they might be brought to God. Jesus' mortal body was killed on the cross, but in the resurrection Jesus, the living Christ, was made alive in order that they might be brought to God.

The basic tenet of our faith is simply too good and to important to allow us to miss it in the midst of arguments among various denominations or points of view over abortion or homosexuality or baptism or communion or ordination policy. The basic truth of our faith is that Jesus Christ was sent to us to bring us to God. What we need in any sort of suffering is to know "Emmanuel," God is with us. If we know that, we can even stand before death, as Jesus did and as countless martyrs have done over the centuries. The fact that we have not known such sacrifice very much in our country does not take away the truth of that possibility.

What we need to see through our suffering is the presence of God, caring for us and loving us and crying with us. Too many people interpret every flash of light and bump in the night as God snooping around with angry, punitive intentions. How sad.

I read the following story recently.

> *A little girl walked daily to and from school. Though the weather one morning was questionable and clouds were forming, she made her daily trek to the elementary school.*
>
> *As the afternoon progressed, the winds whipped up, along with thunder and lightning. The mother of the little girl felt concerned that her daughter would be frightened as she walked home from school, and she herself feared that the electrical storm might harm her child.*
>
> *Full of concern, the mother quickly got into her car and drove along the route to her child's school. Eventually, she spotted her little girl walking along, but at each flash of lightning, the child would stop, look up at the sky, and smile.*
>
> *As the next flash lit up the sky the little girl just stopped, looked at the streak of light, and smiled. Finally, the mother called her over to the car and asked, "What are you doing?"*
>
> *The child answered, "God keeps taking pictures of me, so I keep stopping to smile for his camera!"*

Somewhere that little girl got a different image of God from that of the boy in C. S. Lewis' book. If she was listening, she would have gotten it from Jesus.

As we suffer the various pains of being human and of affirming faith in a world that just doesn't get it, let us remember the suffering of our Lord, and remember that suffering was for the purpose of bringing us to God, not scaring us away.

So this Lent, we can allow all our fears and guilt and questions to come to the surface in the bright light of God's grace, and by the time we get to Easter, we just may be ready to say with new vigor and new gratitude, "He is risen," for spending time during Lent with our sin, our suffering, and our Savior will have brought us into the presence of the real, authentic, loving God.

Growing Faith

It's an old joke, but an insightful one: A man slipped off the edge of a cliff, and just before he fell the hundreds of feet to the valley floor below, he grabbed a protruding branch. There he was, dangling precariously from that little branch, afraid that any second it would pull out from the side of the cliff.

"Help!" he began to cry. "Help! Is anyone up there?!" Finally, after no answer, he began to pray desperately, after which he heard a big booming voice. "I am the Lord. I am here to save you!"

The man was beyond relieved. "Oh, thank you. Thank you, Lord! But please hurry. Do something!"

The Lord returned, "I will, my son. All you have to do is follow my every direction without doubting or fear."

"Fine. Fine," hollered back the man. "Anything! But please hurry! What do you want me to do first?"

The booming voice came back, "Let go."

The man was silent for a moment. Finally he hollered out, "Is anyone else up there?"

This business of "having faith" in God is a huge issue. It is a huge issue today. It was a huge issue long before Jesus came. It has been a huge issue in the intervening centuries.

Think about your own life. How often have you prayed and prayed, hoping against hope that God's will and yours would be in sync? And how often has it turned out that they were not?

I don't have to give examples. You are even now reeling them off in your memory. There are many who would be sitting here in this sanctuary were it not for a prayer that was not answered in the way they had hoped, and something snapped inside, and faith was no longer a possibility for him or her.

The early church, struggling not only with the everyday stuff of life and death and relationships that face you and me in our time, also had other issues. Their whole religious life had been turned on its head. They had been taught from birth to follow the law, and things would be cool. Follow the law and God would smile. Follow the law and you could be at peace.

Of course, there were two problems with that. Number one, there were just too many laws on the books. Hundreds. Too many for anyone but the professional religious folks to memorize, to say nothing about follow.

And secondly, even following the ones they did know brought little peace, for two reasons. First of all, they knew they were leaving some out, so God might still be upset about one they were not following. And secondly, it's hard to be at peace and feel totally accepted and loved when you know that that love is conditional upon doing something.

And along comes Jesus! As Saint Paul writes in his letter to the Romans, just a few verses after our scripture reading for this morning: "But God shows his love for us in that while we were yet sinners Christ died for us" (Romans 5:8 RSV).

Can you begin to fathom how different that concept must have been for those first Christians? Think about what that would feel like today: "My daddy gave me a new bike while I was in litigation for burglary." "My boss gave me a raise after stealing from the company." "My grandmother took me to the movies after I broke her favorite vase." "My teacher came over to my house on Saturday to tutor me after I had stolen her purse."

Do you get it? Can you feel the difference? What kind of love is this? What kind of God is this, who sent us the means of salvation, of coming back into relationship with God, right while we were knee-deep in sinning against God?

What can you do to be sure you are right with God? Saint Paul was well aware of this struggle when he wrote his letter to the Romans. Some folks were so captivated by Jesus' understanding of God's grace that they went way to the other extreme, thinking that all one had to do was have faith, to believe in God, and what one did didn't mean a thing. Others were still stuck with the idea that what matters is simply what we do, and so we can easily judge each other by our works, by our actions.

Saint Paul jumped into the fray with both feet and said you can't divide the two. They are just as tightly connected as the two sides of a coin. To make his point he lifted up Abraham, who was seen by the Jews as their ultimate forefather. Everyone knew the poignant story of Abraham who heard God direct him to sacrifice his only son Isaac. After his wife Sarah had been barren for so many years, she had finally given birth to Isaac and it looked like God's promise to Abraham years back that his descendants would be as the dust of the earth or the stars in the sky would finally come true.

Then this. It made no sense at all. Yet, Abraham was obedient, and took Isaac to the land of Moriah (Genesis 22), fully prepared to sacrifice him on an altar there. At the last moment God stayed his hand, and a ram appeared to be sacrificed instead. This dramatic event was never forgotten and Saint Paul referred to it again and again in his letter to the Romans in his discussion of faith.

Can anyone imagine the kind of faith in God Abraham must have had? To be willing to sacrifice his son, assuming that if such a thing was somehow a part of God's will, it had to be okay? He did not holler out, "Is there anyone else out there?" It is to this faith that Saint Paul referred, saying that doing what Abraham did and that faith which enabled him to do it, were absolutely one and the same thing. To talk of his faith without the action would be senseless, and vice versa.

Now we come to the point for this morning. First of all, am I being unfair to say that not everyone in this sanctuary feels that he or she has the kind of faith Abraham exhibited? I suspect there are many of us for whom this is precisely the issue in our lives. To trust God, really to trust God, is so difficult, especially when we face terribly difficult decisions and experiences.

So how do we get such faith? How did Abraham get such faith? Saint Paul gives the answer in Romans 4:20: "No distrust made [Abraham] waver concerning the promise of God, but he grew strong in his faith as he gave glory to God...."

145

There it is. His faith got strong "as he gave glory to God." Simple. Give glory to God and your faith will grow. So what does it mean to give glory to God?

It means not to glorify ourselves. Not to glorify our wisdom, our creativity, our money, our job, our good looks, our situation. It means not to glorify our country, our party, our way of life. It means only to glorify God. To praise God as the all in all, the *sine qua non* of our lives. The one whom we most long to know and understand and be with, more than wanting to watch *Who Wants To Be A Millionaire?*, more than working on our finest car, more than sitting at our new computer.

The Greek for the English word "glory" is *doxa*, which means that which is bright and magnificent and radiant and powerful and majestic and mighty. Remember the song we sing as the offering is being brought up? It is called the "Doxology." "Praise God from whom all blessings flow."

Saint Paul said that the more Abraham gave glory to God, the more his faith grew. How would that work for us?

I believe we grow faith, which seems to be something that cannot be directly acquired (like happiness) by doing what we *can* do, namely glorify God. If we focus on the glory of God, instead of the glory of all the other things that get our attention, our spirits have the possibility of beginning to consider God first, to trust God more, to have more faith in God. It's still not proof, of course; it's still faith. We will always have to trust without seeing, which makes it tough for us scientific folks.

Saint Paul wrote in his second letter to the Corinthians that "we walk by faith, not by sight." Remember that verse in that beautiful hymn, "It Is Well With My Soul"? Remember that last verse, "And, Lord, haste the day when my faith shall be sight, the clouds be rolled back as a scroll..."? Ah, how we long for that day, but it is not yet. My, how true that is!

We can grow our faith, like Abraham, by giving glory to God, by focusing on God's glory, God's power, and God's works in the world. And faith then has the possibility of growing in our lives.

I read a fascinating article in the February 1999 issue of *Scientific American* (p. 86). The authors wrote about space tethers. They

146

spoke of a theoretical means of getting things in and out of orbit, or of moving satellites or space craft from one orbit to another. They said that the concept was that of having a strong tether, ten or twenty miles long, which would be cart-wheeling in orbit. By attaching an object to one end of the tether, the cart wheeling effect would swing it up and into a higher energy orbit, with no fuel expended! Sort of like David using his sling shot to hurl a rock at Goliath.

A tether, with one end in one orbit and the other end in another orbit. And because it is one tether, it connects the energy of both orbits and enables objects on one end to be moved to the other as the tether turns in space.

What an image. It's like giving glory to God being directly connected to one's faith! So you can't lift your faith by yourself? You've been trying all your life? Well, grab hold of the tether of giving God glory, and your faith may just be lifted in spite of yourself. Like Abraham. Just by focusing on God's glory. Just by training your mind and heart to rejoice over life and every moment as a glorious gift of God. Every part of God's world and most especially the gift of God's love we have seen in Jesus, are all gifts of God. To be filled with, overwhelmed with the glory of God, to bring glory to God, instead of putting it elsewhere. And then feel yourself being hurtled to new levels of faith.

It could happen. It did to Abraham. It just might happen with you.

Lent 3
1 Corinthians 1:18-25

The Holiness Of The Sacred

In the April 7, 1999, issue of *The Upper Room,* Merial Scott of South Dakota wrote the following:

> *One summer morning when I was very small, Mother woke me with the words, "Get up and dress quickly now. I'm frying trout for breakfast." Astonished, I wondered how we could have newly caught fish when the day had just begun. At the table, I learned that my father had driven at dawn to one of his favorite streams and gotten a strike on almost every fly he cast.*
>
> *The unexpected breakfast was less of a surprise than the startling realization that my parents lived a life quite separate from mine. Their activities were not limited to my waking hours. A whole world operated without my knowledge.*
>
> *As an adult, I find that God also moves in ways and places of which I am totally unaware.*

Did you hear that? The writer was shocked to learn that his parents lived a life quite separate from his. Their life was connected intimately with his, but there was a whole part that was unknown, and the realization jolted him into a new awareness of his world and theirs.

"Separate." What an eye-opening thought it was for me when I learned that the fundamental meaning of the word "holy" in Hebrew and Greek is "separate." Something that is holy is separate from the common things of life. Therefore in the scriptures we see holy rituals and traditions which depended on disciplines of separateness as a means to glorify God. Separate dishes for separate foods. Separate leaders for separate, holy functions. Clean, separate from unclean. Holy. Separate.

Unfortunately, over time, these traditions became human devices, human laws defining what and who was holy and worthy before God. Such laws and traditions began to exclude more and more of God's creation. Instead of promoting the holiness of God by setting aside separate places and rituals, such rituals began to separate people from people and people from God.

Clean and unclean became clean people and unclean people. For example, those with leprosy were unclean, and with the undergirding of the religious establishment lepers were ostracized from the community. The poor and the tax collectors and the adulterers also began to be separated out of community, with the support of, if not by the very initiation of the religious community. It all seemed so right; after all, God is holy and clean and righteous, and hates sin.

And then along comes Jesus. And what does he do?

Well, take those, for example, who suffered from that terrible disease called leprosy. How did Jesus relate to them? It was crystal clear what he was supposed to do. Jesus knew the law. Listen to the "holy" law about how to deal with lepers:

> *The leper who has the disease shall wear torn clothes and let the hair of his head hang loose, and he shall cover his upper lip and cry, "Unclean, unclean." He shall remain unclean as long as he has the disease; he is unclean; he shall dwell alone in a habitation outside the camp.* — Leviticus 13:45-46 (RSV)

It was the religious establishment that set up those rules. And many in the church today still want to follow some of those old laws which cut people off from the community.

Ah, but what did Jesus do? Listen.

> *Behold, a leper came to him and knelt before him, saying, "Lord, if you will, you can make me clean."*

150

And he stretched out his hand and touched him, saying,
"I will; be clean." And immediately his leprosy was
cleansed. — Matthew 8:2-3

Jesus touched the leper. His compassion was greater than the law which required separation. Do we cut people out of our lives because they are "unclean" according to society or an old church tradition?

Jesus was able to stand with those who were either different or sinful, and love them. In so doing, he unleashed a power for healing and change that came straight from the heart of God.

You see, Jesus showed us that the holy life consists in recognizing how separate God's way is from our ways. Jesus lived a life that clearly articulated the fact that the holiness to which we are called involves embracing the amazing way of God. This way assumes that God will work in ways totally different from the way we might expect. God's ways are separate from our ways, as the prophet Isaiah said so beautifully (Isaiah 55:8). They might include a tiny baby. They might include using someone seen by the world as repulsive. They might include a moth shutting down a whole computer system, or a man on a cross shutting down a whole system of "doing religion," of relating to God.

My what a stir it causes when we follow God's radical ways. Society and friends and family call us naive. We are do-gooders. We are fools. Loving our enemies. Turning the other cheek. Emptying ourselves of power so God can use us in powerful ways.

Saint Paul said very plainly that "the word of the cross is folly to those who are perishing, but to us who are being saved, it is the power of God. For it is written, 'I will destroy the wisdom of the wise ...' " (1 Corinthians 1:18-19 RSV).

And then he nails it down further with these words, in verse 25: "For God's foolishness is wiser than human wisdom, and God's weakness is stronger than human strength."

Someone who lives according to Jesus' way will be seen by the world as a fool. Have you ever felt like a fool when you have followed the way of Jesus? Have you ever been kind to the nerd at school and felt the eyes of your classmates on you?

151

God's way is so different, so extraordinary, so separate from that which we are encouraged to accept as normal. God's sacred, holy ways which Jesus lived out, are astounding, astonishing, and unexpected.

In fact that was why the Jews simply could not accept Jesus as the Messiah. They had certain expectations of what the Messiah would do. Because Jesus did not fit that expectation, they could not see him as the Messiah. As the rabbi said in a recent *Newsweek* magazine article about Jesus, "Jesus didn't obey the Torah, so of course he could not be the Messiah!"

The way of Jesus is different. The way to holiness, to God, to the abundant life, is not to be discovered simply by thinking it through. It comes from a separate realm. It is of God. It is holy. Which is why the scriptures call us to pray constantly (1 Thessalonians 5:17) and remain an intimate part of the Body of Christ, the Church (Acts 2:42). It's the only way we will have the wisdom and the strength to live the Christian life.

The way of the cross, such things as radical compassion for all people, voluntary weakness, and crushing defeat, all of these, when offered to God, can bring new life. That, to the world is utter foolishness. But if we can stand the ridicule of our friends and maybe even our family, it is the way to the meaningful and exciting and fulfilling life which we all long for.

As Michael Card wrote: "When we in our foolishness thought we were wise, he played the fool and he opened our eyes."

Jesus calls each of us now not to figure it out — but to live it out.

So Great A Love

I've been trying to decide whether it's good or bad that one cannot fully appreciate what others are going through in life, either their joys or their sorrows, until one has experienced them oneself.

It's probably more on the bad side, if we are not as sensitive either to people's joy or pain, leaving them feeling lonely, either in need of more compassion or celebration than is being offered.

On the other hand, one could probably make a case for it being a good thing, because to appreciate fully and to take in all the world's despair and horror and grief and disappointment fully, as though it were one's own, would do one in. By the same token, to absorb fully all the world's joy might be a sensory overload and short out all of a person's nerve endings and brain parts!

But however you may come down on that question, one thing I know: experiencing the birth of a child by your child is not a feeling you can fully anticipate. The long months of hoping and wondering about health, is it a boy or a girl, the long hours of waiting to hear what is happening in that hospital thousands of miles away across the ocean after you have heard that the process of birth had taken a more imminent turn; and then the ring of the phone, the sound of that familiar voice, and the hearing of a name you had never heard before, spoken by a mere child, your own daughter. *Marc André Christophe Randy.* Hmmm. That'll work. I like it. And then to hear the tiny cry of your own grandson drift through the phone as a mysterious harbinger of exciting, poignant things yet to come ... Ah, so that's what it's like to be a grandfather.

There are so many folks in the world who are so caught up in that which is dragging them down. There are so many people of all ages who live in a place where only hopelessness and death are known. There are so many human beings who cannot imagine what it would be like to have hope, to be loved, to be shown mercy, to know a God who has so great a love, that even their hell is not the last word.

How to communicate such a God, such a love, without first having experienced it is quite a challenge. But Saint Paul would say it is worth the effort, for the God he had come to know in Jesus was worth getting to know.

In his letter to the church at Ephesus, in the second chapter, he scrawled these words with quill pen on parchment: "But God, who is rich in mercy, out of the great love with which he loved us even when we were dead through our trespasses, made us alive together with Christ; by grace you have been saved (Ephesians 2:4-5 RSV).

Hollow words these are, if the only God you have been introduced to in your life is the God who is most likely responsible for your cancer, for "somewhere in your youth and childhood, you must have done something wrong." Hollow words these are, if worship and prayer and good works, instead of being eager responses to a God who cares, are instead desperate attempts to get that all-seeing, wrathful God off your back.

I heard just yesterday about someone who was behind a car at an E-Z Pass tollgate. The driver obviously didn't have an E-Z Pass and didn't know what to do. Finally, she opened her door and started throwing money at the closed window of the tollbooth, nickels and dimes hitting the glass and flying all over the place! Utter frustration had apparently caused her to lose her senses!

Sometimes I think that people do that with God. They throw prayers and money and good works and promises and worship attendance at God, mindlessly hoping it will call off God's supposed wrath or cause God to heal a son or change a boss or get her a job or stop the affair.

Paul speaks in this verse in Ephesians of a different kind of God, the Father of our Lord Jesus Christ. A God who brings life in the midst of death, hope in the midst of despair, love in the midst of hatred, generosity in the midst of selfishness. So great a love, that doesn't wait until one deserves mercy to offer mercy. So great a love, a love which, when experienced by one person, can trigger a domino effect of caring and love. And our job as followers of Jesus Christ is to help others experience that wonderful love of God.

I'll never forget it. I was visiting a Sunday school class. The teacher had passed out cookies shortly before I had arrived. Being the playful person I am, I went over to one of the children and pretended to try to take his cookie. Instinctively he pulled the cookie away. I then went to the next child who did the same. It went that way, playfully of course, around half the table until something happened. You know what? Suddenly a little girl reached out her hand, offering me her cookie. Everyone was stunned. "Why hadn't I thought of that?" you could see on their faces. And suddenly there were a dozen hands with cookies in them reaching out to me. An astounding experience.

Who will be the one to reach out the cookie at work, at school, in the car pool? Who will change the pattern and draw forth the goodness waiting to be lived out in all of God's children? Who will live out the image in which she was made, the image of God, and live out mercy and generosity? Who will enable yet another person to know the depth of God's love seen in Jesus Christ?

You did it when you walked, even for a few steps, in the footsteps of Jesus, in your life, in your family, at work. We do it in the One Great Hour of Sharing offering. Jesus did it in sacrificing himself on a cross.

Now it is your turn, my turn, to reach out the cookie, to help someone experience for themselves the richness, the fullness, the overwhelming joy of God's great love.

The Source

One of the most precious and indispensable needs you and I have is to be able to have at least one person in the world who truly understands us. How often have we known folks who try to be such a one for us, but we know they just don't understand.

Surely there are many of you here today who carry great burdens of worry or anxiety or fear. Just the words *job* or *spouse* or *child* or *cancer* or *finances* or *death* bring up such an overwhelming baggage of emotions. (And for some of you, you are already gone and will hear little of the rest of the sermon because of one of those words I just used.)

We are a people who need one who knows and understands.

I read recently of one who does not understand. In the December 2000 issue of the *U.S. Catholic* magazine there was the following article:

> *Last summer the [Catholic] Madonna Rehabilitation Hospital in Lincoln, Nebraska, had reached an agreement with pornographer Don Parisi, who wanted to donate his Internet domain name madonna.com to the hospital. But the agreement was voided because the singer Madonna filed and won a complaint to claim the domain name. Her publicist boldly asserted that she "happens to be the most famous Madonna in the world."*

Something must have happened, though, because the address madonna.com does take you to the Madonna Rehabilitation Hospital.

Of course the actress Madonna is better known than the Mother of Jesus in many pockets of culture, but the combination of presumption and lack of awareness of a broader reality on the part of Madonna's publicist is remarkable. And sad.

There are some who feel that way about Jesus. About God. About the church. About faith. Empty, well-meaning words by pastors and priests at times of terrible pain have left a question mark about the ability of the Divine Reality to understand truly. Not everyone sings the song with feeling, "Nobody knows the trouble I've seen, nobody knows but Jesus. Nobody knows the trouble I've seen, glory hallelujah."

The scripture reading this morning sounds heady — theological — removed from your life and mine. But, in fact, it's close. Quite close, indeed.

Not a lot of folks pick up and read the book of Hebrews. It's close to the end of the New Testament, hidden nicely between Philemon and James. If you're going to hide, that's the place to hide! We don't know much about the author or to whom this piece of literature was written. But it's well worth the read, for it is specifically about this Jesus, who knows our troubles.

Chapter 5, verse 5. What kind of a person is this Jesus? Well, for starters we need to remember that "Christ did not exalt himself to be made a high priest, but was appointed by" God. Does that ring a bell? It should. Remember those words from Philippians?

> *Have this mind among yourselves, which is yours in Christ Jesus, who, though he was in the form of God, did not count equality with God a thing to be grasped, but emptied himself, taking the form of a servant, being born in the likeness of men. And being found in human form he humbled himself and became obedient unto death, even death on a cross. Therefore God has highly exalted him and bestowed on him the name which is above every name ...* — Philippians 2:5-9 (RSV)

The way the writer of Hebrews puts it is he "did not exalt himself ..." but was appointed by God.

So we've learned a bit about the early church's understanding of Jesus Christ, haven't we? He was not an ego maniac who volunteered to be the Messiah, like a child thrusting her hand in the air to volunteer for something in the children's moment. No, Jesus was appointed by God. I think I can relate more to someone like that, someone who is being obedient, rather than cocky. Such a one might be able to understand me ...

But the writer of Hebrews goes on. He says, "Thou art a priest forever, after the order of Melchizedek."

Wow. Now that tells us a lot, right? Might as well have said it in Chinese, right? Well, actually, in that one sentence he told us a bundle. It's just that the bundle has to be unwrapped a bit.

Melchizedek. A mysterious, now-you-see-him, now-you-don't figure in the Old Testament. We have to turn a lot of pages and go back, back to the first book of the Bible, Genesis, to the fourteenth chapter to meet up with this guy. Abraham (actually called Abram at the time) had just returned from rescuing his nephew Lot from having been captured by King Chedorlaomer (you remember him, right — actually there's not enough time to tell the bloody story leading up to this moment) and was about to have a brief meeting with the king of Sodom when Poof! That's right. Poof! Right out of nowhere, with no introduction, pops Melchizedek. Listen:

> *After his return from the defeat of Chedorlaomer and the kings who were with him, the king of Sodom went out to meet [Abram] at the Valley of Shaveh (that is, the King's Valley). And Melchizedek king of Salem brought out bread and wine; he was priest of God Most High. And he blessed him and said, "Blessed be Abram by God Most High, maker of heaven and earth; and blessed be God Most High, who has delivered your enemies into your hand!" And Abram gave him a tenth of everything.*   — Genesis 14:17-20

Just like that. Melchizedek brings Abram something to eat and drink and blesses him by *El Elyon*, "God Most High," who had delivered Abram's enemies into his hand. And Abram gave him a tithe of all the spoils of the battle. Abram stood in the presence of

Melchizedek and whipped out his checkbook on the spot. Amazing. He felt an immediate connection, an immediate sense of trust.

This is the story. The folks to whom the book of Hebrews was written knew about old Melchizedek, though, so they knew what the writer was saying when he said that Jesus Christ would be a priest forever "after the order of Melchizedek."

"After the order of Melchizedek," someone unique, someone who entered history, knew the specific needs of God's people, and fed and blessed and received a remarkable immediate response of worship and, yes, even a willingness to tithe their money. (But that only came after they were fed and blessed.)

Jesus is a high priest "after the order of Melchizedek," and, continues the writer of Hebrews, "became the source of eternal salvation to all who obey him...."

The source.

I'm not really into cars. Oh, I can drive them and I can put oil in them if I have to, and windshield washer fluid, and I can even change a tire. But when I look under the hood ... well. It's like looking into the pile of spaghetti in the strainer after it's been cooked. You know what I mean? I just don't really understand it.

But I did just recently learn what a manifold was. Oh, I had heard the term all my life, but I finally asked someone. "What's a manifold?" And I learned that it's a sort of fat pipe off of which several other pipes go. You can have a manifold in the concrete floor of your basement which routes hot water to heat your whole house.

The source. Jesus Christ is the source of eternal salvation, the dependable source of hope for this life and the next. He is the manifold, from which the riches of heavenly food and drink come, as steady as seed time and harvest, flowing into every corner of your life and our world. He is the one who truly understands, and thereby enables us to go on with courage and hope.

Eating out is generally fun. But do you know the feeling when the shadow of the waitress falls across your napkin and you know it's your turn to order? You know the feeling. Well, today you may feel the shadow of decision time falling across your shoulders. You may finally feel that the old striving to please God, that old scratching and itching is just too exhausting. You need a High Priest along the order of Melchizedek.

It may be for you time to plug into the source, hook up to the manifold, and experience the warmth of a new thing, an everlasting, dependable Savior who is more than going through the motions of ritual. Like John Wesley, founder of the Methodist movement in England, you want a heart "strangely warmed."

We really do have a Savior after the order of Melchizedek, the eternal source of life, the One who truly understands. Therefore we can sing with faith and trust: "Nobody knows the trouble I've seen, nobody knows but Jesus. Nobody knows the trouble I've seen, glory hallelujah!"

The Amazing Holy Week Equation

One of the typical difficulties of days like today is connecting the ritual and annual stories of Palm Sunday with the stuff you came in here today worrying about!

Okay, so Jesus rode into Jerusalem on a donkey 2,000 years ago. Hey, that's cool. But, you say, I'm worried about paying for repairs to my Chevy so I can ride into Buffalo to go to work!

Okay, so the people were all excited about Jesus and waved palm branches at him. That's a neat image, you say, but I'm more concerned about whether the insurance company will wave the deductible!

I believe, in fact, that Palm Sunday, maybe even this Palm Sunday, has a message for us all. In fact, I am hoping that this Palm Sunday may be the one you look back on as having been decisive in your life.

You see, Palm Sunday meant one thing for those shouting, "Hosanna!" and something very different for Jesus. The disciples and bystanders were caught up in the excitement and thrill of the beginning of Passover and the potential new leader Jesus, who might free them from Roman rule.

For Jesus, on the other hand, his entry into Jerusalem was the beginning of a go-for-broke divine plan to break the back of an understanding of God which was keeping people from God and keeping them stuck in their sin. It was the first step in his final course of action to reconcile humanity with their Creator. From the time of his childhood when his relationship with God began to dawn he had been inexorably moving toward this day. Palm Sunday. The die was cast. As the Gospel writer Luke put it, " ...he set his face to go to Jerusalem" (9:51). It was Palm Sunday. The time had arrived.

Palm Sunday was the day when a long-percolating vision of obedience began to take its final form. Palm Sunday was the day when a string of events began that would change Jesus' life and the life of the world. Palm Sunday was the day when obedience won out over any hesitation or doubt, though there may well have been lingering, human fear of what obedience might bring in pain or suffering. But it would be worth it, to say the least.

Jesus was unique in his relationship with God and with his sacrifice for all of humanity. However, Jesus also was part of a long line of splendor of those who have been obedient to the call of God on their lives.

Abraham heard the call of God (Genesis 12:1 RSV): "Go from your country and your kindred and your father's house to the land that I will show you." Surely he had been feeling nudges and wondering if this was really God. But finally it was Palm Sunday, and obedience was the only way. And he went, not knowing where he was going, totally depending on the Lord.

The prophet Isaiah had an overwhelming experience of the power and majesty and glory of God while worshiping. At the end of that experience he uttered those words which have been said in a variety of ways by countless faithful people of God over the centuries. "And I heard the voice of the Lord saying, 'Whom shall I send, and who will go for us?' Then I said, 'Here am I! Send me' " (Isaiah 6:8 RSV). And he went. For him, it was Palm Sunday.

We Protestants tend to ignore one of the most faithful persons in our religious history, the mother of Jesus, Mary. After she was told she was going to have a baby, out of wedlock and by the power of the Holy Spirit of God, even with all the questions lingering in her mind, Luke reports: "And Mary said, 'Behold, I am the handmaid of the Lord; let it be to me according to your word' " (1:38 RSV). It was Palm Sunday for Mary.

Then there were others who were faithful but needed a little more encouragement. Remember Jonah, the reluctant prophet.

164

Called by God to speak words of warning to the sinful city of Nineveh, he instead fled by ship, found himself in the belly of a whale, and was rerouted to — you guessed it — Nineveh. It was Palm Sunday, with a watery circuitous route on the way to his obedience.

And there was Saint Paul. Before he became Saint Paul he was Saul, the Christian hater. But to Paul's credit, he really was trying to do the will of God. He thought this Jesus was a blasphemer and his followers heretics. He had a mid-course correction, however, and his Palm Sunday occurred on the way to Damascus, in the northern part of Palestine.

Paul's conversion must be an important story because Luke tells it three times in the book of Acts. Acts 9, Acts 22 and finally, listen to how he quotes Paul as Paul tells his story to King Agrippa.

> *Thus I journeyed to Damascus with the authority and commission of the chief priests. At midday, O king, I saw on the way a light from heaven, brighter than the sun, shining round me and those who journeyed with me. And when we had all fallen to the ground, I heard a voice saying to me in the Hebrew language, "Saul, Saul, why do you persecute me? It hurts you to kick against the goads."* — Acts 26:12-14 (RSV)

It was Palm Sunday for Paul, and he became the first and greatest missionary of the gospel who ever lived.

And then there is you. And there is me. And there is today, Palm Sunday. Anything perking in your life that you feel God has been calling you to do or to be, perhaps for years — perhaps for a few months, or weeks or days?

This could be your Palm Sunday. It could be mine.

Listen to Saint Paul again. The scripture we read today helps to put Jesus' actions on Palm Sunday into context.

> *Have this mind among yourselves, which is yours in Christ Jesus, who, though he was in the form of God, did not count equality with God a thing to be grasped, but emptied himself, taking the form of a servant, being born in the likeness of men. And being found in human*

165

*form he humbled himself and became obedient unto
death, even death on a cross.*

— Philippians 2:5-8 (RSV)

The amazing Holy Week equation that we see in Jesus is that, when it comes to doing the will of God, less is more. Jesus, writes Saint Paul, "emptied himself" and thereby became obedient. Jesus did not fill himself up with pride and drive and determination. Rather, Jesus emptied himself, and allowed his spirit and mind to be filled with God.

Here is the meeting place of Palm Sunday, A.D. 33 and Palm Sunday 2003. It is in the conscious making room in our minds for the Mind of Christ in order that we might be eager to do the will of God. It is in the emptying of all that would get in the way of God so that it becomes possible to think thoughts that lead us to paths of righteousness and holiness and joy.

Think how important that is. Remember the words of the prophet Isaiah:

*For my thoughts are not your thoughts, neither are your
ways my ways, says the LORD. For as the heavens are
higher than the earth, so are my ways higher than your
ways and my thoughts than your thoughts.*

— Isaiah 55:8-9 (RSV)

Saint Paul wrote to the church at Rome. "Do not be conformed to this world but be transformed by the renewal of your mind ..." (Romans 12:2 RSV).

To have the mind of Christ is to have an empty head — well, sort of. At least there is the intent of leaving room, the intent of filling it, or making it available for God's thoughts, not just our own.

So what is it for you today? If we stay in A.D. 33 and wave palm branches, but don't make the connection of our obedience to God's will today, then this will have been a hollow event, an empty diversion on a gorgeous day.

You've thought about it. You've prayed about it. You intend to do it for God. It's Palm Sunday. For you and for me. It could be the most important day of our lives.

166

Stop The Offerings!

Go with me to the year 1968, to the basement of Good Shepherd United Methodist Church in Silver Spring, Maryland. I was the student assistant at that church, while attending Wesley Theological Seminary in Washington, D.C. One Sunday morning, immediately following the Sunday school hour, the senior high teacher came hurrying into the fellowship hall and engaged me in an almost desperate conversation. The question had been raised in his class that morning, "How could the death of a man 2,000 years ago actually serve to do anything about the sin of someone in 1968?" The teacher had been confused and speechless before the class. Today I don't remember what I told him, but I remember clearly the question — and I've heard it many times since.

As we celebrate this profound watershed day in history, I would like to reflect on this awesome, mysterious, paradoxical symbol of the Christian faith. I am making the assumption that there just may be some of you who also have struggled with this mystery, this often-spoken article of faith that "Jesus Christ died for our sins." And central to this question is the cross.

One of the golden oldies in our hymnal is "The Old Rugged Cross." It's a great song to sing and I wonder what people are thinking when they sing it! Remember?

> *On a hill far away, stood an old rugged cross,*
> *the emblem of suffering and shame.*
> *And I love that old cross, where the dearest and best*
> *for a world of lost sinners was slain.*

167

So I'll cherish the old rugged cross,
till my trophies at last I lay down;
I will cling to the old rugged cross,
and exchange it someday for a crown.

What does it mean to "cherish the cross"? I mean, the cross was the means of execution back then. It would be like saying, "I will cling to the electric chair," or "I hold the hang noose close to my breast," or "I keep a syringe in my pocket." Why would someone cling to the old rugged cross?

This scripture reading from the tenth chapter of Hebrews deals directly with this issue.

It's hard for us today to feel or understand the radical nature of what the writer of Hebrews was saying. Remember, up to this time the sacrifice of doves and lambs and bulls and goats was the only way people knew to please God, to rid themselves of the guilt that plagued them. The words in this tenth chapter really were revolutionary to the ears of the Jews of his day. Listen.

If the worshipers had once been cleansed, they would
no longer have any consciousness of sin. But in these
sacrifices there is a reminder of sin year after year. For
it is impossible that the blood of bulls and goats should
take away sins. — Hebrews 10:2b-4 (RSV)

Can you imagine the impact such words had? It would be like someone saying today that washing your hands does nothing to rid your hands of dirt and germs. What?! What do you mean? It is *the* way of doing so! But then the writer of Hebrews goes on, "Where there is forgiveness of [sins], there is no longer any offering for sin" (Hebrews 10:18 RSV).

In other words the writer of Hebrews is saying, "Stop the offerings! Jesus has made the one offering of himself and that is enough!"

Think of it. Growing up, knowing the pang of guilt, just like we do, but then regularly going to the temple with a dove in hand or buying one there, giving it to the priest and watching the blood fly, hoping that this time that nagging guilt would go away, the

168

heaviness of spirit might disappear, peace might finally come. But if the report of Luke in the book of Acts is any indicator, it didn't happen. The law and associated guilt from not being able to carry it all out was a burden, not a pathway to God. Listen to the words of Peter at the Council of Jerusalem, as Luke reports: "Now therefore why do you make trial of God by putting a yoke upon the neck of the [new] disciples which neither our fathers nor we have been able to bear?" (Acts 15:10 RSV).

Peter is referring to the myriad of laws which the Jews had tried to follow, and which some of the leaders of the new Christian community were insisting new, non-Jewish converts had to observe when they became disciples of Christ. Like circumcision for example.

It wasn't working for us, said Peter, so why do we want to insist on it for others? Peter had experienced for the first time the thrill of freedom from compulsive offerings to try to get God to approve of him. And you will recall, he really tested that truth after he denied his Lord. And once more Jesus was found faithful.

It was Jesus' death on that cross which showed how much God loved humanity. It was the cross that got their attention, that revealed the lengths God would go to on behalf of his children. Are you brokenhearted? God really does know your pain.

Are you feeling distant from God? Jesus cried out on the cross, "My God, my God, why have your forsaken me?" The muck and the horror and the death and the chaos of this world has been experienced by God's Son. Like stopping a flaming oil well with dynamite, the world's sin was blasted into eternity at the cross, and in the calm that followed God calls us to believe God would never leave us or forsake us, no matter what, in this world or the next.

And yet ... and yet. Is your guilt gone? Is mine? Did Jesus die on that cruel cross in vain for you? For me? Are we still trying, still working at God's approval? Still holding out on loving others till they measure up?

Have you ever known a child or adult who never got the love and affection and affirmation from a parent that she so desperately craved? Do you know of the effort, the striving, the work required to live a life trying with every action, every phone call, to get

169

approval and love from a father or a mother? Not a pretty way to live. Are you one such child?

The great Leslie Weatherhead wrote a book the year I was born, 1945, called *The Meaning of the Cross*. In that book he wrote this paragraph which speaks so stirringly about the power of God's action in Jesus through the cross and resurrection:

> *In some moods — the mood, for example, in which I find myself on each Good Friday morning — one feels it almost a sacrilege to argue and to discuss. One desires then only to bow in adoration before the mystery of a love whose depths no one can sound and the range of whose august purposes is like that of a shooting star. It sweeps in from the Infinite and the Unknown, and comes near enough to earth so that we may see something of its shining glory. We watch with awe and wonder; but when all that can be seen by human eyes has passed into the darkness, and a cry is heard, "It is finished," we still know that a purpose goes on, beyond our vision, in the Infinite and the Unknown, and we cannot even imagine its scope....*[1]

You see, the power of the Gospel of Jesus Christ is not what we tend to make it and what those outside the Church assume it to be. Jesus' power was not just in his teachings of love, as central as they were. Why? Because the problem that afflicts us, the pain that dogs us, the reality that anyone can see in each of us is that so often we cannot love! Not consistently. Not fully. Not radically.

Instead we have to say with Saint Paul my personal theme-verse: "I do not understand my own actions. For I do not do what I want, but I do the very thing I hate" (Romans 7:15 RSV).

If this is true, then our real need is not more information about what we should do, how we should love, though it does give us a mighty goal and a great compass for our lives.

What we really need is a way to deal with our terrible failure at loving, a way to deal with the ugh in the gut, the whoosh of adrenaline rush as we realize we did it again, or we know we are about to.

For until we do feel at one with God again, we will be like the 400-pound man who has given up on dieting, for the way back

170

seems just too far. Only when we know of God's unfailing love toward us, will we have the energy to recommit our lives to serve and follow in the footsteps of Jesus.

But the author of Hebrews knows how hard that is, and so he adds these words at the end of this scripture paragraph. Listen:

> *Let us hold fast the confession of our hope without wavering, for he who promised is faithful; and let us consider how to stir up one another to love and good works, not neglecting to meet together, as is the habit of some, but encouraging one another....*
> — Hebrews 10:23-25 (RSV)

What I love about these verses is not that they seem to be an argument for more church meetings, but that they recognize the real, honest-to-goodness challenge that faces all humans when it comes to holding on to our hope that God really does forgive us. We really do not have to press and stress to make God smile. These verses remind us that an isolated Christian is a very vulnerable disciple. One little puff of negative energy or temptation at just the right time will throw us into guilt or sin. Is that not our situation?

We must not fail to meet together for encouragement and on-going learning. The mysterious event of the cross and the powerful and even more mysterious event of the resurrection are so totally foreign to the mind-set and assumptions of the world in which we work and play and live, that getting together is a vital discipline, not an optional activity when we have the time. Worship, small groups, eating together in our homes — all of these become the amplifiers which enable us to hear the too-good-to-be-true sweet voice of God, which said, "I love you," from the cross of Jesus — and says it still.

It is in fact, amazing grace, the sweetest sound there is to the human ear and the most healing and empowering gift to the human heart.

---

1. Leslie Weatherhead, *The Meaning of the Cross* (Abingdon Press), p. 21.

Easter
1 Corinthians 15:1-11

Do You Hear What I Hear?

I'm a bird lover, and spring time is prime time to get excited about our feathered friends. This past week I watched as robins and other birds scrounged bits of straw and other stringy things from my garden. It is nest building time!

If you've ever built a house you know the amount of time and effort it takes. Countless hours examining huge books of wall paper samples, floor plans, paint colors and on and on. So many decisions. What sort of house will it be?

Birds have it much easier. Each species of bird only makes one kind of nest. One kind. I have often thought, when peering through a pine tree at a robin's nest, that here I am, a reasonably intelligent man with lots of schooling and degrees, yet I could never make a robin's nest that would hold together and stay in a tree, unless, of course, I was allowed to use duct tape! The passing on of the skill of building a particular kind of nest from generation to generation of birds is truly an awe-inspiring miracle. If that skill were to be lost somehow — well, it would be catastrophic.

Since the crisis with China over the airplane incident, the Olympics have been talked about a lot, especially regarding China's desire to host the 2008 Olympics. One of the most dramatic moments that happens again and again in the Summer Olympics is the passing of the baton during relay races. What an exciting and anxious moment it is when the athletes exchange that baton! A sloppy hand-off loses precious seconds. A dropped baton will most likely cost the team the race altogether.

Passing on genes for nest building and the passing of the baton are great images symbolizing the important process of passing on vital skills and traditions and information.

One of the most difficult and in some cases discouraging things about being a parent is the tremendous challenge of passing on precious traditions and truths to our children, especially matters of faith. In fact, one of the most typical ways for children to rebel is precisely by rejecting the traditional celebration of our faith and involvement in the church.

This process is not new, of course, nor is its difficulty. We might wish that the passing on of faith in God might be as automatic as the process of building a nest for a robin or a hummingbird or a Baltimore oriole. But we know that the passing on of faith is a personal thing, and cannot be forced on someone. That includes passing on the old, old story of the resurrection of Jesus Christ.

Saint Paul was concerned about this matter of communicating the gospel message when he wrote to the Corinthians, "Now I would remind you, brethren, in what terms I preached to you the gospel, which you received, in which you stand, by which you are saved, if you hold it fast — unless you believed in vain" (1 Corinthians 15:1-2 RSV).

Saint Paul understood the process of transferring the life-changing Good News of the living Christ, which centered in the Easter story, the resurrection of Jesus, to others who knew nothing about it.

He divided this process up into five different phases. Think about how this process has worked or has not worked in your life: preaching, receiving, standing, being saved, and holding fast.

First there's the preaching of the Gospel. It needs to be communicated. He speaks of this basic task in his letter to the Romans, chapter 10. "How," he writes, "are they to believe in him of whom they have never heard? And how are they to hear without a preacher?" (v. 14). The task of clearly communicating the gospel is critical to passing it on to others. This includes preaching, small group studies, retreats, and the full repertoire of opportunities the church affords.

174

Secondly there is the receiving of the message. If a tree falls in a forest and no one is there to hear it, is there any sound? If the gospel is preached and no one is there to hear the message, has anything of significance happened? It is a worthwhile enterprise to find effective ways of securing a hearing in these days. It is a valid focus to question the assumption that it's "normal" for two thirds of a typical Christian congregation not to be present on a typical Sunday to hear and celebrate the message of God's saving action in Jesus Christ.

Thirdly, writes Saint Paul, after one has heard or received the message of the gospel, one must stand in it. There's a great German phrase, "zur Kenntnis nehmen." It means "to acknowledge something." It often is a way of deflecting a criticism or warning. "Okay, I hear you, but don't expect me to take any action on it or be affected by your words."

To stand in the gospel is to receive it *and allow it to influence your life*. To stand in it is to stand against that which would deny the gospel. To stand in it is not to go with the crowd. It is tough for a teenager to stand in the gospel today. The pressures are enormous to move in every other direction but the Christian walk. And of course one could say the same for adults.

Fourthly, the process of passing on the gospel is to have that wonderful joy of knowing you have been saved from a life of dead-end materialism to a life of hope and vitality and meaning, both in this life and the next, a life that will not lose its luster no matter how many toys you have or do not have, a life that finds meaning in loving and serving God and neighbor above all else.

And finally, Saint Paul says, all of the above will only happen if we hold fast to the gospel message. I hate to interrupt the flow of our thinking with something like football, but it's almost impossible to think about holding fast to something without thinking about "job one" for a running back on a football team. What is job one? That's right: it's simply holding on to the ball. And what is the job of the defense? To try to knock the ball out of the runner's grasp.

There is a whole world of influences today trying in subtle and not so subtle ways to pry our grip loose from the gospel by which we live, the gospel which Jesus' resurrection validated and brought

175

to life again. Saint Paul wrote, "For I delivered to you as of first importance what I also received...." He was saying it was now the responsibility and the privilege of those who heard that message to receive it, to stand in it, to rejoice in having been saved by it, and to hold on to it for dear life!

I am reading a great book by Jerry Linenger called *Off The Planet*, the story of his five months in the *Mir* space station. Listen to what he wrote in his introduction:

> *I wrote this book mainly because five months in space aboard Mir was one great adventure. I want my children to be able to read about it someday, to know what their father did, stood for, and was willing to sacrifice. I want them to be able to feel what it was like up there. My goal was to take them there with me.*

Mr. Linenger wanted his children to hear what he heard, to feel what he felt. It was that life-changing for him.

This is the kind of enthusiasm Saint Paul was calling for among the Corinthians. It had changed his life and he couldn't stand the thought of the message of new life in Christ being taken casually. Our task and our joy today is to stand boldly in that faith when we walk out of these doors and into the emotional, complicated, and stress-filled days of our lives. By the grace of God and the support of the community of faith, we can do it.

He is risen! He is risen indeed. Thanks be to God.

The Joy Of Shared Truth

The chasm between the realities in which two different people live can be vast. Such was the case in July of 2000 in Pompano Beach, Florida. Jamie Dean Petron, aged 41, had killed and injured two victims in a robbery there, when he then forced his way into the home of seventeen-year-old Althea Mills, who was there with some younger relatives.

Althea was threatened by the gunman, but she said that she kept taking comfort from a verse of scripture she had learned, 2 Timothy 1:7: "... for God did not give us a spirit of timidity but a spirit of power and love and self-control."

In the midst of this horrifying circumstance, Althea quietly began teaching her eight-year-old cousin to pray. Overhearing what she was doing, the gunman began to ask Althea about repentance and forgiveness. She then told him about God's forgiveness offered in Jesus. For 51 hours Jamie Petron held this family hostage, apparently even making some attempt to pray. Sadly, the gunman finally took his life to end the ordeal.[1]

Think of the gap between Althea Mills and Jamie Petron's realities and experiences! I have been impressed all my life by the difficulty of transferring hope and faith and truth from one person to another, from one brain to another, from one soul to another. Have you noticed that, too?

I will never forget that walk across the bridge over the Barge Canal by the locks in Baldwinsville, New York. I was a young teenager returning from a summer ecumenical service at the Baptist church. I had my Bible in hand and suddenly a humbly dressed man stopped me on the sidewalk and said, "Son, can you tell me what's in that book?" From the mind of a youth to the mind of an elderly man, toughened and hardened by the rough edges of his life, is a far piece. I felt it then, and I felt it some years later, only from a different direction.

When I was going through my most difficult spiritual desert, when faith seemed an inaccessible goal, I turned to people who seemed to possess faith. Those who knew me well eagerly turned to me to share their faith. Yet, not much of their enthusiastic sharing of faith made it across the gulf, even when I was eagerly reaching out for it. That, I found, was primarily God's business.

Do you know what I'm talking about?

The author of the first letter of John is trying with all his might to bridge that chasm between him and his readers. You can see some of that in the fact that he dispenses with the usual salutation at the beginning of his letter and plunges right in immediately:

> That which was from the beginning, which we have heard, which we have seen with our eyes, which we have looked upon and touched with our hands, concerning the word of life — the life was made manifest, and we saw it, and testify to it, and proclaim to you the eternal life which was with the Father and was made manifest to us — that which we have seen and heard we proclaim also to you....
> — 1 John 1:1-3a (RSV)

Do you hear that? He's trying in every way to convince his readers that what he's talking about is real. He and other disciples have heard and seen with their very eyes and touched this word of life, this Jesus. Such enthusiasm, yet such awareness of how impossible it must come across to others — just too good to be true. Will anyone ever believe it?

Have you ever had such an overwhelming experience that when you begin to tell someone about it you realize that there is no way to get it across to them? As you earnestly recount this great event, you notice the glazed look in their eyes, confirming your worst fears. They want to understand, but ...

I really believe that this is the basic issue we face today in the church as we seek to get the gospel message out. The words of scripture and our experience of the Holy God are light years from what's going on in the minds of those young adults driving cars with the "thump, thump, thump" bass sounds we hear a half mile away.

The gap between these words of scripture and the world you children and youth sitting here in church today live in is huge! The question is whether the church is willing to take the time and energy to do whatever it takes to bridge that gap and enable the message to get through to you.

The author of First John had the motivation to do so, and verse 4 tells us what it was: "And we are writing this that our joy may be complete." There really is a tremendous joy in finally connecting with another person with the truth of the Gospel of Jesus Christ. There is a great exhilarating rush of joy in knowing that another person has gotten a glimpse of the possibility of hope and peace through putting one's hand in the hand of God through Jesus Christ.

Our world is desperately searching for the real and the true. And one of the things that makes the search so difficult is the media and Hollywood, which are making the unreal so real that no one is sure what is real and what isn't. This spills over of course into the spiritual, as well.

A recent special issue of *Forbes Magazine* had as its theme, What Is True? It reminded me of Pilate's question spoken when dealing with Jesus, "What is truth?" (John 18:38). This issue of *Forbes* was a fascinating compilation of articles about what is real in the digital age. One of the articles was by Danny Hillis, a designer of one of the fastest supercomputers in the world. He told of going to Disney World with his children. His young son Noah made the intriguing comment: "Dad, this is a fake Disneyland." A fake Disneyland. Does that make Disneyland real? Is it?

He also told about his five-year-old daughter, India, who one day showed him her craft project, an animal made from fresh fruit. "It's a dog," she told him. Sensing his puzzlement she added, "Well, actually, it's a banana. If you make a banana into a dog, it's a dog.

179

But it's still a banana." Did you follow all that? Danny Hillis concluded his article with these two sentences: "I have learned to relax, and enjoy the ambiguity. I no longer believe in the Real."

Danny Hillis does not have a corner on that mindset. The world is coming to assume that when you get down to the basic structure of things there may very well be just a Star Trek holodeck, and what seems real is just a bunch of zeros and ones in a computer or just a bunch of chemicals randomly forming things, as beautiful crystals are formed on a string dangling in a supersaturated solution of salt and water. Is that really all there is, as the old song goes? People today hover between a fear and a belief that that is so. If we as disciples of Jesus Christ do not share the Good News, who will?

Remember that hymn: "What a fellowship, what a joy divine leaning on the everlasting arms...." It is a great joy and leads to great fellowship, when instead of hesitantly leaning on technology and layers of images, one "gets it" and is able to cross the great chasm, take the leap of faith, and dare to lean on the everlasting arms, the real, present Holy Spirit of God.

Saint Paul wrote in his letter to the Philippians, "... complete my joy by being of the same mind, having the same love, being in full accord and of one mind" (Philippians 2:1 RSV).

Being of one mind does not mean that we will all agree on the details of the great mysteries of life and death. But it does mean that we will be a fellowship that stands joyfully and faithfully under the guidance and love and challenge of the Holy Spirit, ready and eager to walk in the footsteps of Jesus, as best we know how.

That, my friends, is the Church at its best. What a fellowship, what a joy divine, leaning not on drugs or hype or a Sabres or Bills win, or a good salary or even a job; leaning not on the good life, the test coming out well, or the pet surviving; leaning not on good weather for the party or a good outcome of the conversation with a child or parent or boss.

The fellowship the writer of First John is talking about is a fellowship that deepens by leaning together on the everlasting arms of God, seen, heard and touched in Jesus, and proclaimed by those first disciples. Those first disciples were hoping and praying that those who have not touched or seen or heard with their own eyes might believe their testimony, even as Jesus told doubting Thomas, "Blessed are those who don't see and yet believe...."

Those first disciples are rooting for you and for me today. Do you hear them? Will we respond with faith? Ah, the joy of sharing the truth of God, even across the eons of time.

---

1. Found in *The Interpreter*, November/December 2000, p. 20.

Learning From The Spider

I've always been amazed by spiders. I love to watch them spin their webs and catch their prey. I remember as a child we had lots of spiders in our garage and we would catch flies and other bugs and throw them into a web to see the spider come rushing out along the strands to plunge in the paralyzing digestive juices. It would then wrap the prey up in a nice little bundle, for a late-night snack.

Some spiders stay at the middle of a web that is stretched between branches or boards. Other spiders have a tunnel that disappears into a corner of a bush or a building. In either case, the spider stays at that center spot or waits at the mouth of the tunnel, waiting for the slightest movement of the web, indicating supper!

I know preachers' minds make sometimes unlikely connections, but the truth is that this image of the spider and the web came to mind as I was preparing for this series of sermons over the next few Sundays which deal with the powerful gospel message as told in the first letter of John.

Let us not confuse the three short letters of John near the end of the New Testament with the Gospel according to Saint John, situated early on in the New Testament, following the first three Gospels, Matthew, Mark, and Luke. Scholars are not certain whether the writer of the Gospel of John also wrote these three letters, though much of the wording and flavor are the same. For our purposes it really doesn't matter. It is interesting to note, however, that the author of Second and Third John refers to himself as "the elder." It is fairly safe to assume that it is this same "elder" who wrote First John as well.

As I said, the image of a spider came to mind as I was reading 1 John 3, and I'll tell you why. In the first verse of chapter 3, the elder writes that "the reason why the world does not know us is that it did not know God." And then in 2 John and 3 John, the elder admonishes his readers to "abide in him." Abide in God.

What an image. There are so many things we are called to do as followers of Jesus. John, the elder, says that the main one is to "abide in God."

And here's where the spider crawled onto the web of my brain. I pictured the spider, staying in the comforting, safe home, either at the center of the web or in the dark cavity at the end of the tunnel. Only when there is something very important to do does that spider venture forth. And when the job is done, back home it goes.

Think how the spider would be unable to focus on its purpose if it were wandering about on the web, rather than staying at home.

I thought about us. I thought about myself. Scampering about on the web, doing so many things, important things, good things, but not necessarily the most important thing, which is "abiding in God," absorbing the mind of God. For Christians that means coming to know the mind of Christ.

You see, according to the author of 1 John, the reason those who stand outside the community of faith don't know us, and don't understand us, is that they do not know the God we worship. Those who have not heard of or come to know the God revealed through Jesus Christ, only know a God who pats you on the head and answers your prayers if you are good, and sees that you are run over by a back hoe or get cancer if you're bad. For such uninformed folks, talk of forgiveness and loving your enemies just sounds naive and stupid.

That's not to mention those who can't relate to a loving Father because of all that their own father did to them or because their father was absent for them, either emotionally or physically. There are many images of God. Just to say the name God doesn't mean that we're talking about the same entity.

Jesus came to introduce us to who God is. And while many of the struggles in this world, such as with morality and the existence of pain and suffering and evil remain the same, knowing who God is, knowing with whom we are dealing, makes all the difference. Jesus was always saying, "You have heard it said, but I say ..." — six times in Matthew alone.

If that is true, then our task is clearly to continue to focus on maintaining a relationship with God. If the challenges of the world seduce us into just running around the web of life, putting out fires and doing lots of seemingly good things, and forget our center, forget our motivation and our mentor and our power and our guide, we will find ourselves out of gas, angry at those who don't respond to the gospel, and judgmental in our approach.

The elder writes in verse 3 that if our hope is in God, we are purified. Our motivations are purified, our minds and hearts are purified, and we find more energy to live and serve as we place our hope and trust, not in our own efforts and creativity, but in the secret, powerful, mysterious, sometimes agonizingly slow activity of almighty God.

The disciples were often irritated and confused about Jesus. He would be off praying when people needed him (Mark 1), or he would be asleep in the boat when the waves and wind were raging (Matthew 8). That's because Jesus knew all about spiders. He stayed "at home," at the center, in the heart of God, and from that center found the peace that passes all understanding, which enabled him to function out in the web of life, out in the challenging world of sin and selfishness, with peace and courage, confident in the power and ultimate victory of God.

Learn from the spider. Follow Jesus.

Training The Heart

Not long ago I heard about one more study done with rats. This particular study seemed to indicate that the amount of stress experienced by baby rats in their first ten days set their bodies for the rest of their lives as to how the rats would react to stressful situations. As I recall, there are at least two factors at work. First of all, in a stressful situation a chemical is produced that triggers the stress response throughout the body. Secondly, there are receptors throughout the body which sense that chemical and alert the appropriate glands and organs to get ready for "fight or flight."

If during those first ten days of life the baby rat experienced a lot of stress, especially from the mother, then the brain is programmed permanently to produce a lot of the stress chemical and a higher than average number of receptors are produced throughout the rat's body. In other words, not only is there more chemical screaming *stress*, but the rat is more sensitive to and responsive to that stress chemical.

On the other hand, if the baby rat experiences a low level of stress during that same period of time, the brain is permanently programmed to produce lower levels of that chemical when stressed, plus fewer receptors for that chemical appear throughout the body. In this case, the rat would be less reactive and more calm in a stressful situation because less chemical is poured into the body and fewer receptors are there to respond. Whether this plays out the same way in the early days of a human baby is not known, but it gives us pause.

I find this a fascinating study. It reminds me a bit of that song from *South Pacific*. Remember the words? "You have to be taught before it's too late, before you are six or seven or eight, to hate all the people your relatives hate; you have to be carefully taught; you have to be carefully taught."

There are very basic things that are learned psychologically and built in physically and emotionally at an early age. And such learning, or "programming," if you will, has profound implications for the rest of a person's life.

The Bible is full of references to one's heart, which is often referred to metaphorically as the seat of one's intellect, will, and conscience. In the scripture for this morning, the author of First John speaks a very important word about the place that the heart has in a person's relationship with God and others.

But long before this writer took quill pen to parchment, the Psalmist had been writing about the heart. Given our rat story and the recognition of the importance of early training to program us for good or evil, for emotional well-being or fragility, Psalm 139 stands out as a very significant word for all time.

Remember some of the verses in that Psalm? Verse 13: "It was you who formed my inward parts; you knit me together in my mother's womb." And then those powerful final verses: "Search me, O God, and know my heart; test me and know my thoughts. See if there is any wicked way in me, and lead me in the way everlasting" (vv. 23, 24 RSV).

The heart. The formation of the heart, which responds to God and others, is vital in a person's life. How important then to see to it that our children and our youth have opportunities to enable their hearts to be trained aright. How grateful we can be when a little one has the blessing of a mother who is not so inwardly wounded that she is unable to train the heart of her child in a way that will bring joy and balance to that life, before God and the world!

How vital it is that the church be consciously about the process of training the hearts of its people, that they might be permanently receptive to God and open to the way of life seen in and through Jesus Christ, relative to our neighbors, near and far.

Psalm 51 has a wonderful message to it which should be our daily prayer. "Create in me a clean heart, O God, and put a new and right spirit within me" (v. 10 RSV).

All of us can think of a person whose heart was not formed well, a person whose heart is filthy and bitter, a heart that is unable to respond to another's pain with compassion.

Or, and this is the insightful gem in our scripture reading for today from 1 John, there are those who have been brought up to feel guilty about everything, who never know peace. There are those whose hearts constantly condemn them, as the writer of John puts it.

Rather we need to pray this prayer: "Create in me a clean heart, O God, and renew a right spirit within me."

How hard it is for us to have balance in our lives when it comes to deciding when enough is enough, when we have cared enough, when we have sacrificed enough. Of course, you and I know that we don't sacrifice very well or very much. But I am also convinced that God does not call us to a life of constant guilt, which keeps us from the abundant life to which Jesus specifically calls us (John 10:10) or keeps us from knowing when guilt should be listened to, as a word from God. One can be so caught up in little compulsive guilt trips that, like the boy who hollered, "Wolf!" too often, we are emotionally unable to respond to those times when guilt is real and appropriate and should be listened to.

I think I have told you before about the preacher who caught a fly ball at a baseball game and felt so guilty that he hadn't paid for it that he wrote a letter to the commissioner of baseball offering to pay for the ball! The commissioner responded: "Shame on you for worrying over such petty, silly things. I would hope that a leader of the church would have better judgment and would be spending time and energy on truly important matters." This preacher's heart was not properly formed in its early stages. One wonders what parent or teacher or preacher taught him such unhealthy, compulsive responses.

The writer of this first letter of John says that we should love not just in word but in deed, yes, but that there are also those times when we should reassure our heart when it unjustly condemns us, for God is greater than our early programming. God is greater than the guilt trips which tend to be passed on as the Christian gospel.

Rather we should pray this prayer: "Create in me a clean heart, O God, and renew a right spirit within me."

It's not easy to develop a clean heart and a right spirit. Martin Luther, the German reformer who tried early in the sixteenth century to reform the Roman Catholic Church, spoke to this issue. He wrote, "The conscience is one drop; the reconciled God is a sea of comfort."

In a commentary on 1 John, the writer says this as he quotes these words of Luther: "Our supreme court is not the human heart, whose feelings are fickle and manipulable by fear to self-condemnation. Our court of final appeal is God...." The author of this commentary goes on to say that these verses in 1 John "amount to a repudiation of any attempt by any Christian to lay a cheap guilt trip on anyone."[1]

I would challenge us all today to examine our hearts this coming week. When we feel the pangs of guilt, is it truly something that comes from the heart of God that needs to be responded to, or is it unhealthy guilt, thrown up by our subconscious or an old tape recording of compulsive guilt recorded in our formative years by wounded or misguided or misinformed mentors, falsely condemning our heart?

Or is it the word of God, calling us to take loving, courageous action, to repent, change directions, and walk more faithfully in the footsteps of Jesus?

In order to listen attentively and rightly, we will need to train our hearts. The good news is that by the power of God, through Jesus Christ, experienced through worship and small group study and fellowship with caring members of the Body of Christ, the Church, malformed hearts can be healed and renewed!

Let us say once again our prayer for ourselves and all those whose task is to form young hearts in the likeness of Jesus Christ: "Create in me a clean heart, O God, and renew a right spirit within me."

---

1. *The New Interpreter's Bible*, Vol. XII, p. 424.

Easy To Say; Hard To Do

"Love is a many splendored thing...." Or so we heard Don Cornwall and the Four Aces sing time and again. Of course you or I might have other words to describe love, depending on our situation.

Love. "I love you." "I love to play golf." "I just *love* pistachio lush!" "It's tough to love some people." "Jesus loves me, this I know."

Love.

What can be said about love that has not already been said? The writer of the first letter of John obviously thought deeply about love and did his best to write about it. Saint Paul had a similar piece on love which he wrote to the church at Corinth. We know it as the Love Chapter, 1 Corinthians 13. Remember? "If I speak in the tongues of men and of angels but have not love, I am a noisy gong or a clanging cymbal ... Faith, hope, love abide, these three; but the greatest of these is love" (RSV).

Great things have been written about love and wonderful things have been done and are still being done motivated by love. Yet, we can still sing with great fervor another popular song: "What the world needs now, is love, sweet love, that's the only thing, that there's just too little of...."

Need I list the horrors of Sierra Leone and countless other places on this Good Earth where violence still stalks daily life? Need I list the hopelessness and violence in our cities and poor rural areas and plush suburbs in our own nation, where meaninglessness is a daily companion to millions, and violence of all sorts is commonplace?

191

Indeed, it is surely true, that "what the world needs now, is love, sweet love...."

Why could it be, 2,000 years after God gave us the Prince of Peace, Jesus Christ, to teach us and live before humanity the truth that God loves us with an everlasting love, as Jeremiah had said years ago (Jeremiah 31:3)? Not only that, but Jesus also made it clear that God loves us even in our sin; we don't have to offer a sacrifice to approach God and be right with God. How could it be that such a great and life-changing salvation, such a great love, could still elude so many in so many places in this world?

I think a brief two words in our scripture reading this morning might help us. To get the relevant verses in our heads, I'd like us to remind ourselves of a song I used to teach the campers in our summer church camp.

> *Beloved, let us love one another, love one another.*
> *For love is of God, and everyone who loveth is born of*
> * God,*
> *And knoweth God.*
> *He that loveth not, knoweth not God, for God is love,*
> *God is love.*
> *Beloved, let us love one another,*
> *First John four, seven and eight.*

What I want us to note are the two words in verse 7. The author writes, "For love is *of God*." The *New Revised Standard Version* states that "love is *from* God." *The New International Version* says that "love *comes from* God."

The first statement the author of 1 John makes about the specific relationship between God and love makes it clear that God is not an ephemeral, mysterious force field of goodness which we call love. Rather love is a quality of being, a quality of relating which comes *from* God; it's a gift from God.

In other words, the selfless, sacrificial, other-centered love we know from Jesus, which calls us and enables us to forgive those who have wronged us or even to love our enemies, that kind of love cannot simply be passed on from person to person. That kind of love must be grown fresh in each human heart from contact with and living with God, the God we have come to know through Jesus Christ.

Let's listen to the words again:

Beloved, let us love one another, love one another.
For love is of God, and everyone who loveth is born of
*   God,*
And knoweth God.
He that loveth not, knoweth not God, for God is love,
God is love.
Beloved, let us love one another,
First John four, seven and eight.

In trying to think through how to communicate the significance of this seemingly obvious point, an example came to mind from the computer world. When you install a new computer software program, there are many complicated programs which really need to be installed from the original installation CD or disks. Just copying the program from one computer to another does not install it properly. Sooner or later, and probably sooner, you will find that the copied program just doesn't work properly. It's not properly integrated with all the files, something the installation process does automatically. Frustrated, you have to go searching for the original installation disks or CD to install it properly.

My friends, Christian love, the sort that moves mountains, the kind Jesus died to reveal, is not just a nice feeling or set of good intentions. Real love, which enables one to forgive the unforgivable and causes people to do things that look foolish to those who do not understand, such love needs the direct "installation" and support and nurture from God. And to be anything less than honest about that will only lead people into deep waters and great disillusionment if they try it on their own thinking, "Oh, I see. I can do that." It's like seeing a runner loping down the road and saying to yourself, "Hey, I could run that fast!" unaware of the years of daily training required to do what she does.

Recently I ran across the notes from a Pastor's School I attended back in 1977. Listen:

*A man was badly deformed from birth and was angry
and sinful as he was growing up. He hated himself and
others and was bitter toward God.*

*Then there came a time when one of his neighbors
invited him into a Sunday school class. This was a class
that taught and learned, that shared fellowship at other
times than just during the church school hour, and which
was also involved in service projects.*

*Over a period of months this man began to be
touched by what he was experiencing. One day it really came over him how much that group of people really loved him. It seemed impossible.*

*Another day he was struck by their Bible study which
revealed again and again that God loves you as you
are. "In Jesus Christ, know that God loves you." "Impossible," he thought.*

*Another day he was touched by the joy of the shar-
ing of skills, money, and effort with others in meaningful, difficult service and mission projects. "I can't be
doing this," he thought. "Impossible."*

*And suddenly, one day, he got up in the morning and
looked in the mirror and realized that for the first time
in his life he could say to the one looking back at him,
"I love you." And he became a new man.*

*Were it not for the church and the gospel it carries,
that never would have happened. It took regular involvement in study, fellowship, and service in the church,
which enabled the love of God and the love of God
through persons, to enable that man to love himself.
And then everything was different.*

The speaker concluded this way: "I'll bet that the church he
was in was not perfect. But the love which that man came to know
was."

Way back in 1930 Dorothy Day said these words:

*... it is love that will burn out the sins and hatreds that
sadden us. It is love that will make us want to do great
things for each other. No sacrifice and no suffering will
then seem too much.*[1]

194

That kind of love comes from and is maintained only directly from the heart of God, whom we know in Jesus Christ.

So what does that mean for you today? For me?

Let's sing again:

Beloved, let us love one another, love one another.
For love is of God, and everyone who loveth is born of
  God,
And knoweth God.
He that loveth not, knoweth not God, for God is love,
God is love.
Beloved, let us love one another,
First John four, seven and eight.

---

1. Dorothy Day, *House of Hospitality*, ca. 1930.

The World's Still Point

Just this past week I received an e-mail from a gentleman I do not know. He was obviously sending this e-mail out to a long list of people. In essence his message was that I should go to a web site he listed and read the essay there about abortion. At one point in his e-mail he wrote the following:

> *Remember, abortion is not just a political issue. It is very much a religious one. It drives straight to the heart of our beliefs. I am going to do everything possible to tell believers about this essay and I ask for your help also.*

Now my point this morning is not to talk about abortion. This morning, rather, I would like us to focus on a sentence in this marvelous first letter of John, imbedded in the fifth chapter, verses 4 and 5:

> *For whatever is born of God overcomes the world; and this is the victory that overcomes the world, our faith. Who is it that overcomes the world but he who believes that Jesus is the Son of God?*

What the author, called "the Elder" in one of the other little letters of John, writes here affirms that what has the ability to bring victory over evil is faith, and not just some generic faith in the goodness of humanity or the inevitability of social improvement.

Rather the Elder writes that this faith is centered in the person of Jesus Christ.

How strange it is that in the course of our lives we easily allow that which is not central to become in fact central in our time and emotions and expenditure of energy.

Surely you have heard the story of the young sailor on board a small ship that was sailing the ocean. The captain asked him to take the helm while he took a brief nap. It was in the middle of the night and the stars were shining brightly. "All you need to do," explained the captain, "is follow the North Star," which he carefully pointed out to the young man. "Do you think you can do it?" said the captain. "Yes, sir!" said the sailor proudly. "You can count on me." And he put his hands on the big wheel and the captain disappeared below.

Several hours later the captain woke up from his nap and came up to the helm. Glancing at the sky he knew immediately that something was wrong. "Hey, sailor. What are you doing? Why aren't we headed toward the North Star?"

"Oh," said the sailor, puzzled at the captain's amazement. "We passed that an hour ago!"

The captain knew that the only reliable point in the midst of the wind and the waves, the only steady point in the world of confusion and emotions and guess-work over direction and currents and relationships, was the Polar Star, the North Star. To stray from that star was to stray off course, period.

Did you ever notice that what thrills and confuses, excites and mystifies, inspires and challenges someone who is new to the Christian faith is not all the traditions and morals and commandments about which we often spend so much time arguing. What grabs the attention of new Christians is Jesus.

I have noted in my own life that it is so easy to get caught up in all sorts of very important matters of life and church and theology. I find all that stimulating and it has a way of consuming one and making one think one is doing something very important.

But I have also noticed that when I focus on Jesus, interest turns to awe and stimulation is replaced by inspiration.

T. S. Eliot wrote of the search for "the still point of the turning world." The Old Testament from the beginning to the end affirms that there can be no other center of our lives than God. From the beginning of the New Testament to the end we read a witness to the fact that Jesus provides a face and a way to know God.

Those who have grown up with Jesus can easily forget that without Jesus there would be no Christian faith and no center and no peace. We would still be trying to find a way to get an unpredictable, punitive God off our back with sacrifices and laws.

How critical it is for us to remember to focus on our common commitment to God known in Jesus, rather than on the very important, but still *secondary* issues that commitment to the Lord leads us to grapple with, such as war and peace, abortion, homosexuality, welfare, and a host of other vital issues of our time.

If we are to avoid more wars, then we as Christians must gently argue about how best to do it, but keep our eyes on Jesus. We must put our shoulder to the wheel and work for peace at home, at school, at work, at play, but we must keep our eyes on Jesus. We must struggle against racism and greed and immorality as we understand them, but we must keep our eyes on Jesus.

The writer of a commentary on 1 John wrote this: "If Christ occupies the center at which faith comes into focus, then other things, however important, do not."[1]

Mother Teresa was speaking to a group of people who had come from around the world to see her and her work. When she asked for questions, one person from a religious order asked, "How is it that your religious order is gaining members by the thousands and most of our orders are losing members?"

Without hesitating, Mother Teresa answered, "I give them Jesus."

"Yes, I know," pursued the woman. "But take habits, for example. Do your women object to wearing habits? And how do you set up the rules of your order?"

"I give them Jesus," Mother Teresa replied.

"Yes, I know, Mother, but can you be more specific?"

"I give them Jesus," she repeated.

"Mother," went on the questioner, "we are so very much aware of your fine work. I want to know about something else ..."

Mother Teresa said quietly, "I give them Jesus. There is nothing else."

Mother Teresa was able to stay focused on "the least of these" and was able to inspire others to do the same because, while she was not afraid to speak out on matters of policy and root causes, she had a center. She had a still point.

A good question for us this week might be this: What is our still point around which everything else turns in our life? Is it our anger over violence? Is it our anger over the youth of today ... or the adults? Is it our upward mobility and the stock market? Is it our health?

"Where our treasure is, there will our heart be also." I do believe Jesus uttered those words, did he not! And if our heart is set on anything — anything — that can die or rust or be taken away, then we are living on a fragile foundation.

God whom we know in Jesus is the only foundation that will never shake and never fall or fail. So I think it might be a good thing to focus on the Polar Star, to spend some time with Jesus.

The world's still point. Still.

---

1. *The New Interpreter's Bible*, Vol. XII, p. 437.

Height Advantage

One of the key inventions of the modern world is the geostationary or geosynchronous satellite, many of which are now orbiting the earth today. The fancy term "geostationary" means that the satellite's orbital velocity exactly matches the rotation of the Earth under it. Therefore it remains stationary in the sky, typically orbiting about 22,000 miles above the earth. The first operational geosynchronous satellite (Syncom 2) was launched back in 1963, the year I graduated from high school.

Many of you can still remember the challenge of the early space flights when the astronauts could only be in contact with the earth when they were directly over a ground station. Such contact would only last a few minutes and in a crisis that got really interesting for both the astronauts and the ground controllers!

Today, with the need for constant communication for transmission of television and radio signals, having a satellite lodged in one spot in the sky that can cover virtually one whole side of the earth is an obvious critical need. With several such satellites in orbit, one can be in constant communication with any part of the globe, something we saw firsthand in dramatic fashion during the hours of television transmission as 1999 turned to the year 2000.

Imagine today one of the networks being willing to limit its communication range to line of sight transmission, or around seven miles. No matter how wonderful the programming, only those within a radius of seven miles or so would be able to see or hear it. As odd as it sounds, this is exactly what God was willing to do in coming to Palestine as a human being. As long as Jesus was in the

201

flesh, his influence was limited to those few people around him in time and space. Today I want us to look at Jesus' Ascension, when Jesus' physical presence left the earth, in only a few days to be replaced by the Holy Spirit. The impact of the ascension, to use the network television analogy, was like filling the skies with geostationary satellites, in terms of humanity's ability to communicate with the Spirit of God in Jesus Christ.

Now I am fully aware of how removed this may seem to be from your everyday life. It may not seem relevant to the exam coming up this week or the bills that remain unpaid or the problem you are having with your boss or spouse or child or parent, but it is, in fact, directly related to all of these matters.

Is it not true that the natural reaction to hitting a brick wall of fear or anxiety or frustration is to close the eyes or look up and think or say, "Oh, God ..."? We're talking about our human need for guidance, comfort, and strength for the living of our days. And the Ascension is all about exactly that.

Arnold B. Rhodes has written that "the Ascension is the dividing line between the appearances of the Risen Lord to eyewitnesses and the coming of the Holy Spirit upon the church."[1]

What does that mean? To explain that let me very briefly remind us of four terms in scripture: the resurrection, the post-resurrection appearances, the Ascension, and the coming of the Holy Spirit at Pentecost.

The resurrection which we celebrate on Easter Sunday is the event of God's raising Jesus from the dead following the crucifixion on Good Friday.

Following the resurrection there were a number of appearances of the risen Lord to his disciples and to others, the most memorable ones being his appearance to Mary Magdalene near the tomb, to Doubting Thomas, and to the two followers on the way to Emmaus (cf. Luke 24:13ff, John 20:11ff and 26ff, Acts 1:3, 1 Corinthians 15:1-8). Often people saw him but didn't recognize him at first, making it clear that his resurrected body was something very unique.

Then there is the Ascension, which took place around forty days after his resurrection, when he disappeared into a cloud at the top of a mountain, leaving the disciples stunned and confused and anxious.

Assuming the Ascension took place about forty days after the resurrection, one could say it was about ten days later when the disciples were gathered together in one place in Jerusalem, during the Jewish feast of Pentecost, still waiting for something to give them directions, a "power" Jesus indicated would be given them some time soon (Acts 1:8a). It was then that they had a dramatic encounter with the presence of God, appearing to them like the rush of a violent wind and tongues of fire on their heads. From that time on they were filled with courage and direction. From the time of Pentecost, the Church began to do what Jesus had called them to do at the time of his Ascension.

Remember? He told them that after they had received power, they should be his witnesses "in Jerusalem, in all Judea and Samaria, and to the end of the earth." In other words, they were called to witness to God's love in Jesus at home (Jerusalem), in nearby familiar towns and villages (Judea), among people they typically hated (Samaria), and around the world (Acts 1:8).

Do you see now how "the Ascension is the dividing line between the appearances of the Risen Lord to eyewitnesses and the coming of the Holy Spirit upon the church"? As of the Ascension we have the ever-present contact with the Spirit of God known through Jesus Christ.

As Augustine put it: "You ascended from before our eyes, and we turned back grieving, only to find you in our hearts."

And now the scripture Saint Paul wrote to the church at Ephesus comes alive: "... the working of his great might which he accomplished in Christ when he raised him from the dead and made him sit at his right hand in the heavenly places" (Ephesians 1:19-20).

What was accomplished by God's "great might" enables the Spirit of Jesus Christ, which was available in the flesh so long ago, to be available to you and me today. What a privilege!

I was surprised back in April of 1994, at the strong reaction I received to something I said in a sermon that day. I spoke of the beautiful song which came out early in '91, "From A Distance."

The song concludes with these words: "God is watching us, God is watching us, God is watching us ... *from a distance.*"

What I said at the time was that the song taught a terrible untruth, namely that God is "out there" watching us "from a distance," the very idea which the coming of Jesus was to counter. It was, I said, nothing less than heresy. God is, rather, closer than our very breath!

Well, this morning, for those of you who love that song (and I really do enjoy most of it!), I would say that, for our human minds, it may be helpful for us to picture God above the earth in order to communicate at all times with all people, in the same way a geostationary satellite does. I'll buy it — sort of. As a matter of fact, one could say that is what the Ascension is all about. Jesus ascended into Heaven, so that "from a distance," the Spirit of God in Jesus could be available in the heart of every person on earth.

Of course, we need to remind ourselves that these "up" and "out there" physical images are only feeble attempts to speak of our mysterious and loving God whose character and being we have glimpsed through Jesus Christ.

Ascension Day is celebrated on the fortieth day after Easter, or the sixth Thursday after Easter. That's this Thursday. Mark your calendar. Get out of bed this Thursday with joy and gratitude, for Jesus has ascended into heaven, and his Spirit is therefore available today to warm your heart and enable you to walk in his footsteps and live even your challenging life with courage and hope.

Thanks be to God.

---

1. Arnold B. Rhodes, *The Mighty Acts of God*, 1985, p. 324.

Spelling Doesn't Count

How many of you know what BASE jumping is? BASE jumping is the very scary sport of jumping off *B*uildings, *A*ntennae, *S*pans, and *E*arth objects. If you want to do it more than once, you jump with a parachute or perhaps a hang glider. Some of you may have seen examples of this daring sport on television.

An example:

> *Austrian extreme sportsman Felix Baumgartner, 30, took a sunrise swan dive off the outstretched hand of the Christ the Redeemer statue overlooking Rio de Janeiro. BASE jumpers, who parachute from fixed objects, often run afoul of the law. So Baumgartner had to smuggle his chute and kit (including the crossbow and steel cable he used to climb the 100-foot concrete-and-soapstone structure) onto a train carrying tourists up the 2,300-foot mountain, then scale the statue under cover of night. "This was real hardcore," said Baumgartner, who survived the jump and was whisked away in a waiting car. "Now I know why none of my colleagues have tried this before."[1]*

Timothy F. Merrill, author of *Learning to Fall: A Guide for the Spiritually Clumsy*, wrote this about falling:

> *Unlike myself, many people enjoy the emotions of falling. They jump from airplanes, hot air balloons, bridges, skyscrapers, and high mountain cliffs. They*

*dive off 30-meter platforms and oceanside bluffs ... But
if you don't have enough altitude, grabbing a parachute
isn't going to help much! It is important to gain altitude in life, rise above the battle, get beyond the irritations you have hitherto felt were so important.*

He then quotes Ray Bradbury who says that ...

*if we listened to our intellect, we'd never have a love
affair, we'd never have friendship, we'd never go into
business because we'd be so cynical ... That's nonsense.
You've got to jump off cliffs all the time and build your
wings on the way down.*[2]

Wow! Sounds like risky, exciting business, this jumping off
things and building wings in flight!

What I'd like to suggest this morning is that it is just such out-
of-the ordinary, pushing-the-envelope stuff which enables us to experience the fullness of life for which God created us, and to which
we are called in Jesus.

Over the last few weeks we've been looking at that marvelous
little letter called 1 John, nestled between 2 Peter and 2 John in the
New Testament. Last week we read from the first few verses of the
fifth chapter, in which the author made it clear that it is a faith
centered in an understanding of God we have come to know through
Jesus, which enables us to tackle the challenges of the world.

Today we continue in the same fifth chapter. Here the author
focuses on what he calls "the testimony" which God has made
through Jesus. It's one of those precious verses in the Bible where
the writer seeks to condense the whole message, or "testimony" of
God to humanity, in a few words. Here is what the author of 1 John
says in the eleventh verse of chapter 5: "And this is the testimony:
God gave us eternal life, and this life is in his Son."

The testimony of God is that God has given us eternal life, and
this life is seen and explained and revealed in Jesus Christ.

So what is this eternal life? There is a place in the Bible where
eternal life is defined. Here is what Jesus says in the Gospel of

John: "And this is eternal life, that they may know you, the only true God, and Jesus Christ whom you have sent" (3:17 RSV).

So eternal life is more than just life after death or immortality. This verse would indicate that we're talking about a quality of life that can begin now — a life that is marked primarily by knowing and relating to God. And further, and this is what I want us to note today, this knowing of God is to be found in Jesus (v. 11).

So what does that mean? I believe it has a very practical and vital meaning for you and me in our Christian lives. Eternal life is to be found in Jesus because it is through walking in his footsteps that we learn to trust in God and thereby know God.

What does it take to get a glimpse of this thing called eternal life? It just doesn't seem to work very well just to think about it, right? It goes back to that great line that "you can act your way into thinking much easier than you can think your way into acting." I believe that is why John writes that "eternal life is in God's Son." It is Jesus who is always BASE jumping, always doing crazy, unexpected things. And as we walk and jump in the footsteps and hang gliders of Jesus, we get our wings, we experience eternal life. We learn to trust and learn the joy of the life with God we were created to experience.

Life with God that we access through Jesus is not a life where we are always worrying about whether we've done this or that wrong. Life with God, eternal life in which we know God, is not trying to communicate with a God who is always looking for the corrections, the grammar checks. Life with God, eternal life, is not just an anxious life, wondering whether, after we've done our best piece of work, the Great Spell Checker in the sky will ignore our effort and instead see our mistakes. Ever have a love letter to your parents returned with the misspellings underlined? That's what many people feel any effort to be faithful to God will result in.

The testimony of God, says the writer of 1 John, is that we have been given eternal life, and if you want to know what that is, don't sit at home pondering. Go BASE jumping with Jesus! Do what Jesus would do, who *lived* eternal life! Go on a work camp. Go serve food in a soup kitchen. Work with youth. Visit the elderly. Teach a Sunday school class. Tell your boss to stop using the

Lord's name in vain. Tell your best friend to cool it with the swear words. Find new ways to love and forgive friends and members of your family, beyond what is expected. Go BASE jumping with Jesus, and you will find eternal life. And even if you fall, God's Spirit and the Body of Christ are there to catch you.

What would eternal life look like? I'll give you one example:

> *Two brothers worked together on the family farm. One was married and had a large family. The other was single. At the day's end the brothers shared everything equally, produce and profit.*
>
> *One day the single brother said to himself, "It's not right that we should share equally the produce and the profit. I'm alone, and my needs are simple." So each night he took a sack of grain from his bin and crept across the field between their homes, dumping it into his brother's bin.*
>
> *Meanwhile, the married brother said to himself, "It's not right that we should share the produce and the profit equally. After all, I'm married, and I have my wife and children to look after me in years to come. My brother has no one, and no one to take care of his future." So each night he took a sack of grain and dumped it into his single brother's bin.*
>
> *Both men were puzzled for years because their supply of grain never dwindled. Then one dark night the two brothers bumped into each other. Slowly it dawned on them what was happening. They dropped their sacks and embraced one another.*[3]

Those brothers tasted eternal life.

Pray that this week you might be led to do some BASE jumping with Jesus, the out of the ordinary, the thing you can only do by God's power, and in the process, find the wings of eternal life.

---

1. Art Koan, "The Big Picture: Brazil," *Life*, February 2000, p. 22.

2. Timothy F. Merrill, *Learning to Fall: A Guide for the Spiritually Clumsy* (St. Louis: Chalice Press, 1981), pp. 81-85.

3. Jack Canfield and Mark Victor Hansen, *A Second Helping of Chicken Soup for the Soul* (Health Communications, Inc., 1995), p. 37.

Sermons On The Second Readings

For Sundays
After Pentecost
(First Third)

Glenn W. McDonald

To Mark, Katy, Jeff, and Tyler
Growing disciples
Bearers of God's grace
To their own Mom and Dad

Preface

A ministry colleague of mine once sat with an anguished young man. "I just don't have enough faith to endure a crisis," said the would-be disciple. My friend asked, "Do you need such faith right now?" "Well, no," came the answer. "But when hard times come, I'm afraid I won't have the ability or the spiritual resources to trust God." My friend wisely answered, "The reason you don't have such extraordinary faith today is that God hasn't called you to such a challenge today. Don't worry: God will provide, right on schedule."

Part of the graciousness of the grace of God is that it cannot be stockpiled. We have no ability to fill a reserve tank with trust or grace, because reserve supplies are unnecessary. God's grace arrives *in the midst* of life's most daunting moments — in the midst of suffering, weakness, shame, loss, hopelessness, and exasperation. Whatever realities we are facing this day, may we have the grace to affirm that assurance from God that so gripped Paul the apostle: "My grace is sufficient for you, for power is made perfect in weakness" (2 Corinthians 12:9).

Glenn W. McDonald

Grace In The Midst
Of Hopelessness

Submarine accidents are rare. Successful submarine rescues, unfortunately, are rarer still. The complex variables of depth, pressure, temperature, and time conspire to doom most trapped sailors. During one celebrated rescue attempt a message could be heard reverberating through the hull of a downed sub. It was tapped out in code from the inside, metal clanging against metal: *Is there any hope?*

At the beginning of the twenty-first century the world is waiting for an answer to that question. Opinion guru George Gallup has concluded, "People in many nations appear to be searching with a new intensity for spiritual moorings. One of the key factors prompting this search is certainly a need for hope in these troubled times."

What the world needs now is hope. Thinking people crave assurance that there are good reasons for waking up tomorrow morning — that our presence and our efforts are not meaningless — that our being here is actually making a difference in the outcome of world history. Sadly, the grounds for hope on which too many of us stand are unable to endure a serious shaking.

All too often our response to the seemingly endless deluge of global change and conflict is what amounts to "hope against hope." We turn away from CNN and sigh, "I don't have a clue how to solve these crises. I hope someone will figure it out." We spend our adult years succumbing to a dependence on credit cards, then say, "I hope there's a surprise financial windfall in my future so I can retire." But real hope is not lottery-level optimism. Authentic hopefulness isn't an irrational shot in the dark that someone, somewhere, will come through.

A good portion of America is comfortable with the idea that hope is self-generated. "I make my own breaks." Winston Churchill once accepted an opportunity to address the British schoolboys at Eton, the scene of his own childhood education. The prime minister rose from his seat, grasped the lectern, and proceeded to deliver one of the most electrifying speeches of the last century. It was precisely five words. Churchill said, "Never, never, never give up." He then sat down. Given the chance to say anything, Churchill urged an assembly of students never to surrender. Indeed, his own unyielding resolve, dominating physical presence, and inspiring words were monumental factors in the maintenance of Allied hope during World War II.

Nevertheless our dearest dreams and our deepest commitments are vulnerable in a fallen world. "Never give up" doesn't always win the day. One only has to think of the two American sprinters who invested four years in training for Olympic glory. When it came time to run their first heat, they were nowhere to be found. Their coach had accidentally told them the wrong time. They were physically, mentally, and emotionally capable of peak performance. Yet something — something insanely easy to have been prevented — stole their dream.

In a world where there are countless "somethings" just around the corner, is there any hope? On what basis can we believe that what we most value and most need can never be snatched away from us?

In the eighth chapter of his letter to the Romans the Apostle Paul provides the answer. Christians have grounds for hope. Our hope — this confidence that our existence in both the present and the future is completely secure and utterly meaningful to God — is experienced most significantly through God's gift of the Holy Spirit. The third person of the Trinity takes up permanent residence within every true follower of Jesus. The Spirit is God's guarantee that there is an amazing future awaiting us, and that we haven't been abandoned to hopelessness and weakness in the meantime.

Hope is no small matter on the pages of the Bible. The word itself appears more than 160 times, in dozens of contexts. Peter writes, "Blessed be the God and Father of our Lord Jesus Christ! By his great mercy he has given us a new birth into a living hope through the resurrection of Jesus Christ from the dead" (1 Peter 1:3). What God offers to us is a *living hope* — a renewable spiritual resource that is "living" because it connects us to a living Savior.

Because of the mercy of God and the life of Jesus, Christians are granted an altogether hopeful picture of the future. It's called heaven. That's what Peter describes in the very next verse: "... an inheritance that is imperishable, undefiled, and unfading, kept in heaven for you." Our destination is a guarantee. What might happen between here and there is not. Being a Christ-follower is not easy. Many times we will be powerfully tempted to give up. Peter is transparently honest about this, beginning in verse 6: "... even if now for a little while you have had to suffer various trials, so that the genuineness of your faith — being more precious than gold that, though perishable, is tested by fire — may be found to result in praise and glory and honor when Jesus Christ is revealed."

At the doorway to our text in Romans, Paul declares the same truth: "I consider that the sufferings of this present time are not worth comparing with the glory about to be revealed to us" (8:18). The present may seem hopeless. But take heart. God is gracious. Our future is secure. The *invisibility* of our ultimate security may appear to be cause for concern. But Paul counters in verse 24, "Hope that is seen is no hope at all. Who hopes for what he already has? But if we hope for what we do not yet have, we wait for it patiently."

Reinhold Niebuhr wrote, "Nothing that is worth doing can be achieved in our lifetime, therefore we must be saved by hope." The Lord of the cosmos is working out a plan that is bigger than our abilities and infinitely longer than our spans of life. Therefore our trust is not in what we may or may not appear to accomplish in this world, but in God's promise of wholeness in the next world. As Paul puts it in verse 23, "We ourselves, who have the first fruits of the Spirit, groan inwardly while we wait for adoption, the redemption of our bodies." Today we may groan. But our future shall be full of rejoicing.

Therefore, in hope, we are afforded the luxury of taking a longer view of things. Consider the early American pastor Jonathan Edwards and his wife Sarah. They parented eleven children, a sure formula for several decades of celebration and tears, laughter and frustration. On the days in which the milk was spilled twice and half the children had colds, it would have cheered the Edwards considerably if they had had the power to look down the road. By 1900 the family had grown to include 1,400 descendents — among them thirteen college presidents, 65 professors, 100 lawyers, thirty judges, 66 physicians, and at least eighty prominent public officials, including three governors, three senators, and a U.S. vice president. Living in hope means knowing that a God of grace is able to multiply our present modest efforts at faithfulness to bless generations to come.

While today we may groan, our future will be glorious. That's not to say that God has abandoned us in our present need. The Holy Spirit who lives within those who trust Christ is forever calling out and reaching out to God — even when our natural minds, on this side of heaven, are preoccupied with pains and distractions. That's what Paul affirms in verse 26: "Likewise the Spirit helps us in our weakness; for we do not know how to pray as we ought, but that very Spirit intercedes with sighs too deep for words."

The continuing development of the 911 Plus emergency telephone system in counties around the United States provides some insight into the power of intercession. A Midwestern emergency dispatcher was asked, "How often do you have people call who are completely unable to put into words what they need?"

"We get calls like that all the time," he said. He went on to describe families experiencing frightening moments of domestic violence. One person in the house might simply dial 911, then leave the phone off the hook. Help will be sent immediately. The dispatcher described people with asthma so severe that they cannot catch their breath; they are barely able to speak. With 911 Plus they don't need to. The call itself is a cry for help. "Listen," he concluded, "even if you dialed 911 and then immediately hung up, we would know who you were and where you lived, and would send someone to investigate."

Paul says that when we don't know how to pray — when we're fumbling for the right words, or are simply crying out our hearts to God — the Spirit within us is interpreting everything perfectly. Help is on the way. God knows our address and God knows who we are. Ann Lamott, who has written with searing honesty about her battle to survive alcoholism, reveals that she has two favorite prayers. Both are six words in length: "Help me, help me, help me," and "Thank you, thank you, thank you." We need not pray in greater detail. The Spirit will fill in the rest.

In verse 27 Paul continues: "And God, who searches the heart, knows what is the mind of the Spirit, because the Spirit intercedes for the saints according to the will of God." Christian history is replete with stories of God's people who have been suddenly awakened in the middle of the night or startled by strong impressions in the middle of day that someone is in need of their prayers. The Holy Spirit quite literally recruits us to intercede for each other.

Disciples of Jesus are called to experience and to share God's grace, even in circumstances that seem to scream out a reality of hopelessness. Author and church leader Lee Strobel, in his book *God's Outrageous Claims,* recounts an incident from his days as a reporter for the *Chicago Tribune,* where he helped bring to light the sometimes-deadly consequences of riding in a Ford Pinto. From time to time this compact car would burst into flames when struck from behind. One of the landmark accidents took place in northern Indiana. A Chevy van ploughed into the back of a Pinto and killed three teenage girls. Two of them burned to death within moments. The driver, an eighteen-year-old girl named Judy, was thrown clear of the accident but was burned over 95 percent of her body. Somehow she was still alive when the paramedics arrived.

The doctors at the hospital where Judy was taken quickly realized that they were powerless to save her. They elected to send her by ambulance to a burn center 75 miles away so at least she might receive some comfort. A nurse agreed to ride along with her.

The trip unfolded as a nightmare. Because of damage to her nerve endings Judy didn't feel much physical pain. But as the reality of her situation began to sink in, Judy was overwhelmed with anxiety and sheer emotional anguish. She grasped that these were her last hours. She was separated from family and friends. She sobbed to the nurse beside her, "I'm not ever going to have children, am I?"

What words of hope could possibly comfort this teenage girl? Nothing seemed to penetrate Judy's personal agony — until she mentioned the name of Jesus. Discovering then that both she and Judy were Christians, the nurse came alongside her and provided the one medication that quieted her fears. From memory she recited these verses from Isaiah 43:

> *Do not fear, for I have redeemed you;*
> *I have called you by name, you are mine.*
> *When you pass through the waters, I will be with you;*
> *And through the rivers, they shall not overwhelm you;*
> *When you walk through fire you shall not be burned,*
> *And the flame shall not consume you,*
> *For I am the Lord your God,*
> *The Holy One of Israel, your Savior.*

Strobel writes that it was in the hearing of those words that Judy slowly took on a calmness and courage that lifted her through the last difficult hours of her life. Once again she grasped that she belonged to God, and that no fire is able to destroy what really matters.

If we belong to God, then God's gift to us is a living hope. Through the Spirit we grasp whose we are. No frailties in the present can keep us from the Lord, and no fears about the future can prevent God from blessing us. Most importantly, we discover that whatever power we have to never, never, never give up is ours only because God will never, never, never give up on us.

Grace In The Midst
Of Exasperation

Spiritual storytelling (a.k.a. "my testimony") is often an inspiring experience for a gathered group of Christians. It is also inherently risky. The risk is that the story will sound wonderful. Whenever the overwhelming number of details of someone's garden-variety life are squeezed down to a significant few, it can seem that that four-minute abridged version of existence is fabulously more exciting or meaningful than anything the rest of us have experienced in the previous forty years. We may say to each other, "How awesome it is that God is at work in your life," when in fact what we're really thinking is, "Why isn't God doing things like that in *me?*"

Over the years it's hard for a growing disciple not to wonder, "Where is the proof that my life is different because I am a Christian? What hard evidence can I muster?" We may even muse, "If only I had come from the rough part of town. If only I had been in prison. Then the changes would be obvious and I could tell a better story than Compliant Suburban Teenager Meets God, or Light Finally Comes On For Dim-Witted Accountant." To write his book *Reaching For the Invisible God*, Philip Yancey asked a number of people how they knew their lives were different because they had trusted Christ. His most poignant response came from someone whose name he chose not to share, except to say that he hosts a national radio program and dispenses solid biblical advice every week. That man wrote:

I have no trouble believing God is good. My question is more, what good is he? I heard a while back that Billy Graham's daughter was undergoing marriage problems, so the Grahams and the in-laws all flew to Europe to meet with them and pray for the couple. They ended up getting divorced anyway. If Billy Graham's prayers don't get answered, what's the use of my praying? I look at my life — the health problems, my own daughter's struggles, my marriage. I cry out to God for help, and it's hard to know just how he answers. Really, what can we count on God for?

That *is* the question. If we're trusting that God is here, at work in our lives, actually changing us, what exactly can we expect? Does Christian discipleship deliver real power for real change? Before such real change in our lives can come about, we have to understand why change is necessary ... and why our search for the evidence of spiritual progress can be so exasperating.

The Bible provides a fascinating assessment of the condition of humanity. God's Word asserts that every human being is a slave to desire. Every person is born with a particular set of desires — desires that lead us away from God and into lives of sheer frustration. If we choose to receive Christ as Savior, however, we are given a brand new set of desires — desires that lead us to please God and ultimately to be fulfilled and contented.

The important thing to note is that our slavery to desire is not negotiable. The only choice we have is which kind of desire we will obey. Does this mean that humans aren't free? Aren't we at liberty to choose whatever we want to do at a given moment? The fact of the matter is that our choices are always determined by our desires — *and we always end up doing what we truly desire at any given moment.*

For example, there is abundant evidence from physicians, sociological research, the testimonies of friends and family and our own experience that quality of life is enhanced by exercise. The case has been made. Few individuals are likely to say, "Being out of shape has been a major asset in my life, and I hope to prolong my time on the couch." Investments in exercise equipment, work-out plans, personal trainers, and specialized clothing have skyrocketed within the last quarter century. A majority of those polled on January 1 annually indicate their resolve to pursue a more vigorous regimen of exercise.

However — take a snapshot of your neighborhood. More than fifty percent of America is overweight, and 25 percent is technically obese. What has happened to the expressed and even fervent desire for physical conditioning? It is routinely overwhelmed by a greater desire — to eat whatever happens to taste good, and not to "sweat it" when it's time to work out. Day by day we obey our greatest desires at any particular moment. It's just that our cognitive resolutions to be in better shape stand little chance if we continually hang out at buffets. As millions can attest, this reality is nothing short of exasperating.

Nevertheless, as theologian R. C. Sproul argues in *Chosen by God,* most of us intuitively reject the notion that we are slaves to our strongest urges. We believe ourselves to be captains of our own souls and directors of our own agendas. We protest, "I don't always do what I desire. In fact right now I'd much prefer being on a golf course in Hawaii than sitting here reading about theology." That being said, we are still doing what we *most* desire. Tickets to Hawaii are expensive. So are greens fees. We may daydream about making the sacrifices necessary to chuck it all and head west, but when push comes to shove, reading this page at this place and time has risen to the top of all of our available alternatives. People always choose to do what they most want to do at any particular moment.

What does this have to do with following God? This has everything to do with following God. Scripture consistently declares that every human being is endowed with a set of desires that automatically steer us away from God. The Apostle Paul calls this a sin nature. It is the irrevocable legacy of being born into a fallen world. Ponder your highest and purest intentions: "I promise to be a holy person; I vow to think affirming thoughts; I resolve to stop hating those who have hurt me; I swear I will stay away from pornography; I promise I will no longer go through life feeling afraid." What happens when we send such good intentions to war against our sinful desires? The result is a spiritual catastrophe — precisely what Paul chronicles in Romans 7, beginning at verse 15: "I do not understand my own actions. For I do not do what I want, but I do the very thing I hate." Verse 19 continues, "For I do not do the good I want, but the evil I do not want is what I do." It is exasperating indeed. The climax of frustration arrives with the despairing cry of verse 24: "Wretched man that I am! Who will rescue me from this body of death?"

Who exactly is this "wretched man"? This is no mere spiritual wannabe. This is the early Church's greatest thinker and missionary. Paul's best intentions are being stampeded by a herd of his own desires that he has no ability to control. If Paul feels this frustrated, what hope do we have that *we* can ever change? What makes us think that we can kick habits or resist temptations? The very next verse presents the answer: "Thanks be to God through Jesus Christ our Lord!"

It is through the Second Person of the Trinity that God pours out grace in the midst of exasperation. Jesus alone delivers power to change. How? It is no accident that Romans 8:1, 2 are among the most cherished verses in scripture: "There is therefore now no condemnation for those who are in Christ Jesus. For the law of the Spirit of life in Christ Jesus has set you free from the law of sin and of death."

Have you ever been riding in an airplane and suddenly started wondering, "How in the world is this thing staying up in the air?" Think about it: Planes are a great deal heavier than air. They cannot float. The law of gravity declares that whatever is heavier than air must be drawn directly toward the center of the earth. For centuries philosophers and inventors concluded that flying was a privilege reserved only for creatures born with wings. So how is it that over the next 24 hours more than 200,000 passenger flights will take off and land somewhere in the world?

The answer is Bernoulli's Principle. Airplane wings are curved in such a way that air flows faster above the wing than beneath it. According to Bernoulli's principle, if water or air is flowing faster along one side of an object than the other, the pressure along that side will decrease, and force will be exerted toward the low-pressure side. That's what gives airplane wings their lift. Every time a jet is ready to take off the air traffic controllers don't have to say to the pilot, "You'll be cleared for take-off just as soon as we suspend the law of gravity." The law of gravity is *never* suspended. It is always operational. Planes are able to fly simply because they are empowered by a *greater law* — one that supersedes gravity.

Paul writes, "For the law of the Spirit of life in Christ Jesus has set you free from the law of sin and of death." In this world God does not eradicate our sinful desires. They still reside within us and they remain exceedingly powerful. But Christians can experience victory over those desires because of a higher law, a greater power. That greater power is mediated by the Holy Spirit.

Whenever someone chooses to become an intentional imitator of Jesus Christ, a brand new set of desires is placed inside them — and so is the Holy Spirit, God's own Self living inside our hearts. Christians receive an entirely new nature — a whole new level of passion and insight concerning spiritual things. That new set of desires is what often makes young disciples virtually intoxicated with excitement about pleasing God.

All too soon, though, reality sets in. Exasperation returns. Inside every Christian the old desires are still lurking. People who follow Jesus routinely feel "Balkanized" in their inner worlds. Old desires battle new desires. That's why disciples still sin. Rarely does a week go by that someone with a heart for God doesn't resolve to be warm, caring, and grace-giving to every person they meet. That would reflect our conscious desire. But other desires — to be petty and small-minded and cynical — are never very far away. Sometimes the darker desires win an overwhelming victory. Then we think, "Why did I do that? What's wrong with me?" The answer is that our inner natures remain a bundle of contradictions. We agonize, "Am I really a different person? Has anything about me actually changed? How can I truly say that I belong to God?"

For this reason it is crucial to remember, every day of our lives, God's guarantee that we are able in the here and now to experience life's most important change. What's the most important change in my whole life? It's not getting rid of a particular habit. There may be some habits that I never finally kick. It's not smoothing all the rough spots in my personality. I will undoubtedly reach the end of life still in a pitched battle against some form of selfishness. But there is one change that I can know has already taken place — that I have moved from being someone who is spiritually lost to someone who has been adopted into God's own family.

Paul exults, beginning in verse 14: "For all who are led by the Spirit of God are children of God. For you did not receive a spirit of slavery to fall back into fear, but you have received a spirit of adoption. When we cry, 'Abba! Father!' it is that very Spirit bearing witness with our spirit that we are children of God."

The Holy Spirit whispers to us, "Don't lose heart. You belong to God. You are God's child. You have been rescued by grace and you will never be rejected." Yet how can we believe that, especially when we continue to make the same stupid mistakes and surrender to the same sick desires of our old natures? Here is the wonderful answer: God has already given us the *status* of righteousness. But we still don't have the *reality* of righteousness. God looks at Christians right now as God's perfect children, even though, in reality, we aren't even in the zip code of *acting* like perfect children. We can summarize our situation this way: "Even when we foul up, we don't foul out."

Imagine what it would be like if you were awarded the Olympic gold medal in the 50-meter freestyle — which every four years showcases the world's fastest aquatic athletes — even though you don't know how to swim. All you would have to do to claim the status of "fastest swimmer on planet earth" is show up at the medal ceremony, cry a little bit during the National Anthem, and then head for the post-race party. That's what God has done for us. If we enter a relationship with Jesus, then we are given the ultimate status in the universe — we are God's own children — even though we have done nothing to *earn* that status.

In our hearts we know that this simply can't be the whole picture. Who could possibly feel good about accepting a gold medal under such circumstances? That's why the Holy Spirit instructs us, "Keep the gold medal. It's really yours, and it will never be taken away. But now it's time for your reality to catch up with your status. Get in the pool and let's work on treading water."

Our call, in other words, is to keep changing. God's grace is an invitation to grow into the likeness of the One whose name we bear. As Paul puts it in verse 12, "So then, brothers and sisters, we are debtors, not to the flesh, to live according to the flesh — for if you live according to the flesh you will die; but if by the Spirit you put to death the deeds of the body, you will live."

Bernoulli's Principle allows airplanes to overcome the law of gravity. That's very reassuring. But Bernoulli's Principle has never once pried an airplane off the ground. That's the pilot's job. For a plane to fly, somebody has to start its engine, taxi it to the runway, and gun the engines to reach sufficient speed to become airborne. *In principle*, God has provided everything we need to live a spiritual life — but we will never get off the ground unless we make the right decisions and take the right steps to walk with God.

What are the right steps? We must decide to feed our new desires to follow God, and starve the old desires that make us want to run away. The Holy Spirit is the key to winning that battle. God promises that the Spirit who lives inside us will remind us of the right things to do, will strengthen our desires to carry them out, and will never let us forget that as God's children we *are* going to become what God has called us to be.

Stuart Briscoe, pastor of Elmbrook Church outside Milwaukee, illustrates the power of feeding and starving with an observation about cuckoo birds. Cuckoos aren't merely the obnoxious noisemakers heard at the top of the hour in certain clocks. They are certifiably real. Two species, in fact, nest in America. To be more accurate, cuckoos rarely make their own nests. When it's time for a female cuckoo to lay her eggs, she will scout the local territory until she finds the nest of another bird that already has eggs — often the nest of a thrush — and wait until that mother bird is absent. Then she will dart in to the nest and deposit at least one egg of her own.

Thrushes are apparently not overly skilled in algebra, for when the mother returns, she doesn't notice that there is an addition to her nest. She continues to go about the work of hatching the eggs.

What happens when the nestlings appear? There are four tiny thrushes and one lumbering cuckoo, two to three times larger than the other birds.

What happens at mealtime? The big bird gets the worm. The cuckoo continues to grow while the thrushes fight for survival. Briscoe remarks, "When I was a kid, you could always find a baby cuckoo's nest. You walked along a hedgerow until you found dead little thrushes, which the cuckoo throws out one at a time."

God's children have two sets of desire in one nest. Which one shall we feed? We must feed the new desires and starve the old ones. We must feed the ones that strengthen our walk with Christ and starve the ones that have always taken us down. The more we choose the new desires, the stronger the Holy Spirit grows our personal resolve to choose the new desires the next time as well. We won't always succeed. Trying to become a spiritual person in a fallen world — trying specifically to think, feel and live as *Christ's* person — will always to some degree be exasperating. But through God's gift of grace, Christ's victory over sin, and the indwelling presence of the Spirit, we can know that we truly have the power to change.

Grace In The Midst
Of Weakness

Over the centuries rank and file church members have grown up in the presence of stained glass saints. Sanctuary windows throughout Europe and America have featured thousands of them — monumental, brightly colored portraits of men and women whose lives were right with God. Their faces are placid and trusting. Their heads are often enveloped by golden auras or haloes. All of them were heroes of the faith, either from the Bible or from Christian history. They are spectacular representations of spiritual victory — but also intimidating. How can an ordinary person grow up to become a stained glass saint?

We sense that our weaknesses disqualify us. Generic frailties cling to us. We wonder how God puts up with our erratic attempts to jump-start our own spiritual lives, and wonder how long God can possibly be patient with our efforts at mastering something as basic as sustaining a life of prayer.

Three ministers once sat together in a church study to discuss their views regarding the most effective ways to pray. In an adjoining room there happened to be a telephone repairman who was working on the lines. The first pastor said, "When I pray, I find it helps to hold my hands together like this, as a personal expression of worship." The second suggested that real prayer ought to be conducted on one's knees. The third pastor corrected him, saying, "The most biblically authentic posture for talking to God is to lie stretched out on one's face."

At that moment the telephone repairman, who'd been eavesdropping, poked his head around the corner and said, "I'd have to say the best prayer I ever prayed was when I was dangling upside-down by my heels from a power pole about forty feet above the ground." The most cursory venture into the stories of scripture reveals that most of the stained glass saints who filter the light of the world's great cathedrals prayed a lot more like the telephone guy than those pastors. In the Bible, the Big Names get into Big Trouble. Weaknesses abound in God's chosen servants.

Consider this excerpt from the book of Numbers, chapter 11. A key leader asks the Lord, "Why have you treated your servant so badly? Why have I not found favor in your sight, that you lay the burden of all this people on me? Did I conceive all this people? ... If this is the way you are going to treat me, put me to death at once — if I have found favor in your sight — and do not let me see my misery." This seriously depressed man feels so flattened by circumstances that he literally prays, "God, if you love me, please kill me." Who prayed that prayer? Moses.

Here's a paraphrased cry of the heart from 1 Kings 19: "I have had enough, Lord ... I'm the only one left who really cares about you, I've done everything that you asked me, and what do I get for my trouble? Right now there's a posse out hunting for my head." Who is this whiner? The prophet Elijah.

Another prophet's name is attached to one of the longest books in the Bible. God worked through him in dramatic ways during difficult times. Yet he prayed, "Cursed be the day I was born! May the day my mother bore me not be blessed! Cursed be the man who brought my father the news, 'A child is born to you — a son!' Why didn't he just kill me in my womb? Why was I ever born to see all this trouble and sorrow?" This is exasperation at a level beyond Prozac. Have you ever seriously concluded that the world would be a better place if you had never entered it? Then you can relate to the prayer life of Jeremiah.

The big names of the Bible frequently relate to God out of emptiness, not out of anything that resembles fullness. Where spiritual courage and trust are demanded, they routinely display weakness. By grace God's champions were destined to become whole people — but only because they first were broken people.

Consider the opening lines of Psalm 32: "Happy are those whose transgression is forgiven, whose sin is covered. Happy are those to whom the Lord imputes no iniquity, and in whose spirit there is no deceit ... I said, 'I will confess my transgressions to the Lord,' and you forgave the guilt of my sin." Who offered that prayer? He was a politician who had had an affair and then used government employees to arrange a cover-up. His name was David.

Over in Ephesians, chapter 4, we read: "Speaking the truth in love, we must grow up in every way into him who is the head, into Christ, from whom the whole body, joined and knit together" (is) ... "building itself up in love." That is a remarkable expression of the heart, especially from a lynch mob organizer and murderer of members of Christ's Body like Saul of Tarsus.

In 3 John verse 2 we read: "Beloved, I pray that all may go well with you and that you may be in good health, just as it is well with your soul." That's a surprisingly gracious wish from a man whom Jesus once took aside to scold for his outrageous temper, and who, while slouching toward the Last Supper, got into a heated argument as to whether he merited the best seat in heaven. His name was John. The Bible calls him "the disciple whom Jesus loved."

Can we walk with God in the company of stained glass saints? We most certainly can — as long as we follow the path they blazed for us. We must acknowledge our essential brokenness, even as we reach out to receive God's grace in the midst of our prevailing weakness.

Paul frames our condition in verse 7 of our text: "But we have this treasure in clay jars...." In other words, God has chosen to store the riches of heaven in fragile containers. In the first century the most durable containers were carved out of stone. A rich family might keep their prized possessions in a box made of alabaster. Clay pots, on the other hand, were a dime a dozen. In a Jewish home, if a ceremonially unclean animal like a lizard accidentally hopped into a clay pot — even if it held every ounce of dinner — there was no negotiating the next step. That pot itself was now ceremonially unclean, along with everything inside it. Everyone who touched it would become ceremonially unclean. Therefore it had to be broken — never to be used again. It was unthinkable that a clay jar should be the container of anything worth keeping.

Every time Christians gather to ordain a woman or a man to ministry with a so-called capital "M" or pray for God's blessing on the various lower-case "m" ministries that are carried out by every member of the Body, they aren't declaring that perfect servants have finally been identified, trained, and released. A congregation is instead acknowledging the grace of God, who is pleased to work in and through our weaknesses. What is this awesome treasure in jars of clay? At least three descriptions of it emerge from our text.

First, the treasure carried in the breakable containers of human lives is *God's ministry*. How pathetic and dangerous it is to conclude the work that God has uniquely placed within each of us is *our* responsibility — that the kingdom of God is no more than 24 hours away from collapse if we don't keep all the balls in the air.

Die-hard basketball fans know the name of Stacey King, former power forward from the University of Oklahoma and a role player in the NBA who won a world championship ring as a member of the Chicago Bulls. When King announced his retirement from the NBA a few years ago, there wasn't a glitzy press conference. But a reporter did ask him a question. "Stacey, what is your most cherished memory from your days in the NBA?"

"That's easy," he said. "That would be the night that Michael Jordan and I combined to score seventy points." Impressive, isn't it? And how many points did Michael Jordan score that night? Sixty-nine. Stacey King had hit one free throw. It helps when you're playing with the very best.

That's precisely where we stand — except that any time we "score" in ministry it's by grace, not by skill. Those called to bring about God's work aren't so much partners with the Lord as servants who are awaiting their next command. The ministry belongs to God. As Paul puts it in verse 1, "Since it is by God's mercy that we are engaged in this ministry, we do not lose heart." Even on days in which it seems, in our humanness, that we can never possibly make a difference for the kingdom, we can know that God is still going to have God's way with us.

Second, the treasure that's been entrusted to jars of clay is *God's message*. Flawed as we are, we are called to be reporters of the greatest news the world has ever heard.

It's hard to watch television and not feel repulsed when a reporter maneuvers to become bigger than the story he's relating, or a hostess postures herself as an incomparably brighter star than any celebrity she might interview. Paul says that God's person must never go there. We instinctively flinch when evangelists or authors or the guy who lives just down the street somehow imply that the good news is all about them. Look at verse 5: "For we do not proclaim ourselves; we proclaim Jesus Christ as Lord and ourselves as your slaves for Jesus' sake." Obedient messengers never trump the message. Our task is to share the treasure. How do we do that? We choose to be servants.

In the movie *The Blues Brothers*, Dan Ackroyd and John Belushi — ex-cons and sometime musicians who are trying to raise money for an orphanage — have a pat answer when someone asks what they are doing. "We're on a mission from God." They always say it as if it could actually be true. Author John Ortberg observes, "The very idea that two inept, unworthy human beings could be on a mission from God was, of course, the central joke of the whole story." Ortberg then asserts, "Here is the story of your life: You are on a mission from God." We must never fall into such despair about our own weaknesses that we lose the conviction that God will use us. Though we boast all the glamour of a clay pot, God has entrusted to us the reporter's role for the most important news that has ever been heard.

Third, and finally, the treasure that God has placed within the containers of our hearts and minds is *God's power.* Paul draws the essential contrast in verse 7: "But we have this treasure in clay jars, so that it may be made clear that this extraordinary power belongs to God and does not come from us."

In his remarkable book *Great Souls*, journalist David Aikman chronicles the lives of those individuals whom he believes exerted the greatest moral and spiritual influence in the twentieth century. Author Philip Yancey comments that of the six he chose — Billy Graham, Pope John Paul II, Nelson Mandela, Alexander

Solzhenitsyn, Mother Teresa, and Elie Wiesel — only Graham may be said to have had what we might call a "normal," pain-free childhood. Again and again God's power explodes through what appear to be life-defeating circumstances.

God delights to work through unlikely characters. Moses was the original basket case. When he heard the call of God he said, "Here am I, Lord. *Send Aaron!*" Gideon gasped, "You can't choose me. I'm the least of the least of the least in my family tree." Jonah was told to head east, so he immediately jumped on a boast heading west. Peter had the original case of Foot and Mouth Disease, repeatedly putting both of his feet in his mouth at all the wrong moments. Every one of the Twelve seems to have had a bad case of spiritual amnesia. As Tevye, the main character in the musical *Fiddler on the Roof*, puts it, "Lord, I know we're the chosen people. *But* couldn't you choose somebody else every now and then?"

The answer we receive today is the same answer they received: *No.* God places heaven's greatest treasures and entrusts heaven's highest missions to jars of clay. Our adequacy is not the point. Our inadequacy is not the point. God's adequacy *is* the point. As Paul summarizes in verse 16, "So we do not lose heart. Even though our outer nature is wasting away, our inner nature is being renewed day by day." That's why God's people need never feel afraid of fragility or weakness. God is the source of all the power we will ever need. We may think that being a cracked pot disqualifies us from God's service. But the truth is that failure, more than anything else, is what prepares us to receive God's gift of grace.

Ortberg recounts the moment some years ago when a junior executive at IBM went out on a limb in a risky venture and lost the company over ten million dollars. He was called into the office of Tom Watson, Sr., the legendary founder and CEO of IBM. The young man knew what was coming, so he cut right to the chase. "I guess you've called me in for my resignation. Here it is. I resign." Watson replied, "You must be joking. I just invested ten million dollars educating you. I can't *afford* your resignation."

Is there any prevailing evidence that the Twelve could have looked back on the last week of Jesus' life and felt encouraged by their performance? They had fallen asleep in the Garden of

Gethsemane when they should have been praying; they had run for cover when Jesus was arrested and crucified; one of them had shouted out loud that he had never even met Jesus; and when they first heard that the tomb just might be empty, quite frankly they didn't believe it.

Therefore when Jesus stood before them, incredibly real and alive, they knew what was coming. "You've come for our resignations," they were thinking. "Well, here they are. We resign." How might Jesus have answered? "You've got be kidding. I can't afford your resignations. I just invested an incarnation, an atonement, and a resurrection in you. Right now you're all I've got."

A God of limitless power can never be limited by our weaknesses. We can never finally say, with theological accuracy, that we're all that God has. The amazing thing, therefore, is that God *chooses* such self-limitation. God is eternally pleased to work through jars of clay. What Good News — what gracious Good News — that is for every one of us.

Grace In The Midst Of Suffering

For several years an earnest and energetic woman has been attempting to make August 8 a national holiday in the United States. She'd like to call it, "National Admit You're Happy Day." She has canvassed the governors of all fifty states, personally requesting their support. At least fifteen governors have responded positively. A good many others have been less happy with the idea — including George Pataki, the governor of New York, who has said, "The state of New York has no official position on happiness."

Does God have an official position on happiness? What are we supposed to conclude about God the creator as we look around the world — this world that is so incredibly burdened with sadness, pain, and loss? What are we supposed to conclude about God the protector as we consider the hardships endured by his chosen servants? Paul affirms with brutal honesty, "So death is at work in us ..." (2 Corinthians 4:12). Does commitment to Christ actually diminish our happiness quotient?

John Stott, rector of All Souls Church in London, acknowledges the tension: "The fact of suffering undoubtedly constitutes the single greatest challenge to the Christian faith, and has been in every generation. Its distribution and degree appear to be entirely random and therefore unfair. Sensitive spirits ask if it can possibly be reconciled with God's justice and love."

The apparent unevenness and ambiguity of suffering is on display in many of the most familiar stories in scripture. Consider the Bethlehem accounts. We learn that Zechariah and Elizabeth, the parents-to-be of John the Baptist, spend almost their entire lives

237

defeated by infertility. Mary and Joseph endure a whispering campaign in their small town: *She's pregnant, but they're not married.* Joseph, jolted by a dream, uproots his family overnight and is compelled to move them to a distant city in an alien culture.

In the Psalms we find the same mingling of ups and downs. There is immeasurable comfort in Psalm 23: "The Lord is my shepherd, I have everything I need." But the psalm right before it, number 22, begins, "My God, my God, why have you forsaken me?" Side by side we encounter the heights of personal security and the depths of personal despair. Jesus borrowed from Psalm 23 to declare, "I am the Good Shepherd." Then he willingly went to his death on the cross and screamed, "My God, my God, why have you forsaken *me*?" In the Bible, real security is never very far from real suffering.

How are we supposed to make sense of this? One day the evidence for God's presence and power seems to be everywhere. The next day God appears to have vanished from the radar screen. C. S. Lewis in all likelihood delivered the gift of intellectual spiritual certainty to more people over the last century than any one other apologist. Then his wife died. Shattered by grief he wrote, "Not that I am (I think) in much danger of ceasing to believe in God. The real danger is coming to believe such dreadful things about him. The conclusion I dread is not, 'So there's no God after all,' but 'So this is what God's really like. Deceive yourself no longer.' "

So what is God's official position on happiness? From the perspective of those who follow Jesus, *there is no guarantee of happiness in this world.* Period. "Happy" comes from the English word "hap," which means "chance." It's related to the word "happening." This makes perfect sense: "Happiness" is a momentary and unpredictable sense of well-being that comes and goes, depending on what is happening to us at a particular moment. People are happy in relationship to their circumstances.

Second Corinthians is one of those books in the Bible that makes it clear that Christians are often in the middle of very difficult circumstances. Chapter 1 opens with Paul's frank admission of a recent brush with death. The outcome appears to have generated a serious bout of spiritual depression. N. T. Wright comments in his book *Following Jesus*, "Depression is what happens when one particular little clutch of fears gets together in a circle, and it forces us to go round and round the circle, worrying about one thing, which leads us to blame ourselves for the next thing, which leads us to be anxious about the third thing, which takes us conveniently back to the start of the circle, and round we go again. And one of the key features of depression is that we put ourselves on trial, produce lots of evidence for the prosecution and none for the defense, find ourselves guilty, and pronounce sentence. Paul says in 2 Corinthians 1:9, 'I felt as if I had received the sentence of death.' " There's not much happiness in that picture.

But Paul has something else to say: Happiness is seriously overrated. What happens to us isn't remotely as important as how we respond. Instead of a fixation on the "Why?" of our pain, scripture is considerably more committed to the question, "What now? Where do we go from here?"

Where do we go, indeed? God is good and God is powerful. Yet suffering happens. God frequently chooses not to intervene to take our suffering away. This is where understanding fails us. God is infinite, while we are finite. We are required to endure hardship with far less information than we crave. God promises that in the next world everything crooked will be made straight, and every injustice will be made right. But now, in the midst of pain, it takes courage to live out those familiar words from Proverbs: "Trust in the Lord with all your heart, and don't rely on what you think you know" (3:5, 6 TEV). When it comes to suffering, only God knows the fullness of what is being accomplished in our lives.

From time to time, however, we are granted clues. Every now and then the doors of understanding are nudged open. So it is with Paul's personal reflections in the first five chapters of this epistle. In our present text he acknowledges the nearness of pain. God's grace, however, will win out — both *present grace* and *future grace* in the midst of suffering.

Present grace includes the blessings that are received by people in the here and now, even when things go wrong. Reminiscing on his own recent trials, Paul says in verse 15, "Everything is for your sake, so that grace, as it extends to more and more people, may

239

increase thanksgiving, to the glory of God." What is startling is the sheer number of parties who are deriving benefit from Paul's hardships: the Corinthian readers, "more and more people," and God Almighty are specifically mentioned. Paul clearly includes himself as on that list in the previous sentence.

In verse 16 the Apostle cites another example of present grace: "So we do not lose heart. Even though our outer nature is wasting away, our inner nature is being renewed day by day." Hardship takes its toll. But for the Christian, inner reconstruction more than counter-balances outer erosion.

The Bridger Wilderness Area of Wyoming is one of the most rugged and beautiful sections of the Rocky Mountains. Those who manage this area periodically ask hikers and tourists to make comments and recommendations as to how their visit might have been improved. Here are some actual suggestions from visitor comment cards.

1. *The trails need to be reconstructed. Please avoid building trails that go uphill.*
2. *Too many bugs and leeches and spiders and spider webs. Please spray the wilderness to rid the area of these pests.*
3. *Please pave the trails so they can be plowed of snow during the winter.*
4. *Chairlifts need to be in some places so that we can get to wonderful views without having to hike to them.*
5. *The coyotes made too much noise last night and kept me awake. Please eradicate these annoying animals.*
6. *A small deer came into my camp and stole my jar of pickles. Is there a way I can get reimbursed?*
7. *Escalators would help on steep uphill sections.*
8. *A McDonald's would be nice at the trailhead.*
9. *Too many rocks in the mountains.*

In the real world, mountains are full of rocks (the Rocky Mountains in particular). Marriages brim with heartaches. Faces degenerate into wrinkles. High school parties hide secret sadness. Offices present close encounters with cutthroat co-workers. And there is no escalator to move us past it all.

So why does God let all this happen? What is the cause of our suffering? Here's an honest answer: The Bible does not tell us. If we choose to spend our time agonizing over the origins and meaning of pain — *why, why, why* — we will inevitably be very frustrated. Here is what the Bible does tell us: God is in charge of the universe. God permits our pain. And God is *in* that pain with us. We never go into a nightmare or through a nightmare alone.

Even more important, we can know that our pain — no matter what we are experiencing — is accomplishing something. On the other side of his depression, Paul writes in chapter 1, verse 9 that it happened "so that we would rely not on ourselves but on God who raises the dead." Ultimately every circumstance is an opportunity for us to strengthen our reliance on God — or rather, to allow God to strengthen a divine grip on us.

All this speaks to the reality of *future grace.* Paul rejoices in verse 14 of our text, "... we know that the one who raised the Lord Jesus will raise us also with Jesus...." And in verse 17 we read, "For this slight momentary affliction is preparing us for an eternal weight of glory beyond all measure."

It takes courage to adopt a long-term perspective on personal pain. What word of encouragement does the Bible have for parents who keep waiting and waiting for a prodigal child to come home, for a husband and wife who feel chained to a loveless marriage, for the one who can almost wrap the reality of loneliness around herself like a blanket, for anyone whose body is steadily eroding from disease? What God tells us is that for those who entrust themselves to Jesus Christ, the universe is an utterly safe place — not because bad things never happen (because they most certainly do) — but because, as Paul writes elsewhere, "Who can separate us from the love of God which is in Christ Jesus?" The answer is No One. We can never, ever lose what life is really all about.

So what exactly does God promise? God never promises supernatural *deliverance* from hardship. From time to time God does indeed provide remarkable rescues. But history, on the whole, informs us that Christians die from accidents and diseases at almost the same rate as non-Christians. Enthusiastic evangelists who say otherwise are dangerously off the mark. They either fail to understand the Bible or reality or both. In fact, some preachers are so eager to get God off the hook when it comes to suffering that they are willing to put *us* on the hook. Whose fault is it if we aren't healed of cancer or saved from a tornado? Why, it's our fault, of course — for not earnestly believing in the God who always delivers disciples from hardship.

But in fact there is no biblical guarantee of deliverance. Instead God guarantees the supernatural *use* of hardship. That's the essential difference in the experience of suffering between those who trust God and those who don't. In chapters like Romans 5 and Hebrews 12 and James 1 we receive the assurance that the pain of those who walk with God is absolutely meaningful. It is not random. It is not unknown to God. It is accomplishing something.

Paul boldly states that our troubles are "achieving" for us an experience of future grace that will one day make them infinitely worth enduring. Before us is the promise of a transformed body: "For we know that if the earthly tent we live in is destroyed, we have a building from God, a house not made with hands, eternal in the heavens" (2 Corinthians 5:1).

In the present moment it is impossible to grasp what heaven might be like. Imagine a group of Polynesian islanders sitting in a circle and reading about midwestern strawberries. They can see the big red one in the picture and they can memorize the scientific classification. But that hardly qualifies as "knowing" a great deal about strawberries.

But what if someone from that island were to take a trip and returned with enough fresh strawberries for everybody to have a taste? That is precisely what Jesus accomplished on Easter weekend. None of us can fully know about death until we face it ourselves. We cannot fully experience future grace while living in the present. But God sent the Son to go before us. Jesus died and came back to give us a taste, a real taste, of what's in store for all those who trust him.

Every person who hurts asks two questions: Why is this happening to me? The answer is, we don't know — *but God can be*

242

trusted. God provides grace in the present and promises grace for the future. Secondly, why doesn't God do something about my pain? The answer is, God already has — *God sent Jesus,* whom we can receive and follow, fully confident that "the one who raised Jesus will also raise us." Until that day, nothing in this world can ever separate us from his love.

Proper 6
Pentecost 4
Ordinary Time 11
2 Corinthians 5:6-10 (11-13), 14-17

Grace In The Midst
Of Judgment

In his book *Making Life Work*, Chicago area pastor Bill Hybels cites a study that was published under an intriguing title: *178 Seconds to Live*. The study concerned twenty pilots, all seasoned veterans in the cockpits of their small planes, but none of whom had ever taken instrument training. One by one they were placed in a flight simulator and told to do whatever they could to keep their planes level and under control. The simulator generated the conditions of a storm, including impenetrable, dark clouds. Even though the pilots had exceptional intuition born of years of actual flying, every one of them "crashed." Their planes went down, on average, within 178 seconds, or less than three minutes after they lost their visual reference points.

It may seem an odd way to put it, but it takes courage to rely on instruments more than intuition. It takes courage and supreme good judgment to rely more on unchanging standards and measurements than on personal instincts that we feel certain are telling us what to do next.

For pilots that's a matter of life and death — and it happens to be doubly true for anyone contemplating an authentic spiritual existence. One of the great dangers of moving forward with God is that our intuition may scream that it knows better than God when it comes to the most appropriate ways to respond to life's joys and challenges.

Facing a personal crisis apart from an appreciation of the principles of scripture (and a determination to obey them) is like flying into a storm without instrument training. What makes us assume that our intuition concerning a particular realm of life — whether sexuality or finances or relationships or morality — is going to keep us from hitting the ground? And what has led us to conclude that no matter what the seriousness of our personal missteps, we can surely handle the consequences?

Paul offers a more ominous perspective. He opens the fifth chapter of his second letter to the church at Corinth joyfully enough — with assurances that God's people will always have an embodied existence, and that whatever we happen to do with our bodies in this world *matters*. Our decisions and our actions are never trivial. His line of reasoning culminates, however, in verse 10: "For all of us must appear before the judgment seat of Christ, so that each may receive recompense for what has been done in the body, whether good or evil."

Research consistently reveals that neither church attenders nor the unchurched in our country are particularly concerned about the possible negative ramifications of that verse. Most of our neighbors are glibly confident of a happy outcome in the next world. In the mid-1990s when *US News & World Report* asked a large group of Americans whom they thought was worthy of going to heaven, Mother Teresa of Calcutta topped the list, receiving the support of 84 percent of those polled. Oprah Winfrey received a thumbs-up from 66 percent, Bill and Hillary Clinton merited 52 and 55 percent respectively, and O. J. Simpson brought up the rear at 16 percent. What was most revealing was the answer to the final question in the poll: Do you think you personally are going to heaven? A stunning 86 percent of the respondents felt confident about their chances — that's 2 percent more than Mother Teresa, who perhaps more than anyone in recent times has been revered as a living saint. It's hard to imagine more outlandish spiritual self-assurance than that embraced by the typical American.

According to the authors of scripture, however, a Day of Reckoning awaits us — one that will turn out to be considerably more challenging than a spiritual pop quiz. Appearing before "the judgment seat of Christ" connotes a courtroom atmosphere. Jewish and Christian teaching affirms the existence of an aggressive prosecutor who goes by the title Satan, which means "adversary." The cumulative data of our lives — everything that we have ever said, done, or thought that has not been in conformity with the absolute holiness of God — will be presented as evidence against us. In other words we will all be judged as to whether we have navigated our lives by God's "instruments" or chosen to fly by the seats of our pants.

Needless to say, this is a profoundly uncomfortable picture. It's no wonder that the marketplace spirituality of our times — the ideas about God that we might pick up on talk shows or discover in *New York Times* best-selling paperbacks — rarely, if ever, mention the possibility of giving an account of our lives to a higher power. We would much prefer a God who is adjusted to our behavior. Contemporary spirituality offers a therapeutic vision of the world. It promises resurrection without death, joy without sorrow, Easter Sunday without the messiness of Good Friday. The blessings and the promises that are associated with the Bible are offered at no cost and in exchange for modest commitment. In the words of cultural critic Kenneth Myers, we all become clients in the hands of a Smiling Heavenly Therapist who is there for us. We're certainly not here for God.

The difficulty with this non-judgmental-everybody-is-wonderful view of the cosmos is that beyond our personal imagination, it's genuinely hard to produce evidence that it's true, and there's a great deal at stake if it's not true. As C. S. Lewis reflected, "One cannot go against the grain of Reality without getting splinters."

How did Jesus portray reality? Over the course of his ministry Jesus consistently described his listeners as servants in a household who will have to stand one day in the presence of the master and own up to their performance or lack thereof. At that time there will be no distinction between public life and private life. Everything hidden will be revealed. Every word we have ever voiced, whether shouted aloud or whispered in secret, will be recited. In verse 10 Paul points out that our personal participation in this exercise will not be optional. "All of us must" have our day in God's court. This will surely be a moment when the availability of a great attorney will be crucial. Left to ourselves, we would be in the direst of straits. But in the grace of God, all will not be lost. In the

247

grace of God, we ourselves (those who have trusted Christ) will not be lost.

Everyone who has enlisted as a lifelong learner of Jesus Christ — not on his own terms, but on Christ's terms — will be represented by a whale of an attorney. Our defender will be Jesus himself. 1 John 2:1 affirms, "If anyone does sin" — and that would include the person currently on your left, the one on your right, and the one sitting in your chair — "we have an advocate with the Father, Jesus Christ the righteous." The amazing fact is that when the record of sins of any Christian is opened in the next world, the angels will proclaim, "Lord, this file is *empty*. There is nothing written on it. Everything that was once recorded here has been erased."

The digital age has introduced us to the amazing power of a tiny bit of real estate on the computer keyboard. It's the Delete key. With one touch of the keyboard we have the power to alter reality. For that matter someone else — with a quick, mindless, and unintentional keystroke at the IRS or the county board of records, for instance — has the power to alter *my* reality. It's as if the document or the data on the screen that was just there a second ago ... never existed.

Something like that will take place in heaven, with an eternally happy outcome. I will discover the degree to which Someone Else has altered my reality. Jesus Christ erased my file. He canceled the prosecutor's best stuff. But it wasn't quick, mindless, or unintentional. The Son of God gave up his life so there would be no case against me.

How did that happen? It happened on the cross. Paul writes about Christ in another context (Colossians 2:13), "And when you were dead in trespasses and the uncircumcision of your flesh, God made you alive together with him." When did Jesus help me? When I was right there, working alongside him for the good of the kingdom, pitching in and earning gold stars for my performance? On the contrary, Paul affirms that I was *dead*. Spiritually dead. Legally dead. The case against me was open and shut. No chance for a hung jury. No possibility of appeal to a higher court. There is no higher court than the court of heaven.

248

But when that court demands an accounting for my performance in this world, the miracle is that Jesus' performance will stand in for mine. All my debt sheets will have been erased. Paul continues in Colossians, saying that Christ's work erased "the record that stood against us with its legal demands. He set this aside, nailing it to the cross."

When a first century criminal was spiked to a cross to hang there and die, it was customary to post a small placard that indicated the charges on which he had been convicted. In other words, something in his private record was made public. "Murderer." "Thief." "Insurrectionist." We recall that the words "King of the Jews" were posted above Jesus. That was the "blasphemous" claim of Jesus that according to the Pharisees merited his death.

Colossians 2:14 makes an extraordinary statement. When Jesus died, he took something with him to the cross. He took your record of failure and sin. He took mine, too. Jesus willingly accepted all the junk in all the files in all of human history and let it be posted on his cross, *as if he were personally responsible for all of it.* He died for it. That means justice has been served. That means our sin records, in principle, have been erased.

What do we mean, "in principle"? Jesus has acted. Now it is our call to act. The case against us is canceled when and if we are willing to say, "Thank you, Lord. You rescued me. You gave me my life back. Now I will live a brand new life — not for me this time, but for you." That is the background of the wonderful words in 2 Corinthians 5:15: "And he died for all, so that those who live might live no longer for themselves, but for him who died and was raised for them."

Paul summarizes in verse 17, "So if anyone is in Christ, there is a new creation; everything old has passed away; see, everything has become new!" The newness of the Christian life includes a certainty of our status before God. We are clean. It's as if we never sinned. What is my essential identity? I am a person who is loved by God. I am a forgiven person. I am not someone who *was* forgiven up until two minutes ago when I nurtured that degrading thought and sacrificed the acceptance of God. I don't have to try to figure out how to make things right again. By God's grace, *things already are right.* Jesus made them right on the cross. A Christian is a new creation. The old grounds for being terrified of judgment are gone. A new emotional and spiritual freedom has arrived.

Because God has received payment in full, he doesn't require additional sacrifices on our part to preserve our forgiven status. In 1811 the United States government established the so-called Conscience Fund. American citizens, as they feel led, may send money or payments in kind to atone for mistakes of the past. Every year approximately $50,000 is received, and nearly four million dollars in all has been added to the fund over the years.

The letters and objects that have been sent to the government are astonishing. Early in the 1970s an ex-G.I. sent ten dollars to cover the cost of two blankets that he took at the end of World War II, an event about which he still felt guilty. A man sent several coins along with the confession that he had once placed some coins on a railroad track to see how the train would smash them. He wanted to atone for defacing American currency. A woman sent two brand new postage stamps, admitting that once she had received a letter with a stamp that had not been canceled, so she had peeled it off and used it again. Now she wanted to make things right. An anonymous note read, "I have not been able to sleep because of money that I failed to pay on my taxes. Enclosed is one hundred dollars. If I find that I still cannot sleep, I'll send you the rest."

In our relationships with others it's vital, when and where possible, to make restitution. But we are utterly incapable of settling accounts with God. Our nickels and dimes and most desperate sacrifices could never add up to more than Jesus has already done for us on the cross. Our debts are canceled. Period.

As forgiven people, then, we have a new identity. We have a new freedom. We are free because the greatest threats against us have been erased. Just one more question must be addressed. How should we respond?

In *Saving Private Ryan*, the character played by Tom Hanks makes the ultimate sacrifice for another soldier. As he lies dying, Hanks' eyes meet the eyes of his living comrade. "Earn this," he gasps with his final breath. Earn this? How could such a gift possibly be earned? Only one equation makes sense: a life for a life. We are called to surrender all former claims to our own existence so that we might be reborn to a new kind of life — one lived not for ourselves but for the One who graciously gave his life for us.

Proper 7
Pentecost 5
Ordinary Time 12
2 Corinthians 6:1-13

Grace In The Midst
Of The Crush Of Time

In the year 2000 *Forbes Magazine* featured a special edition on a single topic that it called "the biggest issue of our age — time." The editors wrote, "We've beaten, or at least stymied, most of humanity's monsters: disease, climate, geography, and memory. But time still defeats us. Lately its victories seem more complete than ever. Those timesaving inventions of the last half-century have somehow turned on us. We now hold cell phone meetings in traffic jams, and 24-7 has become the most terrifying phrase in modern life."

While many of us experience time as a source of distress, the Bible clearly presents time as a gift. It is, in fact, the only means by which we can receive the grace of God. Time and space are God's chosen media for self-revelation — as evidenced by the arrival of Jesus at a real moment in history at a real place on this planet — and they are the only media through which God may be encountered this side of heaven. Why then has time seemingly become a crushing burden?

For one thing, time is limited, and chronically busy Americans chafe at such an unyielding limitation. We may discern inequalities in certain gifts that God has given to us — financial resources and Spirit-given empowerments come to mind — but time is different. With regard to time, people are truly equal. We all are charged with managing exactly sixty minutes over the next hour. In a culture that seems increasingly panicked about such a basic responsibility, what is the call of God? Let's consider a trio of responses.

First, our call clearly is to embrace *God's perspective on time.* What is God's perspective? *It is that time is not our enemy.* We may complain that we don't have enough time or that our time is going too fast. But God's perspective is that we already have at our disposal exactly the number of hours we need to do what *God* wants us to do — and never to feel rushed.

The call of God is to slow down, to be present at each moment as it arrives. Time is a gift to be opened one minute at a time — and no faster. Psalm 90 informs us that God is uniquely able to experience a "telescoping" of time — that for God a thousand years are like a day, but even more intriguing, that a day is as rich and meaningful as a thousand years. Quite literally every moment matters eternally — which means that this present moment counts forever.

One of the great human obsessions of the modern age is to make time jump through more hoops — to force time to be more productive. That's why so many of us are suckers for the next generation of computers, date books, and palm pilots. Even ESPN has endeavored to fit more than one hour of sports highlights into a one-hour show. That's why NFL kickoffs that are returned for a touchdown (without doubt one of the most dramatic moments in football) are now being replayed as if the fast-forward button is stuck. Instead of presenting the play at normal speed, which consumes all of twelve or fourteen seconds, the action is frequently speeded up — now consuming just six or seven seconds — so viewers can quickly move on to see another highlight, and then another, and then another.

First-time visitors to London frequently conclude that they may have only one chance to explore such an historic city. Therefore they sign on for one of those everything-included-hurry-up-and-keep-moving tours. "Now here's The Tower of London, there's Big Ben, and just over your right shoulder is Buckingham Palace." You know the drill. Hurry. Stand over there and let me get your picture in front of the lions at Trafalgar Square. Wow, there sure are a lot of pigeons. Hey, look at the time. *Let's go.* That is all too often an out-of-towner's only exposure to the city of London.

By contrast, Americans who *move* to London have a completely different encounter with the city. They don't rush from place to place as tourists. They are residents. Experienced Londoners know that years are required simply to begin to comprehend what this place has meant to human history. A tourist cannot possibly appreciate that perspective in a four-hour sweep across town.

With all of our hearts, we must resist the temptation to become tourists in our own lives. "I'd like to take the four-hour highlight tour of parenting, please." "Come on, kids, it's time to do third grade. Stand right there and let me get your picture. Okay, on to the next stage in your life." We must refuse to buy tickets for the quick walk-through of the Museum of Religious Experiences. God calls us not to rush through the time that has been given to us, but to be fully alive to God and to each other — actually to become residents within these moments we've been provided. Why? Every one of these moments counts forever.

Second, our call is to embrace *God's shape to time*. There is a God-ordained shape to human life. This shape is what gives our lives a meaningful rhythm. Mornings and evenings, mornings and evenings — it's like a tide. When we rebel against that rhythm, there are consequences.

What time is it any more? The boundaries and shape of daily life are rapidly becoming blurred. One can now shop on-line any hour of the day. A television commercial portrays a group of stunned consumers standing in the middle of the night outside a conventional store at a mall. No lights are on. The customers are puzzled: "It's *closed*. Man, that is so weird." We are taught to expect that everything should be available every hour of every day. What season is it any more? We no longer have to wait for summer to get strawberries and watermelons. We can find ripe peaches year-round in Snow Belt stores. Contemporary culture clearly wants to remove the boundaries customarily imposed by the more classic shapes and rhythms of time.

In an act that is flagrantly counter-cultural, the guides of certain spiritual retreats demand that weekend participants give up their watches. Giving up one's watch is tantamount to giving up control — which is precisely the act of faith God asks of us moment by moment when it comes to time. Our call is to trust God

255

and to pay attention to three important rhythms connected to our experience of time.

The God-given shape of time, first, invites us to *Divert Daily.* That means that we must stop every day for rest. A key component of the management of time requires us to get the sleep our bodies need. For some of us (who seemingly have taxi meters for brains and are always counting the cost of every squandered minute) the very idea that we sleep away one third of our lives seems like an incalculable waste. But it is during those sleeping hours that our bodies carry out something like eighty percent of the biological processes required to maintain basic health. At many junctures, God's Word challenges us to commit a portion of each day to the experience of simply being in the presence of God. The goal of that quiet time is not to be productive. We are simply called to *be.*

The shape of time that God has provided, second, also invites us to *Withdraw Weekly.* This speaks to the notion of the Sabbath. God worked for six days at the beginning of creation — then God rested. For us to cease our work one day out of seven is to be like God. God doesn't *suggest* a Sabbath. It is mandated as one of the original Ten Commandments. Our Sabbath doesn't have to be on Sunday nor even on a weekend. But one-seventh of our time during each week should be reserved to pray and to play.

God's design for time also invites us, third, to *Abandon Annually.* In Old Testament times there were prescribed festivals for God's people. Whole families were compelled to walk all the way to Jerusalem three times each year. These became annual opportunities to enjoy life and to enjoy each other. Essentially these festivals amounted to divinely ordained vacations. To believe that we shouldn't take a break each year — to assert or to act as if our work is far too important to slow down — is to take ourselves far too seriously and to violate the rhythm and shape of time as God has provided it. As the fractured proverb puts it, *Better to have loafed and lost than never to have loafed at all.*

As we grasp God's perspective that time is not a monster to be tamed, and as we live out the God-provided shape in which human life makes sense, Paul's heartfelt cry at the beginning of 2

Corinthians, chapter 6, takes on a far deeper significance. Our call is to see that *this* is the time to receive God's grace.

This moment may seem like an ordinary moment, but it is the gift of an extraordinary God. This moment counts — forever. If we were asked the question, "Do you want to do something today that will be eternally significant?" our tendency is to sigh, "You know, my day is so full. I really don't have time." To that Paul thunders in verse 2, "See, now is the acceptable time; see, now is the day of salvation!"

Perhaps we are waiting for the crush of time to pass. Then we will turn our attention fully to spiritual questions — when we're not so busy. Perhaps we are waiting for the right circumstances to arrive, or for a hardship to vanish. We're waiting for more money or more education or more insight or more data. First let's have the baby, or wait for the children to get into school, or wait until summer vacation, or wait until the nest is empty. Then we'll have time.

Paul couldn't agree less. In verses 3 through 10 there isn't the faintest evidence that a hardship-free life is just over the horizon. It will never be the "right time" to act. Therefore God calls us to act now. The wise heart is the one that grasps that *this* moment has become a world-changing moment when we let it fully belong to God. "As we work together with him, we urge you also not to accept the grace of God in vain." Will we capture the richness of this moment through an act of spiritual submission — or miss this opportunity altogether?

Henry Stanley is chiefly remembered as the American journalist who, in 1871, having walked into a jungle clearing in central Africa, spotted a pale-skinned man and said, "Dr. Livingstone, I presume?" In his own right, however, he was also an explorer of uncharted territory in Africa. Historians believe that until Stanley's expedition five years later, no one — either inside or outside Africa — had ever been all the way down the treacherous Congo River, with its canyons, gorges, and cannibals. His trip took 999 days and was filled with unimaginable hardships.

One night proved to be so fraught with difficulties and doubts that Stanley realized he had to make a choice — either to keep going forward into the unknown, or to head back toward security.

That night he approached his friend and helper Frank Pocock. "Now, Frank, my son, sit down. I am about to have a long and serious chat with you. Life and death — yours and mine — hang on the decision I make tonight." What should they do?

Pocock and Stanley decided to flip a coin — an Indian rupee. Heads they would go forward; tails they would go home. The coin came up tails. Disappointed, they flipped the coin again. Tails. "How about three out of five?" Once again it was tails. In fact the coin came up tails six times in a row. The two men decided to draw straws — long straw to go forward, short straw to go back. Every time they drew, however, they picked the short straw.

Stanley and Pocock suddenly realized that they had already made their decision. No matter what the coins or the straws "told them," in their hearts all they wanted to do was head down the Congo River into the Great Unknown. That is precisely what they did, making history in the process. Their most significant opportunity for adventure didn't come and go in vain.

This day we don't need to flip coins or draw straws to know what is on God's heart. God calls us to receive grace — to embrace God's perspective and shape of time. We aren't called to wait for the next moment. This is the time to respond. This moment belongs to God. That's why it counts forever. "See, now is the acceptable time; see, now is the day of salvation!"

Proper 8
Pentecost 6
Ordinary Time 13
2 Corinthians 8:7-15

Grace In The Midst
Of Limited Resources

Year after year Stumpy and Martha attended the fair in their home state, and every summer it was the same story: Stumpy was tantalized by the old-fashioned bi-plane in which anybody could take a ride for ten dollars, and Martha was disgusted by such an obvious waste of money. "Ten dollars is ten dollars," she would always say. And Stumpy would go home without his airplane ride.

One year Stumpy said, "Martha, there's that bi-plane again. I am 81 years old and this year I want to go for a ride." Martha bristled, "There you go again. Don't you realize that ten dollars is ten dollars?" At this point the man who owned the bi-plane, and who had heard this conversation as far back as he could remember, intervened. "Listen, you two, I'll make you a deal. I'll give you both a ride *for free* if you promise not to say anything during the flight. If you speak even one word, I'll charge you the ten dollars." Stumpy and Martha thought that sounded fair, and off they went.

The pilot put on quite a show. He took his plane through banks and spins and loop-the-loops, and then did the whole thing over again. Amazingly, he never heard a single word. When the plane landed he looked over at Stumpy and said, "I'll have to admit I'm impressed. You never spoke once." "Well," said Stumpy, "I was going to say something when Martha fell out of the plane, but ten dollars is ten dollars."

If there's one thing that Americans understand, it's the value of money. We know that ten dollars is ten dollars. If there's one thing that Americans fundamentally misunderstand, it's the value of God. In the marketplace theology of our times we may trust

God to be there, and we may trust that God hears our prayers, and we may even trust God with getting us safely to heaven after we die. But the toughest challenge for the person on the street is believing that God *provides* — that God will actually come through by supplying us with what we need, when we need it.

Paul challenges the fledgling church in Corinth, "Now as you excel in everything — in faith, in speech, in knowledge, in utmost eagerness, and in our love for you — so we want you to excel also in this generous undertaking" (v. 7). Excellence in the grace of giving, however, runs headlong into the reality of "limited resources" — the virtually universal self-assessment that since our bank accounts are barely able to support our pursuit of the Good Life, there's not much left to share with others.

Our culture's vision of the Good Life is amazingly easy to understand. It requires us to *get more*. Getting more was clearly the conventional strategy for happiness in Jesus' time, and little has changed after twenty centuries. Jesus warns in Luke 12:15, "Take care! Be on your guard against all kinds of greed; for one's life does not consist in the abundance of possessions." In other words, more is not more.

The New Testament Greek provides two distinctly different words that are translated into English as "life." One is *bios*, which refers to physical life. We can immediately see the linguistic connection between *bios* and *biology*, which is scientific inquiry into plant and animal life in all its diversity. The other Greek word is *zoe*, which refers to a particular *quality* of life. *Zoe* is the word one would use when talking about "real life," or authentic human existence. What's frustrating about being alive? It's possible to have *bios* but not *zoe*. The reason that people buy matching cherry red imported sports cars, risk their lives climbing mountains, collect Ming vases, and drink Mountain Dew while hang-gliding is that at some level they are hoping that these possessions and experiences will yield a rich harvest of *zoe*. Jesus says, "Don't you believe it."

A lot of people would like to play basketball like Michael Jordan. Even more people secretly dream of enjoying a Michael Jordan-sized income. During one of his recent years in the NBA his combined salary and commercial deals were estimated to be at least 58 million dollars. How much money is that? Michael Jordan earned $106 every minute of every hour of every day that year. Whenever he went to an average-length movie he spent $7 for a ticket, $5 for the popcorn and drink combo, and then just by watching the movie earned over $13,700. Every night during his sleep he raked in $50,480.

All of that was meaningless, however, when Jordan's father was murdered. Money had no power whatsoever to repair his heart, to rekindle his vision at that moment, or to bring back the man who had been the most important figure in his life. Money makes promises that only God can keep.

What then is God's vision of the Good Life? It is radically different. God's vision requires us to *imitate the sacrificial generosity of Jesus.* Paul observes in verse 9, "For you know the generous act of our Lord Jesus Christ, that though he was rich, yet for your sakes he became poor, so that by his poverty you might become rich." The Bible's premise is that the good things God has chosen to pour into our lives are not all about *us.* They are all about God. Jesus is the ultimate model of making others rich. Good things come to us because they are on their way somewhere else. The Good Life is discovering the rich fulfillment of cooperating with God in that amazing venture.

But wait just a moment. For what exactly am I accountable? Am I accountable for how wealthy I become? Paul said that Jesus was "rich." At what point do I conclude the same about myself? How much money do you have to have to be wealthy? In the late 1990s a New York Yankees ballplayer signed an $89 million contract. He had held out for a long while before signing, hoping that management would match the $91 million offer of another team. The Yankees refused to budge. In an interview afterward, the player's wife said, "When I saw him walk in the house, I immediately knew that he had not succeeded in persuading them to move up from $89 to $91 million. He felt so rejected. It was one of the saddest days of our lives." Most of us would say that that couple's disappointment is seriously disconnected from reality.

What does the Word say? The writers of scripture refuse to define what it means to be rich. Being wealthy is entirely relative — relative to one's context. For that matter, nowhere does the Bible condemn those who happen to possess a great deal of money. Accountability is related to our stewardship, not to our fiscal bottom lines.

Scripture, in fact, openly states two compelling reasons to work hard and thus to accumulate wealth. The first is providing for personal and family needs. In the second chapter of 2 Thessalonians, Paul declares that it is a worthy goal not to be a burden on other people. Christians must prefer work to welfare, earning enough to take care of the immediate needs of our own households.

But let's be honest. A good many Americans are enjoying surpluses that far surpass our daily needs. We already have what we need to be fed, to be clothed, and to stay dry. Now ... what shall we do with the rest? Sociologists are starting to talk about a new group on the American scene. They're called Children of Rich Fathers. For the first time in our history — for the first time in the history of any country — a large number of men and women, at a comparatively young age, are inheriting great wealth. By and large, there is no public consensus and there has been little family training in how to utilize this wealth. Just after World War II, eight percent of American households were judged to have significant discretionary income. Today that number has risen to 51 percent. After personal and family needs have been met, what does God want us to do with the good things that have come our way?

Our answer begins with the second biblical reason for accumulating wealth, the very one that Paul details in the eighth chapter of 2 Corinthians: *Being free to share with others who are in need.* Jesus was "rich." He chose to become "poor." For what purpose? Paul says in verses 13 and 14, "... it is a question of a fair balance between your present abundance and their need, so that their abundance may be for your need, in order that there may be a fair balance." God's people are blessed so that they might be a blessing. God is uniquely able to coordinate both needs and provisions.

A pastor in Indiana received a call from a man outside his church whose one-and-only car had gone into the shop. The repair was completed but the bill was much greater than he could pay. Would the church be willing to help find the funds — a grant or a loan — that would put him back into his car? It was crucial to have an answer by Friday. By then it was clear that the pastor could round up half the funds. As he headed out of the office for the day, a couple met him at the door. "Could we talk to you for a few minutes?" they asked. The pastor was already late for an appointment, so he said, "To tell you the truth, I can't really talk to you right now." "That's okay," they said. "We'll just walk with you outside. We only need a minute."

Years ago this couple had received a gift from the church to help them through a tough time in their lives. "God's been doing wonderful things for us," they said, "so now we can offer back what you offered to us." They handed the pastor a check. There was the second half of the money for the car bill. God provides, accomplishing wonderful things precisely when they need to be done.

Paul takes pains to point out that *stewardship* is the ultimate issue when it comes to being accountable for our gifts, not the numbers on the checks we write. "For if the eagerness is there, the gift is acceptable according to what one has — not according to what one does not have" (v. 12). The specifics of one person's accountability to God will be different from the specifics of another. But God will ask all of us the same question: What did you do with the good things that I put into your hands? Did you become rich for your own sake, or rich for my sake? This matter of being accountable to God means understanding at least three things.

First, we need to understand *whose* property we are managing. The farmer in Jesus' parable in Luke 12 is extremely confused on this point. He has been reaping bumper crops. In verse 17 he says, "What should I do, for *I* have no place to store my crops?" (emphasis added). That's why God roars in verse 20, "You fool!" In the Bible, even a genius can be a fool. Without so much as a notice in the mail, God is calling in his loans. God says, "This very night your life will be demanded of you." The verb translated "demanded" is part of the language of the first century banking system. The farmer's life is officially *required* by God, because it has always been on loan — something that the farmer has obviously failed to grasp.

Second, being accountable to God means understanding *why* God has entrusted good things to us. We are blessed to be a blessing. God meets our needs, and then some, so that we might meet the needs of others. Why did God specifically choose to bless some of us one way, and others of us in another way? Only God knows — and brooding on the matter can fill our hearts with pain and misunderstanding. Why was she born so pretty? Why couldn't I hit a curve ball and make the high school team? Why was I so inept in chemistry, when everybody else could figure it out? That guy can sell anything. Why can't I do that? How can she be so energetic and organized, when I don't even have the strength to get out of bed? Why were they born into money, while I have to work so hard?

God tells us that in this world we have the privilege of knowing the details of exactly one person's story — our own. I am accountable for the gifts, the resources, and the opportunities that God has uniquely given to me — and not for what God *hasn't* given to me. As Paul reminds us, "The gift is acceptable according to what one has — not according to what one does not have."

Finally, being accountable to God means understanding *what* we need to do to "close the gap" in our behavior. Closing the gap between my version of the Good Life and God's version of the Good Life might mean any number of things. It might involve re-thinking my checkbook. Or readjusting my calendar. Or recalibrating what I value the most. How does my life need to change so that I can become rich toward God?

Some of us will discover that we can live on just fifty percent of what we make, and are in the remarkable position of providing help and support to a wide range of causes around the world. We might fund the education of someone who would otherwise never be able to attend classes. We might help develop Christian leadership in a Third World country. The possibilities are endless. It doesn't take a truckload of dollars to make a difference. *ABC Nightly News* recently featured a Manhattan cab driver who every week has saved just five or ten dollars to send back to the village where he grew up in India. Because of his generosity, and the reality of compound interest, he has single-handedly opened a school for the little girls of his town. His faithfulness and persistence made the difference.

Americans traveling overseas frequently delight in the phenomenon of foreign currency. Paper money from other nations is frequently colorful and comes in variety of interesting sizes. Coins are of different colors and textures and don't "jingle" in one's pocket in quite the same way. Foreign currency may even be said to be fun — but is completely worthless in an American store. You can visit another country and stuff your wallet with its legal tender, but as soon as your jet lands in New York City those colorful pieces of paper or interesting coins can't even buy a pack of gum.

God assures us that our destination is another country. Only a fool would spend his life trying to hold on to the currency of this world, which in the next world will be powerless to buy anything. The currency of heaven is the degree to which we are imitators of the Son of God. Jesus, though he was rich, for our sakes became poor. Are we sharing and investing the good things that God has poured into our lives in such a way that we are looking more and more like him?

In recent years Paul Azinger has been at or near the top of professional golf. As Bob Russell points out in his book *Money: A User's Guide*, he's known for three things: being an outspoken follower of Christ, recovering from a bout of cancer, and being so frustrated with his performance at the British Open in 1996 that he broke his putter over his knee in front of an international audience, leaving him nine holes to play without a putter.

After that event Azinger was embarrassed beyond words. One of the British tabloids shrieked that this man was the model of the Christian life, yet he had lost his temper. Azinger began to grasp the degree to which pride had fed his frustration.

"When I started playing competitive golf," he said, "my hometown paper asked, 'Is Azinger good enough to make it on the tour?' When I made the tour they asked, 'Is Azinger good enough to win?' After I won my first tournament they asked, 'Can he sustain it?' Then when I was the PGA Golfer of the Year, my thrill lasted two days — until I picked up a magazine and read an article that said, 'Is Paul Azinger the best player never to have won a major?' It's never enough."

In the eyes of the world, enough is never enough. People who have received the greatest gifts can become trapped in the deadly undertow of believing it's necessary to earn more, to have more, to accomplish more. Paul Azinger said, "No more." No more falling for a false version of the Good Life. Even though he dreaded the thought of facing the public after his British Open meltdown, Azinger had made a promise to speak at a men's prayer breakfast in Louisville, Kentucky. He came humbly. He led from weakness. He revealed the degree to which he keeps learning that his life isn't all about himself. It's all about God — and it's never too late to go a different way. Several of the 2,000 men in attendance that morning decided to become Christians.

No matter how we've lived, it's not too late to go a different way. If you are reading these words, God hasn't yet called back the living loan of your life. We can still choose to invest wisely the good things that God has given to us.

Grace In The Midst
Of Unanswered Prayer

No one ever really prepares you for your first theological bull session. Usually it arrives without fanfare or advance warning. Usually it happens long before you enter the relative clear-headedness of your adult years, or before you take that philosophy course in college. Usually it happens when you're a junior high school student, up late with friends at a sleepover, or camping out in somebody's backyard. There's just something about a smoky fire and charred food and stars out overhead that turns twelve-year-olds into theologians.

"All right," someone will say, "if God is all powerful, and if he can do anything at all, does that mean God can make a rock so big that even God can't move it?" Everybody's got an opinion on that one. "Of course God can move it," says someone else. "Isn't that what it means to be God?" But someone else will retort, "If God can do anything, can God create a problem so big that even God can't solve it?" And on and on the discussion goes.

The neat thing about being a twelve-year-old is that you can fall asleep out in the backyard without resolving those questions, and when you wake up the next morning the world is just fine. But Christian believers don't get off so easily. Unresolved questions have the power to keep us up at nights. Can God really do everything? Then why is it that we can tick off a laundry list of things that an all-knowing, all-loving, all-powerful God *ought* to do — yet they aren't getting done? Are there rocks out there that are too big for God to move, or does God simply not answer every prayer?

267

Author and evangelist Tony Campolo was still settling into the pastoral role in his first small parish when he was told that a nine-year-old boy in his congregation had cancer. Prayer chains were hastily assembled. All-night vigils were held. Time and again the boy's parents heard fellow believers "claim the victory" and assure them that their prayers would be answered and the boy would be healed. But after many excruciating weeks of suffering, the boy died.

The congregation was disappointed and disillusioned. The boy's parents stopped coming to church. Campolo made a call at their home to urge them to rejoin the fellowship. "Ralph," he said, "you can't stop believing in God because he didn't answer your prayers." Ralph answered, "Oh, that's not it. You don't understand. I didn't stop believing in God. *I just hate him.*" Campolo had been ready with answers to every imaginable theological objection — but he had no answer to that one. He wasn't prepared to comfort a man whose love for God had been vaporized because an all-powerful deity had refused to help his suffering child. If God can do anything, why did those prayers go unanswered?

Jesus himself, just hours before the apex of his own suffering, affirms the unlimited power of God. He pleads in the Garden of Gethsemane, "Abba, Father, for you all things are possible" (Mark 14:36). At the door of death Jesus says, "Father, you can do anything. I know that. You are all-powerful." But Jesus died. God *could* have done something. Yet God didn't. What are the Bible's answers to the scandal of unanswered prayer?

What we learn from Jesus' wrestling in the Garden and Paul's pleading about a thorn in his flesh is that God is limited after all. God is intentionally self-limited when it comes to answering prayers that would grant us comfort in the heat of the present moment — but would thereby defeat God's intention to bless us in far grander and more strategic ways.

God the Father cannot be mistaken for earthly parents. I may have an idea about what is good for my children, but I am predictably inconsistent in giving them only the best. I may know all about the foods that they should eat, but when they pester me for snacks at all hours of the day I may hedge on my commitment to nutrition and supply them with junk food.

God on the other hand is unmoved by his children's prayers for spiritual Cheez Wiz. God is so alarmingly committed to our good that prayers for what God knows is ultimately misguided or pathetic or dangerous stand no chance of being answered. That's grace. We may picture a Plan A in our minds, and cry out to God to make it happen, but God has envisioned a Plan B — perhaps one that we cannot yet understand — that is infinitely more strategic. It is impossible for God to give up on Plan B just because Plan A would get us out of a lot of trouble today.

In Gethsemane Jesus requested a specific outcome: "Remove this cup from me." In other words, "I don't want to go through the hell of this crucifixion. Father, since you can do anything, I know this doesn't have to happen." Jesus follows his plea with the most spiritually mature and eloquent prayer statement in history: "Yet, not what I want, but what you want." Anything is possible, but there is one pathway that will bring about the ultimate good. Jesus gives up a claim on his own comfort, his own way of imagining the future, in order to say, "Father, of all the things that could possibly happen, make the one happen that *you want*."

Let's be honest. Most of the time our prayers tend to revolve around concerns for safety, pleasure, and success. "Lord, take care of us tonight, and give us a good meeting, and bless everyone who is here." That's a fine prayer, but it is hardly the sum of what God desires for us. We may wish happiness to arrive as soon as possible at the least personal expense. But the Son of God didn't come to make us merely happy. He came to make us like himself — and identifying with Christ is never achieved apart from suffering.

Paul knew that. "To keep me from being too elated, a thorn was given me in the flesh, a messenger of Satan" (v. 7). The reference to this "stake" or a "skewer" clearly indicates a serious degree of discomfort. Commentators have never achieved consensus on the identity of Paul's thorn. It might have been a metaphorical reference to persecution by enemies (Gentiles or Jews); attacks of malarial fever; a recurrent affliction like migraine headaches or epileptic episodes; the overwhelming emotional burden of launching young churches (see 2 Corinthians 11:28-29); or compromised eyesight (the preferred choice of a number of sight-challenged preachers).

What we know for sure is that Paul was sufficiently afflicted by this thorn to take up the matter with God on at least three occasions. We may presume Paul is referring not merely to three *prayers*, but to a trio of significant episodes of spiritual pleading. And God's answer to the greatest missionary-evangelist of the early Church? "No." Paul concluded in this case that unanswered prayer meant that God had a more compelling plan for his life than the one he was requesting.

The account of Augustine's early days provides a helpful illustration. A rebellious, immoral, yet brilliant teenager growing up in North Africa, Augustine drove his godly mother to her knees. She begged Augustine to come to Christ, but he rebuffed her at every turn. Ultimately he determined to skip town and sail toward greater adventures in Italy. Monica spent a sleepless night pleading with God to block his path. "Please let him stay here in Africa so that one day he might find and serve you!" Her prayers went unanswered. Augustine sailed away unhindered ... only to come under the influence of Ambrose, bishop of Milan, who mentored him into a spiritual life that would bless and transform the history of the Church.

Later in life Augustine reflected on his mother's sincere prayers that night. He was grateful — grateful that God chose not to answer them. If God had said, "Yes," then her real desire for his spiritual awakening might never have been satisfied. Augustine wrote this prayer of thanks: "Thou, in the depth of thy counsels, hearing the main point of her desire, regarded not what she then asked, that thou mightest make me what she ever desired."

God doesn't always give us what we ask. But God unfailingly provides us with what we need. "You want power, Paul? Power to take away your greatest discomfort? Here's my grace instead. And my grace is sufficient for you, for my power is made perfect — is fully received and fully known — when you are at your worst."

We don't need an instant "out" from every problem. Much of what is vital to our progress as disciples comes about only through what pushes us, pinches us, even crushes us. But isn't Paul taking things a bit too far in verse 10? "Therefore I am content with weaknesses, insults, hardships, persecutions, and calamities." The *New*

270

International Version renders this statement, "Therefore I delight in weaknesses...." Has Paul crossed the line into spiritual masochism and joined the No-Pain-No-Gain school of sanctification?

In fact Paul takes no delight in the reality of his suffering, in the mere sensations of his nerve endings. Rather he rejoices because of the *meaning* of his suffering. Verse 10 concludes, "For whenever I am weak, then I am strong." The essence of God's grace is that Paul's pain has reinforced his dependence on God's strength.

Pain and unanswered prayer that are experienced apart from the context of some overall meaning to the universe are truly unbearable. Such suffering naturally leads to despair. If there is no meaning to what is happening to us, then there is no reason to take courage. It's not surprising that so many people break down. But Paul grasps something of infinite significance. He realizes that suffering and sacrifice are prime ways in which God is repairing a broken world. If things had gone differently in the Garden of Eden, it's a safe bet that pain wouldn't even be in the picture today. But this is a *broken* world, and God powerfully uses suffering to put things back together.

With Paul we can affirm that God never wastes pain. "For Christ's sake, I am content with weaknesses." Suffering never happens arbitrarily. Pain is God's servant. It exists to serve God's purpose and to accomplish God's will. That doesn't mean a God-ordained thorn in the flesh ever feels good. But such a limitation, frailty, or affliction genuinely has meaning. God never wastes pain.

How might this insight change the way we talk to God? Let us pray not so much that our friends and loved ones are free of all pain, but that they are truly free to see the greatness of God. Sometimes we unintentionally cheat the people we love out of the experience of their struggle with suffering. Remember that it was Jesus' friends who pleaded with him not to go to Jerusalem to die, even though his death was crucial for them and for us. Remember that it was Job's wife who said, "Curse God and die! Stop trying to trust God when it's clear he has no intention of answering your prayers." It is vitally important for us not to run away from the challenges of our suffering, but to let God's work be carried through to completion — even when we have no final idea about what is being accomplished.

The legacy of great prayers in the Bible helps point the way. Seldom do we find God's saints pleading, "Lord, keep every bit of pain and suffering off our doorsteps." Instead we find, "Lord, when suffering and misunderstanding and persecution come our way, help us respond the way you would have us respond." Paul doesn't pray that the church in Ephesus, for example, might be problem-free. He knows better. He prays that in the midst of their problems they might see the awesomeness of God. In chapter 3, verse 18, he writes, "I pray that you may have the power to comprehend, with all the saints, what is the breadth and length and height and depth, and to know the love of Christ...." In the midst of the confusion and frustration of unanswered prayers it is always wise to pray that our concept of God may expand to a dimension we have not yet known.

Whenever we are suffering we are not called to put our trust in a plan; we are called to put our trust in a Person. Most of us yearn to know the specifics of God's plan. "Lord, if only I knew why this were happening, I could bear it." That is profoundly untrue. It isn't knowledge or insight that brings comfort. What comforts the heart is the absolute conviction that no matter what is happening Jesus Christ is Lord over everything, and that we can trust him (even when it seems that heaven is absolutely silent) that our pain truly means something.

But how do we know he can be trusted in this area? Our conviction is that God is trustworthy when it comes to suffering because he himself came into this world and tasted real pain.

A story is told of a grandfather who came to the home of his grandson to play. He entered the toy room to find little Jeremy sitting in the playpen. The boy immediately jumped to his feet and shouted, "Grandpa!" whereupon the older man extended his arms and swooped his grandson up into his arms. They had been playing excitedly for about five minutes when the boy's mother walked into the room. "Jeremy!" she said sternly. "You know that you were in that playpen because you have been bad. You shouldn't have made Grandpa take you out!"

The grandfather felt horrible. Unwittingly he had made a tough situation for Jeremy even worse. He lifted up his grandson and placed him back into the playpen. "Please, Grandpa, play with me!" the little boy pleaded. What could he do? It would be wrong to overrule the restrictions that had gotten Jeremy into the playpen to start with. One option remained. Grandpa crawled into the play-pen, taking a little boy's restrictions upon himself.

That is what Jesus did for all of humanity. He came down and experienced the junk of our lives, the thorns that stab human flesh, and the dark drama of hearing the Father say, "No." Why did he do it? He did it for us — so that we'd never have to doubt that he is really there and he really intends our good — even when it hurts.

Grace In The Midst
Of Guilt And Shame

At the beginning of his ministry Jesus had a chance to impress the people he grew up with. According to Luke, chapter 4, Jesus was invited to stand up and read the Bible in his hometown synagogue of Nazareth. And why not? He was the latest sensation. His reputation as a teacher was starting to get around. He was the local kid who had made good. There must have been smiles and gentle ribbing as Jesus got up to read the Scriptures on that Saturday morning a long time ago. "Remember when he was just a child, helping Joseph around the carpenter's shop? Wow, look at him now."

Manuscripts weren't bound like books in the ancient Middle East. Important documents were on scrolls. A very long manuscript would be wrapped around two rods that looked a bit like rolling pins, and one would progressively unroll that long sheet until he found the place he wanted to read. When Jesus got up to speak he was handed the scroll of Isaiah, the Old Testament prophet.

Apparently Jesus could have read anything in Isaiah he wanted. He located the text of his choice and read it out loud. Then he rolled the scroll back, sat down and said, essentially, "You know those words I just read to you? They're all about me. You've been waiting 700 years for the person who would make those words come true. Well, that person grew up just down the street from you. Here I am."

Imagine a kid from your church's high school youth group striding up to the pulpit in the middle of a Sunday service. "May I borrow the mike for just a moment? It's so nice that you all came to worship today — and by the way, you really ought to be worshipping *me.*" We'd say, "Take the car keys away from that arrogant little whelp. What kind of nut case is he?" Actually, things were a lot tougher for Jesus in his own synagogue. Luke tells us that the insulted crowd tried to toss him off the local cliff. But Jesus blew their minds even more by walking away as if he weren't the least bit perturbed.

What exactly did Jesus read to invite the scorn of his neighbors? He chose the opening salvo of Isaiah 61 — words that communicated, "This is the kind of Messiah I'm going to be. I'm here for the poor. I'm here for people with broken hearts. I'm here for people who have smeared ashes on their faces, because their lives hurt so badly. I'm here to give out new clothes — a garment of praise to replace a spirit of despair." *The King James Version* memorably translates the last phrase, "a garment of praise for the spirit of heaviness."

Those pursuing certification in Lifesaving are required to demonstrate a technique that may one day save their own lives. Fully clothed, they must jump into deep water. While staying afloat they must wriggle out of their pants, tie the two pant legs together, then flip the open end (that is, the waistline) over their heads and catch enough air to inflate them, thus creating a crude life jacket. By means of those pants alone they must stay afloat for no fewer than 45 minutes.

Those seeking certification sometimes recall those as the longest minutes of their lives. Their remaining clothes feel plastered to their bodies. They can barely move in all that heaviness. They wonder if those who drown during this exercise at least receive their Lifesaving status posthumously. Isaiah 61's spirit of heaviness — the spirit of despair — is like the entanglement of clinging clothes.

Ours is a culture on the verge of drowning under the weight of unresolved burdens of personal guilt and shame. Despite our claims of post-Enlightenment wisdom and the keenest insights of the therapeutic industry, American society seems singularly ill-equipped to peel these burdens away. Guilt and shame, furthermore, are tricky animals. As *feelings* they are frequently experienced out of proportion to the *realities* that trigger them, and they are frequently confused with each other. Christians, at least, are in agreement on one matter: Jesus came to eradicate both guilt and shame.

What is guilt? It is the reality and/or the perception that we have done something wrong. What is shame? It is the reality and/or the perception that *we ourselves* are the "something wrong." Paul's words in the first chapter of Ephesians make the case that the cross is God's means of forever changing our encounters with these spirits of heaviness. Let's begin by considering God's grace in the midst of unresolved guilt.

Author and rabbi Harold Kushner tells of visiting two families deep in grief. Each home had lost an elderly matriarch who had died of natural causes. At the first home the son of the deceased woman confessed to Kushner, "If only I had sent my mother to Florida and gotten her out of this cold, she would be alive today. It's my fault she died." At the second home the son told the rabbi, "If only I hadn't insisted on my mother's going to Florida, she would be alive today. It's my fault she's dead."

Two homes. Two losses. Two men struggling to go forward under equal burdens of unresolved guilt. Yet ... was either of them actually responsible for his mother's death? Isn't it possible that both of them had saddled themselves unnecessarily with guilt feelings? That would be the assumption of many contemporary therapists. They would try to make a case that guilt feelings are universally inappropriate. They are irrational and destructive. They make us feel responsible for things that have already happened and cannot now be changed. They paralyze us. Therefore we should let ourselves off the hook and refuse to feel so guilty.

That sounds therapeutic — until we open the pages of the Bible. God's Word identifies guilt feelings that are proper and necessary because they connect us with a *status* of guilt that is objectively real. God has planted in every human being a kind of moral seismograph that registers behavioral earthquakes. When we live contrary to God's desires, the seismograph goes crazy. What registers in our minds and hearts is guilt. The Bible would say that one reason we are besieged with guilt-like feelings is that we frequently do things that are truly wrong.

When it comes to this irregular emotion called guilt, Christians have a tough assignment. We need to walk in such a way that we don't veer to the left or to the right and fall off the cliff of one of two extreme positions. On the one hand, we need to avoid the idea that all guilt feelings are meaningless and irrational, and that we should simply find ways to cope. On the other hand, we need to reject the idea that just because we feel guilty we've therefore done something terribly wrong. Finding the middle path is difficult. Sometimes we feel bad when we shouldn't; other times we feel happy-go-lucky when we should be down on our knees before a holy God.

The first chapter of Ephesians has nothing to say about guilt feelings. Paul, however, makes an important contribution to what we know about true guilt. True guilt is a theological problem. It is directly linked to our relationship with God. When we have done something that is objectively wrong, an act that violates the moral laws of the universe, something inside us screams, "I need to be punished or I need to be forgiven. Something *has* to be done!" True guilt demands action. Here's the question: Will we try to erase our guilt through our own actions, or through God's actions on our behalf?

If we opt for the former, we can choose from a legendary list of strategies. First, we can shift the blame. "Sure, I've done wrong things, but it's not my fault. My preschool teacher warped me. It was the environment. It was the unfair way they graded the SATs in the 1970s." Recently several courts have heard cases in which adults are suing their grown parents for "wrongful birth." In other words, those parents should have known better than to bring such unhappy children into the world.

A second strategy is to seek punishment, or, as author Frederick Buechner puts it, "Our desire to be clobbered for our guilt, and thus rid of it, tempts us to do things we will be clobbered for." How else can we explain the incredibly bone-headed ways that would-be robbers, every year, manage to do things that lead police right to their doorsteps? Recently two Midwesterners tried to pull the front off a cash machine by running a chain from the ATM to the bumper of their truck. Instead of pulling the front panel off the

278

machine, however, they pulled the bumper off their pickup. Scared, they left the scene and headed home — with the chain still attached to the ATM, their bumper still attached to the chain, and their license plate still attached to the bumper. If we don't like the idea of God punishing us, we will certainly find a way for someone else to get the job done.

Likewise we can try to serve our guilt away. We'll be as good as good can be, and make up for our mistakes. We'll get forgiveness the old-fashioned way, the Smith Barney way: *We'll earn it.* This much is certain: We'll make ourselves miserable in the attempt. As a young monk, Martin Luther invested as many as six hours a day racking his brain to confess the sins he might have committed during the previous 24 hours. Did this make him feel closer to God? Luther wrote in his diary:

> *Although I lived a blameless life as a monk, I felt that I was a sinner with an uneasy conscience before God. I also could not believe that I had pleased him with my works. Far from loving that righteous God who punished sinners, I actually loathed him ... I always doubted and said, "You didn't do that right. You weren't contrite enough. You left that out of your confession."*

True guilt demands action. Our actions will never be adequate to take guilt away. But God's grace, in the midst of our guilt, is this: God has acted *for us.* Paul declares in verse 3 that God has "blessed us in Christ with every spiritual blessing in the heavenly places." Guilt must either be punished or forgiven. Jesus accepted our punishment on the cross so that we might be forgiven. We read in verse 7, "In him we have redemption through his blood, the forgiveness of our trespasses, according to the riches of his grace."

The miracle of this grace is that Christian disciples — those who have received Christ's gift of new life and enrolled as his intentional imitators — cannot sin themselves out of their relationship with him. Our sins cannot separate us from God. Nevertheless, our *attitudes* toward our continuing failures may create the impression that God has fled — especially if we are unwilling to accept God's solution to the dilemma of ongoing guilt feelings.

Some Christians remain under the spell of the spirit of heaviness. *Feelings* of forgiveness have never come, or at least haven't stayed. Why does this happen? Far too many of us awake in the morning as if the cross never happened, or as if God's actions fell short. We've concluded that our sins are so big or so frequent that Jesus' death wasn't enough. During confession we imagine God saying, "What? You again?" Thus we're paralyzed. We feel just as paralyzed as the young man in the Gospel account who couldn't move until Jesus said to him, "Your sins are forgiven. Now get up and walk."

That's the key. If we wrestle with guilt feelings that seem to hang on and on, it's crucial to take Christ at his word when he declares us forgiven. He is not a liar. Some of us need to ask forgiveness for something else. We need to ask God forgiveness for acting as if we are somehow beyond the reach of grace, and for our unwillingness to believe the promises of scripture. We don't need to *feel* forgiven to believe God's assurance that in Christ we *are* forgiven.

We turn now from the realm of guilt to the even more challenging task of confronting shame. What is shame? It is a feeling — a deep, relentless feeling that I am not the person that I should be, and that I can't wriggle out of the mess that I've gotten myself into. As Lewis Smedes beautifully puts it in his book *Shame and Grace*, "Shame is the dead weight of not-good-enoughness." Shame, of course, can serve the healthy role of demonstrating the gap between our character and the holiness of God. But all too often it settles down into the cracks of our consciousness as the despairing judgment that we will never get things right. Smedes writes:

> *Shame can fall over you when a person stares at you after you've said something inane at a party, or when you think everyone is clucking at how skinny or how fat or how clumsy you are. It comes when no one else is looking at you but yourself and what you see is a phony, a coward, a bore, a failure, a dumbbell, a person whose nose is too big and whose legs are too bony, or a mother*

280

who is incompetent at mothering, and, all in all, a poor
dope with little hope of ever becoming an acceptable
human being.

Unhealthy shame is all about being unacceptable. This kind of
shame is not merely an alert that we are flawed people (which is
certainly true and easily demonstrated). Unhealthy shame declares
that we are unacceptable as human beings. We are not worthy of
being loved. Such a feeling can only be described as a life-weary-
ing heaviness.

We must fear for teenage girls who read the magazines that are
specially designed for them — specially designed to make them
feel as if their skin and their bodies and their boyfriends will never
look like those of the models who are on every page of those magazines. We must fear for the boys who read muscle magazines and
take steroids because that's how to become an impact athlete, and
that's how to impress a girl. We must fear for overly responsible
people — those who have the good sense to realize that the world
is filled with pain, but the misguided sense that it is their job to fix
it. When they fail, they feel devastated.

Sadly, church can be a place where many people experience
the heaviness of shame. Sometimes it's because a congregation
doesn't know how to speak of grace. Other times it's because worshipers can't imagine being embraced by a God who has any standards of excellence. Our ideal is to think like Jesus and talk like
Jesus and *be* like Jesus. But in truth the vast majority of us have
extended periods of time when we don't want to be anything like
that at all. Maybe we sit in church and daydream about punching
out our boss, or wishing that an annoying relative would just die,
or pursuing forbidden sexual adventures, or running away from
the people who are depending on us right now, or simply wishing
that we could get all this over with, and simply be dead ourselves.
Then when it's time to pray we think, "*As if ... as if* God would
reach down and love me right now, since he knows what I've been
thinking about." Thus we conclude that we're not worthy of being
accepted — by God or by anyone else who really knows our secret
imaginings.

How do we escape the heaviness of shame? As Smedes points out, what we have to do is address the lies that we tell ourselves. Nobody gets up in the morning and says, "Boy, I think I'll tell myself a whopper of a lie today ... and then believe it." But that's what we do. We believe the lie that we have to make ourselves acceptable before we can be accepted, and our feelings fall right in line. They back us up all the way.

On the other hand, what does the Bible say? The Bible says that we can be healed. We need to forsake the lies and believe the truth. The truth is that we can replace the heaviness of inappropriate shame with the lightness of God's grace. The same Messiah who read Isaiah 61 in that synagogue also said, "Come to me, all of you who are weary and heavy-laden — all of you who are drowning in the dead weight of not-good-enoughness — and I will give you rest. Get into a relationship with me and you'll find that the way I lead you is easy. The 'burden' that I put on you, by comparison, feels so light" (Matthew 11:28-30, paraphrased).

That's grace. Do we deserve it? Absolutely not. If we deserved the love of Jesus it would be because we had *done* something to earn it. Worthiness, on the other hand, is different. We are worthy of something not because we have *done* something, but because we *are* somebody of incredible value.

That is the wonderful news splayed across the first chapter of Ephesians. God has declared us to be people of infinite value. Paul announces that God chose us before the creation of the world (vv. 4, 11). Our adoption as God's children was predestined (vv. 5, 11). This fabulous change in our identity happened "so that we, who were the first to set our hope on Christ, might live for the praise of his glory" (v. 12). On top of it all we have received the Holy Spirit as "the pledge of our inheritance toward redemption as God's own people" (vv. 13, 14).

Grace doesn't say, "Oh, look, you're not so bad. Here! I've found some hidden personal assets that you overlooked deep in your heart." God, with his eyes wide open, says, "No matter what is in your heart — beauty or ugliness, virtue or vice — you are accepted, because from the moment you were conceived I knew you, and every minute of your life you have been worthy. That is how I created you." *Period*. Christians are truly God's chosen people.

In his book *Dangerous Wonder*, Mike Yaconelli recounts a time he hired a man to lay tile in his kitchen. Yaconelli knew this man to be the alcoholic father of a teenager whom he had come to know through a youth ministry. The father had been emotionally and physically abusive to everyone in his family. Yaconelli determined not to be cheated or pushed around by this fellow. He demanded (and received) a written estimate in advance — $350 for three days' work. When the work was finished the tiler said, "I need to talk to you about the money." Yaconelli braced himself for a battle royal. He writes:

> *I was ready for him and glanced at my wife with the look of testosterone on my face. He started to hand me the bill, but then paused for a moment and said, "A couple of years ago I was drinking too much. I am an alcoholic and was at a very low point in my life. I almost lost my family because of my drinking. I mistreated my wife and my children, especially my oldest son.*
>
> *"But you and your wife spent a lot of time with him at a critical moment in his life when he could have gone either way. Shortly after that I went to AA, and I've been sober ever since. Because of you and your wife, I still have a relationship with my son. I've never been able to thank you, but I'm thanking you now."*
>
> *He handed me his bill for $350. "Paid in full" was written across the page. This abusing, untrustworthy man ... had just shown this arrogant snob the meaning of grace.*

What is the meaning of grace? It's that none of us deserves the love of God. None of us deserves another chance. That's the heavy part. But the lightness of grace is that God, magically, considers us worthy of being in a relationship with the Creator of the universe. The incredible news is that God has written across the debt-sheets of our personal lives, "Paid in full."

Proper 11
Pentecost 9
Ordinary Time 16
Ephesians 2:11-22

Grace In The Midst
Of Dividing Walls

According to those whose job it is to know such things, it only takes three weeks to become blind to the presence of stationary objects in our everyday worlds. Hang a new picture on the wall, and one is likely to notice it for about 21 days. After that it has become part of the scenery. It simply doesn't leap into the foreground any more.

That's why it can be so hard to accomplish the simplest chores of housework before the arrival of guests. We've stopped noticing the screwdriver that's been sitting on the living room mantle for the last three months, or the pile of dirty shirts that has found a semi-permanent home at the end of the hallway. Housecleaning requires a new set of "eyes," eyes that are objective enough to see our surroundings as a discriminating guest would see them, not as we have become used to them.

Over a period of time that is a good deal longer than three weeks, people have become used to the barriers that separate them from their neighbors. We are surrounded and isolated by countless dividing walls, yet, unaided, we no longer have the spiritual capacity to see them. In many regards we have even come to assume that the way we *experience* the world, blind as we are, is normal.

Affluent Americans are used to being separated from lower income families. They don't work with them, worship with them, or go out of their way to attend the same parties. Blue-collar workers are used to a life apart from white-collar management. A wage earner may drive through the neighborhood of his employer, but hardly expect to be invited in for a barbecue. Protestants are used to being separated from Catholics. Pentecostal church members rarely cross paths with those in Orthodox congregations.

Likewise, most of us are used to a degree of separation from certain members of our own families. We don't communicate with them and they don't communicate with us, and that has come to seem normal. Anglos are used to their worlds not intersecting those of African-Americans or Hispanics or Asians. For generations the children in American homes of every color have tended to experience those of other backgrounds or nationalities in the most superficial ways — through television sitcom stereotyping, stand-up comedy, and glances into the private lives of entertainment icons and sports stars. Conversations, working partnerships, and personal encounters are disturbingly rare.

It is the disarming yet gracious promise of God that if I am willing, God will give me eyes to see the world from the perspective of heaven. God will give me eyes to see that there are indeed dividing walls in my life, and that these walls are not God's creation. They are *my walls*. Furthermore by grace I am called to be a disciple of the one who specializes in the elimination of barriers, who delights in tearing down the walls that separate people from each other. On what principle does God do this? Christ claims lordship over everybody, including those on my side of the fence and those on the other side. His grace is available to everybody — even before our spiritual blinders have been removed and we ourselves can see the foolishness of our separation.

The plain teaching of Ephesians chapter 2 is that God intends to vaporize such artificial barriers. Why, then, do so many would-be followers of Jesus find it so hard to get with this program? Why do we live as if it is normal to keep dividing walls in good repair?

One answer is that a majority of the human race flinches at the prospect of conflict or change. Over time we have established peace treaties on our own cherished sides of relational fences, and there is little passion for stirring things up. When faced with the challenge of addressing uncomfortable realities, people vote en masse to "keep the peace" instead.

In his book *The Different Drum*, psychologist and author Scott Peck makes a case that within all of us there is a God-implanted desire to experience authentic relationships. Deep inside we long for true community: for relationships in which we can express our real feelings, be accepted for who we are, and give and receive genuine love. But most of us settle for a pale imitation of the real thing. Peck calls this cheap substitute "pseudo community." Most of us are involved in marriages, family relationships, and friendships that hover safely near the surface. We hesitate to speak what is "unsafe." Open discussions about hurt feelings, frustrations, and difficult questions are rare. The underlying rule in pseudo community is: *Don't rock the boat.* Do what it takes to keep the peace.

Peck affirms that our dreams of living in true community can be fulfilled, but only if we are willing to leave pseudo community in the rear view mirror. There's a price tag attached. To enter true community we have to experience what Peck calls "chaos." Chaos describes the uncomfortable span of time during which one chooses to step out in faith — unburying hurts, revealing hostilities, and asking the tough questions, all the while being entirely uncertain how those on the other side of the wall might respond.

Motorists who drive to Key West soon discover that the only way they can get their car to the southernmost tip of Florida is to cross the long series of one-lane bridges that link key to key. It doesn't matter whether or not one happens to be fond of bridges: if you intend to reach Key West, you *will* be crossing a great number of them. Likewise, the only path from superficial relationships that feature little honest sharing to relationships nourished by authentic intimacy is the path that demands we cross ever-higher bridges of trust.

For many Christians, whose Master excelled in the grace of dismantling walls, this is an exercise frightening even to contemplate. They huddle in the safety of pseudo community. A disturbing number of churches are relationally frozen, with little vision of a thaw. Within marriages, one partner may choose to reach out tentatively, groping to communicate a feeling or a hurt at a deeper level, only to be greeted with defensiveness or hostility as the pseudo peace of the relationship is suddenly challenged. Both partners may end up retreating and saying to themselves, "Building new bridges of trust isn't worth it! Our relationship is at least as intimate as any of our friends'. We should hunker down where we are and make the best of it." Some spouses ultimately take a darker turn and fuel their fantasies of the dream partner, the new mate who will ratchet intimacy to the highest level without all the accompanying pain of bridge-building — someone who, of course, does not exist.

And so we go, maintaining a veneer of cooperation that camouflages our families, our workplaces, and our congregations. But every now and then the veneer is yanked to the ground, and suddenly the world can see that there are walls that divide us and fragile relationships that fail us.

Racial unrest boils to the surface of a community. Suddenly the veneer has been ripped off. Leaders of historic denominations move along warily with each other for years, doing their best to submerge deep theological rifts, until external societal pressures force the most sensitive questions to the surface. A half dozen ethnic groups in the Balkan Peninsula are forced to stay together in a pseudo community called Yugoslavia for most of a century. When the veneer is removed, dividing walls that are older than anyone's great-grandparents are suddenly in plain sight, while peace-keeping troops struggle to enforce the next new version of pseudo community.

But the best-intentioned, most aggressively enforced peace-keeping efforts are doomed to fail. We cannot *keep* a peace that does not exist, and there can be no peace — not between races, or national governments, or theological sparring partners — until the dividing walls in human hearts, not merely veneers, are brought down. The Apostle Paul, reflecting on the centuries-old antipathy between Jews and Gentiles in verse 14, proclaims Jesus to be the world's only source of hope for human reconciliation: "For he is our peace; in his flesh he has made both groups into one and has broken down the dividing wall, that is, the hostility between us."

Jesus is our peace. In what sense is this true? What Matthew affirms in his Gospel is that Jesus' death was accompanied by a significant change in the Temple in Jerusalem. The geography of the temple area was essentially designed to be a show-and-tell of theological, racial, and gender exclusion. At the perimeter was a sign that said, "No Gentiles beyond this point." Beyond the court of the women was a sign that said, "Males only." Entry to the holy

288

place was reserved exclusively for priests. In the temple's interior was the most holy place, which was shrouded from view and from visitation (except once a year by the high priest) by a thick curtain. When Jesus died, the curtain was torn from top to bottom. There is little doubt that Matthew intended the reader to conclude that this was an act of God. Now, through God's own initiative, the doorway to the fullness of spiritual life is opened *to everyone* — male or female, Jew or Gentile, clergy or laity.

What Jesus did once in history at the Temple, and accomplished spiritually for all time on the cross — the eradication of dividing walls — he calls us to live out day by day. Yet this glorious job assignment is hardly an easy one. I would much rather huddle in pseudo community with my closest friends than take risks. I will need new eyes to see the world the way God sees it, not the way I've always sliced and diced humanity. How will I ever reach out to people I don't understand, to those who have intentionally hurt me, to men and women of radically different convictions? How am I going to gain sufficient trust to cross all those bridges — from my various levels of phony tolerance to authentic new experiences of partnership?

There's only one way. I will need to realize that Jesus Christ is Lord over their hearts and Lord over my heart at the same time. The walls that I have erected in my mind and the walls I have put up in my relationships are insufficient to keep the Son of God at bay. Paul, pondering the two groups of people who still have a hard time imagining they have very much in common, writes in verse 18, "For through him both of us have access in one Spirit to the Father." Paul knew that if Jesus could "have at" somebody's heart, that person or that entire people group would never look at others the same way. They would ultimately be compelled to see others as God does.

For many years Dr. Paul Brand served as a physician to the multitudes in India who suffer from Hansen's disease, more commonly known as leprosy. Over the centuries most cultures have erected insurmountable walls between those who are lepers and those who are not.

In a story told by Philip Yancey, Dr. Brand found himself one evening in an open courtyard that was packed with lepers. The air was heavy with the mingled odors of poverty, stale spices, and treated bandages. After a while the patients began to ask if he would speak to them for a few moments. Did the doctor have any encouraging words? As he looked over this gathering of "untouchable" human bodies, his eyes were drawn to their hands. Most of the hands he saw were drawn inward in the familiar "claw-hand" of the leper. Some had no fingers, some were just a few stumps. Many patients sat on their hands or otherwise kept them out of sight.

"I am a hand surgeon," he began. "So when I meet people, I can't help looking at their hands. The palm-reader claims he can tell your future by looking at your hands. I can tell your past. For instance, I can tell what your trade has been by the position of the calluses and the condition of the nails. I can tell a lot about your character. I love hands."

Brand went on, "How I would love to have had the chance to meet Jesus and study his hands." He described what it might have been like to see the hands of Jesus as a little one, childishly grasping in the earliest years, then clumsily holding a brush or stylus in school. Then came the rough, gnarled hands of Christ the carpenter, with the broken fingernails and bruises that inevitably come from working with a saw and hammer.

"Then," Brand continued, "there were his crucified hands. It hurts me to think of a nail being driven through the center of my hand, because I know what goes on there, the tremendous complex of tendons and nerves and blood vessels and muscles. You can't drive a spike through its center without crippling it. In that act Jesus identified himself with all the deformed and crippled human beings in the world. He shared poverty with the poor, and weariness with the tired — and clawed hands with the crippled."

The effect of those words on the lepers was astonishing. Could it possibly be true that Jesus identified with them — those whom no one else would touch? One by one the leprosy patients brought forth their hands and held them high for all to see, not ashamed at that moment that they were deformed and crumpled. For someone else, the Someone who had created their hands, had once known

290

their pain, and even been resurrected with a body that still bore the imprints of those nails.

Jesus Christ is uniquely able to identify with every man and every woman who has ever breathed. There is no "leper" beyond the touch of his love. He is Lord over everyone who has ever been afflicted or misunderstood, and his grace is freely offered to every person who has ever brought pain to *us*.

Jesus is Lord over the man who betrayed your trust you when you were young, from whom you've been separated by a wall of bitterness. He is Lord over the boss who gave to somebody else the promotion that you deserved. He is Lord over the doctor who made the critical mistake. Jesus Christ is Lord over the people who don't share your faith or your enthusiasm for it. He is Lord over every division of opinion or experience or background that we have ever known. What is grace in the midst of dividing walls? It is the assurance that *even while we have remained entrenched on our side of a barrier*, Jesus has declared us worthy of being his lifelong learners, and has dispatched us to be wall-removers in every part of the world.

At the 1996 Promise Keepers gathering of 42,000 pastors in Atlanta, an assembly that represented myriad different church groups and denominational affiliations, author and pastor Max Lucado stood at the speaker's podium and made a simple request. "On the count of three," he said, "would you please shout out loud the name of the group or tradition or church body of which you are currently a member? One, two, three ..." Those present voiced their affiliations. Some were fortunate. All they had to shout was "Methodist" or "Presbyterian." One fellow rattled off "The Church of God of Prophecy Incorporated." What everyone heard echoing through the Georgia Dome was an undifferentiated blob of sound.

Lucado followed with a second request. "On the count of three," he said, "would you please shout the name to whom you have trusted your heart, your soul, your ministry, and your entire spiritual future? One, two, three ..." And there rose, in unison, the sound of just two syllables that filled the entire dome: "*Jesus!*" In the memorable moment that followed there was absolute silence — as if the leaders of God's people were suddenly struck dumb by the realization that perhaps they have more in common than first assumed. Perhaps the walls can fall down after all. For around that name, the name of the One who dares to share his grace with those *on both sides* of our most unyielding barriers, we have more in common right now than we have often allowed ourselves to dream. In Christ alone, by his immeasurable grace, there is power to turn dividing walls into dust.

Sermons On The Second Readings

For Sundays
After Pentecost
(Middle Third)

Harold C. Warlick, Jr.

*For their generous support
and lasting friendship,
these sermons are dedicated
to Tom and Rosemary Keller.*

Introduction

Edgar Allen Poe has written a marvelous short story called "The Purloined Letter." One of Poe's characters is the prefect of the Parisian police. His colleagues always give him a hearty welcome, "for there was nearly half as much of the entertaining as of the contemptible about the man, and we had not seen him for several years."

The prefect had the fashion of calling everything "odd" that was beyond his comprehension, and "thus lived amid an absolute legion of 'oddities.' "

When it comes to examining the epistle to the Ephesians and the epistle of James, many a preacher has resembled the old prefect. Even when following the lectionary in our preparations, we prefer the beauty spots of the Bible as a basis for our sermons. This throws us back time and again to the Old Testament and Gospel lessons. Like the old prefect, a sermon from an epistle text is not seen or heard from us by the congregation for several years. We seldom preach on these "odd" texts. Consequently we live amid an absolute legion of "odd" books whose theological issues we never address. One might ask of us, since the Second lesson sources consume the majority of our New Testament, "Are they really 'odd' or just beyond our comprehension?"

To be certain, the texts which follow are not easy texts to manage in sermons. These texts deal with weighty theological issues. I commend you, the reader and preacher, for considering them. There is little wit and humor in them. They demand deep thought and self-reflection. Yet in these texts are contained issues whose articulations are absolutely essential to the health of a modern congregation. Consequently the potential payoff in terms of preaching effectiveness is tremendous. Thomas Paine is correct: "What we obtain too cheaply, we esteem too lightly."[1] Work hard on these texts and you may just obtain a higher estimation of their preaching power.

To facilitate understanding and enable you, the reader, to have at hand a concise explanation of the author's perspectives, I have included a brief preface to each of the sections (Ephesians and James).

I struggled mightily with these texts. While I usually am assigned some tough lessons (First and Second), at least they have in the past been dealing with the two "high" seasons of Advent and Christmas and Lent and Easter. The former season provides occasions when I can wrestle with a few prophets and John the Baptist. The latter, even Lent, provides plenty of preachable occasions when, to quote Barbara Brown Taylor, "we jump off the high dive into the pool of guilt."

Pentecost 2 falls in that period of time preceding Advent when the sweet theological perfume of Christmas and Easter has long since dissipated into thin air. We become weary. This is the time when we wrestle with summer slump, church members moving out of town, and parishioners taking lengthy leaves of absence to be at the beach or in the mountains. Advent culminates with the celebration of the birth of our Lord at Christmas. Lent culminates in our celebration of the Resurrection at Easter. The season of Pentecost, for many preachers, culminates in the fall of the year when we are desperately trying to pledge the church budget. There is an obvious need, then, to have some good material for this season which focuses on what is called Ordinary Time and lasts almost half the year. This is the period for teaching about discipleship. Ordinary Time is still called Kingdomtide by some pastors. Its green colors symbolize growth and maturity. In trying to address issues of practical Christianity, growth and maturity, not common agreements, are the desired products.

These lessons and sermons are probably going to yank the chains and ring the bells of certain listeners. They take us into complicated places in the mind and emotions where we have to juxtapose our own ideas with the ideas of God they try to present. Whatever the responses to the sensitivities being pricked or the equilibriums being upset, the desired aim is to remind us that God's sense of community is much bigger than ours is. Trying to explain and teach that the son of God was convicted and sentenced to die on a cross may be easier to accomplish than wrestling with the fact that he was mocked, rejected, and forsaken by his own people. The conviction and sentence are not likely to ever occur again. The mocking, rejecting, and forsaking by his own people occurs in every age, often unawares. That's why we teach and preach. In the final analysis we can trust the God that was in Christ to be the ultimate highest bidder for our preaching efforts, however humble and flawed they may appear to be at the time.

Harold C. Warlick, Jr.
High Point, North Carolina

---

1. Thomas Paine, Philadelphia, December 23, 1776.

Preface To The Sermons From Ephesians

Perhaps few books in the Holy Bible have marshalled such contemporary hostility as has the epistle to the Ephesians. Consequently it is a preaching resource ripe for misunderstanding or avoidance. This need not be the case.

Many preachers avoid even the *undisputed* letters of Paul with good reason. Reading Paul is hard going for anyone. The frequent use of philosophical logic and Old Testament citations is a far cry from the easy parables recorded in the Gospels.

Letter writing as a form was a nonliterary, private communication in the Greco-Roman world. As such, letters were meant to issue orders, mediate disputes, nurture friendships, and offer praise or blame.[1] In this regard, a letter from Paul could be quite "preachable" by a contemporary pastor.

Unfortunately the work we call Ephesians is more of an epistle than a letter. As such it is composed with skill and convention. It is intended for a wide audience and is meant to be read and discussed, much like a best selling work purchased from a bookstore in today's world. Its long, ponderous style is different from Paul's writings elsewhere in the New Testament. It is best to assume, as most scholars do, that Paul did not write Ephesians.[2] Apparently it is a work written long after Paul's death by an unknown Christian who borrowed Paul's name. By the time it was put into final form, the church was very much an established institution. Herein is, perhaps, our hope for its having significance for our pulpits in a pluralistic world.

Ephesians is written in a rhetorical style to influence the thought and conduct of a general audience and tell its readers how they should act in a world dominated by mystery, individualism, and heavenly rulers and authorities. As its author counters this kind of shallow charisma with a Christian belief that God through Christ has overcome all heavenly and earthly beings, real or unreal, a preaching relevance leaps at us.

In our world where the "Religion" section of bookstores has been replaced by headings such as "Inspiration," "Religious Fiction," "Angels," and "New Age Belief," the issues addressed in Ephesians have relevance. Carefully and constructively presented, sermons on the lectionary texts from Ephesians can, perhaps, enable the church to hear a *particular* word from God in a fashion that neither borders on the *peculiar* nor degenerates into dogmatic and cocksure veneration of tradition.

In order to hedge against an uninformed veneration of pastoral and male stereotypes, given the text's reverential attitude toward the apostles (quite different from Paul's genuine letters), the following sermons labor to unpack such themes without detracting from the purpose of the primary text. To keep the homiletical style from using unbearably complex and long sentences, information for the preacher is given in the footnotes.

Finally, some of the sermons are longer than they need be for effectiveness with a church congregation. This is done with purpose. Most of the lectionary lessons contain enough themes and pressure points to warrant five or six sermons on each. By providing abundant material, the reader can pick and choose, edit and discard, at will and have enough material to craft a unified sermon on less than the full text. The epistle to the Ephesians is addressed to believers. These sermons are as well.

---

1. An excellent analysis of the difference between a letter and an epistle is to be found in Charles B. Cousar, *The Letters of Paul* (Nashville: Abingdon Press, 1996), pp. 15-45.

2. Earl S. Johnson, Jr., a pastor with the ability to write sound theology in comprehendible terms, provides a good overview of the authorship question in the Basic Bible Commentary, Volume 24, *Galatians and Ephesians* (Nashville: Abingdon Press, 1988), pp. 82-85.

The Highest Bidder

An auction is a fun event, especially when you are the highest bidder for an item you really want to purchase. You register for a number and examine the merchandise that is "up for bid." Then the auctioneer begins the chant and cards with numbers on them start popping up and heads nod at price increments. When the crowd ceases to bid, the item is sold to the last highest bidder. "Last chance. Going once. Going twice. Sold."

A delightful cable television show is the *Antiques Roadshow*. Professional appraisers travel to large cities giving appraisals to people, like you and me, who bring their valued family heirlooms. It is entertaining to watch someone find out their grandmother's old painting is estimated to bring five figures if it were "put up for auction." In a perverse way, it is also entertaining to witness someone find out that their "valued" heirloom is a fake and isn't worth the effort to carry it around the corner. The television host tries to soothe the latter's feelings. The host maintains: "Of course, we can't put a price on the *sentimental* value it holds for you."

The context, or image, for today's text could very well be an auction. It speaks of the value of all people. Every society, human or angelic, owes its origin to God and has its divine prototype in God. We kneel before this crafter of all things as the shaper of every family. The family analogy in Ephesians was drawn from a Jewish background in a Roman world. Given that world's universal acceptance of the primacy of male descent, the male analogy would have made sense to its initial readers.

We no longer assume families to be father headed and can be, rightly so, free to use more inclusive language. God's love surpasses knowledge, including that of human attempts to write or record sacred scripture.

The writer of Ephesians prays that we "might know the love of Christ that surpasses knowledge" (Ephesians 3:19). That Greek verb which means "to surpass" or "go beyond" can also mean "to outbid at auction."[1]

It is a wonderful image. God, through Christ, is in the market for the hearts of human beings. The love of Christ will always pay more for our hearts than anything else in heaven or earth that competes for our devotion. Knowledge will never be able to outbid God. There is no predetermined limit[2] that God is held hostage to in God's bidding. Imagine an auction house where all human and heavenly powers are gathered to bid and up the ante for your life's devotion. Christ enters the room to represent God in the bidding process. The arm of Christ stays in the air throughout the entire process, never coming down as knowledgeable competitors keep increasing the bid. For all practical purposes the auction is over. God will never be outbid. God is always the highest bidder for the human soul.

This wonderful imagery in Ephesians overlaps[3] with the list in Paul's letter to the Romans concerning the heavenly powers:

> *I am convinced that neither death nor life nor angels nor rulers, neither things present nor things to come nor powers, neither height nor depth, nor any other creature will be able to separate us from the love of God which is in Christ Jesus our Lord.*
>
> — Romans 8:38-39

Not only is God through Christ and the church the high bidder for now, but for all generations. This is not a one time, single event, auction. Quite the contrary. Every generation will find the same glory and lavish love expended on it.

This is a message our world needs to hear. Our fullness is not an isolated hiccup on the world's stage. Our completing our God-given task extends to all the future generations. This is a clarion call for indefatigable, confident leadership and work in God's behalf. If we are freed from the worry that some competing claim or power will outbid God for our souls, then we can feel a sense of obligation to the future ages.

The great American historian, Henry Steele Commager, was asked why we have so few great leaders today as opposed to the many that came forth in the eighteenth century. With all our wealth, education, and population, why haven't we been able to produce leaders like Franklin, Jefferson, Washington, Monroe, and the like?

Commager said that the one common denominator of all the great eighteenth century leaders was that they had a sense of obligation to posterity. In short, they were animated by the belief that they were acting for the benefit of the whole world and for the future ages. They were motivated by a moral obligation to serve the highest that they knew so those who came after them would know the full and completely good life.

Doesn't that same attitude come through to you in this text from Ephesians? "High purpose. Power together. Knowledge of a love that is never outbid. A divine power inside us."

These words and images look deeply and listen deeply. They see a strength and beauty that rise above a society turned in upon itself where seeking pleasure is lifted up as the highest purpose in life.

Ernest Becker won a Pulitzer Prize in 1974 for a book he wrote titled *The Denial of Death*. One particular passage speaks to me: "The distinctive human problem ... has been the need to spiritualize human life, to lift it onto a special immortal plane, beyond the cycles of life and death that characterize all other organisms."[4]

Indeed, the Ephesian calls to spiritualize human life, to lift it beyond the cycles of human and emotional bids for recognition, are a great religious challenge.

That religious experiences come and go is so much a part of our culture. Our religious experience has a way of losing its bite. We sweep evil out for awhile and have a clean, fresh taste. Then the empty condition returns and we wonder how to approach wholeness. Again, the concept of spiritual growth and fullness speaks to us. We humans were created with a capacity for the Holy Spirit.

We were given the capacity not to become a moral cork which bobs up and down with every bid of social freedom that comes along. We were given the capacity to build institutions which do not financially and programmatically bob up and down depending on whether or not our attitude at the time is one of commitment or lethargy.

Moses, Jesus, and Paul spoke of willing hearts, of full people, bringing what they have got and offering it before the Lord. The encounter with the living God is not a casual one. We come to this place because we seek fullness. We are free and independent, to be sure, but there is something more to life than freedom and independence. There is fullness.

Gerald Kennedy tells the story of a boy who found a dime in the road. He was so impressed at getting something for nothing that for the rest of his life, he walked with his eyes on the road. After forty years of his precious life he had picked up nearly 35,000 buttons, 50,000 pins, approximately four dollars in loose change, a terrible disposition, and a bent back. That's not much reward for making a career out of looking downward.

You and I sit in this church because we are heirs of a universal vision of the early church which viewed God as the highest bidder for human life. We look up to a vision, not downward at nickels and dimes. We are heirs of that glorious news of the unsearchable riches of Christ that the Ephesians heard. No human limit can be set upon this church. God outbids the human divisions, and resources that would threaten it. Heaven and earth are complete and you and I are called to be complete as well.

Certainly any true religious completeness must consider all three of its dimensions: length, breadth, and height. One of the favorite sermons of Dr. Martin Luther King, Jr., was titled "Three Dimensions of A Complete Life." It was the first sermon he preached before his future wife, Coretta Scott, in a little church in Roxbury, Massachusetts. It was also the initial sermon he preached in Dexter Avenue Baptist Church in Montgomery, Alabama, where he began his pastoral work that was to have such a positive effect on civil rights in our country. And it was the sermon he chose to preach in St. Paul's Cathedral in London when he was on his way to receive the Nobel Prize.[5]

It was King's contention that the troubles of the world "were due to incompleteness." Just as great cities, nations, and civilizations have suffered from incompleteness, so have many great leaders. King contended that the first dimension of a complete life is the development of a person's inner powers. The author of Ephesians hammers this point home from the beginning of his prayer for the Ephesians: "I pray that (God) may strengthen you with power through (God's) Spirit in your inner being" (3:16).

The second dimension of a complete life, said King, is concern for and identification with one's fellow human beings. The author of Ephesians followed his prayer with a plea in chapter 4 for unity in the church through "bearing with one another in love" (4:2).

Finally, posited King, there remained the third dimension, the height, the upward reach of humankind.[6] Loving God with heart, mind, and soul is the height of life.

No one can outbid God for control of human destiny, not now and not ever. God can do more than all we ask or imagine. That is, indeed, the glory that can be the church in Christ Jesus throughout all generations, forever and ever! Amen.

---

1. The verb *hyperballo* is defined in David J. Williams, *Paul's Metaphors: Their Context and Character* (Peabody, Massachusetts: Hendrickson Publishers, 1999), p. 170.

2. The notion that God has no numerical limit may be contrasted with the idea in Jewish thought that there is a predetermined divine number. The number of the "sealed" in Revelation does not originate from the same Greek word, *pleroma*, as the author of Ephesians uses to denote "fullness" or "completeness." See Manfred T. Branch, *Hard Sayings of Paul* (Downers Grove: Inter Varsity Press, 1989), p. 68.

3. The author of the later lists in Ephesians certainly is keeping with Paul's views as expressed in Romans and 1 Corinthians, undisputed letters from Paul's hand.

For more information consult James G. Dunn, *The Theology of Paul the Apostle* (Grand Rapids: William B. Eerdmans Publishing Company, 1998), pp. 104-110.

4. Ernest Becker, *The Denial of Death* (New York: The Free Press, 1973).

5. Coretta Scott King, *My Life With Martin Luther King, Jr.* (New York: Holt, Rinehart, and Winston, 1969), pp. 5-8. Note that King used as his text Revelation 21:16, "The length and breadth and height of it are equal."

6. *Ibid.*

Gifted People

You and I are "gifted" people. We live in a "gifted" country. We gather in a "gifted" institution. Regardless of our relative weaknesses, relative status, and relative talents, we are "gifted" by any reasonable definition of human success. We live in an industrialized nation and our lives are hardly struggling to survive. We enjoy sophisticated imaginations and privileged circumstances. Our talents are many. We do not struggle to survive. We have options — we can speak the truth; we can grow and mature; we can build ourselves up in love; we can enjoy relationships which can draw upon one another's talents. We can also tear ourselves apart and degenerate into cold, calculated insensitivity.

The author of today's text writes to people like us. It is not always an easy matter to get gifted people to work together for a common good. The more options one has, the less one is dependent on others for the necessities of life. Division and selfish immaturity often impede the work of "gifted" people and make relationships tenuous at best. Aristotle was one of the first to maintain that truth telling is the product of a mature relationship. Certainly one must be quite mature to speak the right truth to the right person at the right time in the right way for the right reasons.

Ellen Goodman, a syndicated columnist, wrote an article about a friend of hers who was always "keeping his options open." It seems that this friend was allergic to making commitments. He viewed life as a huge buffet line. Consequently he compared people who made commitments to the person who filled his plate with rather ordinary fare at the beginning of the line and then when his plate was full came upon all types of interesting food which he liked better. Using that example to illustrate his philosophy of life, Goodman's friend let everyone know that *he* was "keeping *his* options open."

Ellen Goodman's evaluation of her friend was that *he was always "coming to the end of the line with an empty plate."* It is virtually impossible to build anything substantial without commitment. Everything that is worthwhile in life requires the making of a commitment. At some point you just have to take a plunge without always straining to see what lies on down the line. If you don't, you'll always come to the end of the line with an empty plate.

In this world where we tell people to not get over committed, to play it cool, to stay on balance, and to keep their options open, the words of the writer to the Ephesians stick out like a stray horse that's wandered into our living room during a party. "I am a prisoner of the Lord."

It takes a mature person to recognize that placing one's gifts at the disposal of the church is a divine commandment. Unity is not often the desired end of competitive people living in a supply and demand world. Building up the body of Christ through love and humility is the only way to keep a bond of peace. Yet we sometimes do not measure growth as a maintenance process where each gifted part is simply doing its job.

Peter Gomes has reminded us that "growth" is Saint Paul's favorite metaphor.[1] From the over-read passage in 1 Corinthians 13, where Paul speaks of mature people putting away childish thoughts, to those who wrote to the Ephesians about growing up into the head of Christ, the body maturing, "growth" seems to be the fundamental metaphor of the early church.

To use the phrase "growth" among gifted people in a church context is a dangerous thing. We have imported the American economic image and called it "the Church Growth Movement." Growth means bigger and biggest. Our conventional understanding limits us. Growth is usually something to do with membership charts, cash portfolios, and future planning graphs.

Growth is *not* size and competence, according to Holy Scripture. Growth is, to the contrary, a response to grace. Growth, for the Christian, is to pull together, to be consistently using one's gifts in holding together the blessed union of Christ with his church. Growth is to be anchored in love instead of being tossed back and forth like a cork on the ocean waves by every cunning human scheme that promises us a new personal option for our life's career.

Lack of unity among gifted people is a lasting parasite on the Christian landscape. We keep trying to build a world in which divisions are passé, only they will not lie down and go away. From the first century to the present day, immaturity, competitiveness, and arrogance keep popping back up again. We bring all our best gifts and talents to the church and are shocked when they are not always welcomed. Then, most of the time, we wall ourselves off from that which has hurt us. After all, we gifted people do have other options. We can stay at home. We can do something else with our time and talent. We can find calmer, purer, and more appreciative places to spend our gifts. Then, when that arena plays out, we can move on again. Like infants tossed back and forth and blown here and there, we can keep bobbing up and down.

The people of Ephesus had a particularly bad habit. They tried to keep their options for life open by using all types of books of magic. They had books of charms that pretended to tell people how to win lovers, books of magic to tell mariners how to avoid storms, and books of magic to tell one how to find treasure. It was all quackery, based on rabbits' feet and prayers and charms. But they were chained to that kind of humbug, just as surely as some people today are chained to every self-help philosophy that raises its head. Scripture says you can't follow Jesus and keep all those options open or you'll come to the end of your line with an empty plate. You've got to say, "No, thank you," and work for the common good of the whole.

The gifted Ephesians apparently grasped the meaning of maturity in Christ. They couldn't keep all their religious options open. They agreed to give up their superstition. The book of Acts records that they gathered their books and their magic together and made a great bonfire out of them. Scripture (Acts 19:19) says that they counted the price of what they had burned and found it to be *50,000 pieces of silver.* Now, my friends, metallurgy was advanced in Ephesus in Hellenistic and Roman times. Lead was separated from silver by heating the molten metal in porous material and exposing it to the air. The silver was fired. The silver coins of Ephesus were 98 percent pure silver. Each coin was the equivalent of two to three troy ounces of silver.

Their effort to preserve unity of purpose cost them a great deal, financially. But they moved into a new realm of unity and peace. They grew in stature and oneness.

History records for us some troublesome and catastrophic breakdowns in unity and peace in our own society. Lives can quickly depart from worthy callings and noble purposes when the unity of spirit and the bond of peace are lost.

Charles Sumner was one of the most celebrated congressional opponents of slavery in America. He delivered an "Oration on Lafayette" in which he called Lafayette, the hero of two revolutions, the greatest person of character who ever lived. Perhaps Sumner was correct. In his old age, Lafayette said that he never would have drawn the sword for America had he known that it was to found a government that sanctioned human slavery.

To be certain, those who often achieve unity of spirit and purpose fail to mature enough to grant it to others. Misuse of gifts often tears apart the very institution those gifts founded.

The call for unity in the body of Christ is no small matter. The whole body needs more than a collection of individual talent. It needs growth as each part comes together and does its work.

---

1. Peter Gomes in "Growing Up," a sermon preached June 4, 1989, in the Memorial Church, Harvard University.

Sweet-Smelling Fragrance

Realtors tell us that an empty house is difficult to sell. Regardless of its physical beauty, a home "shows" better when it is furnished. Sellers are advised to have the home cleaned, have a fire going in the fireplace, turn on lamps, have soft music playing in the background, and place fresh flowers on tables and cabinets. The aura and smells that are presented to the customer are important. In major shopping malls the smells of baked cookies are sometimes injected into the ventilation system to lure customers toward the food court.

Accessories top off a room in a home. In fact, it can be said that the accessories make or break the beauty of a large room. The total ambiance is as important to the eye as the individual pieces of furniture in the room. In like manner, well-known chefs work as hard on "presentation" as they do on cooking food. To attract diners, the food must be more than delicious. It must also be "attractively displayed."

All significant entities have to be made to reconcile with one another to create an attractive image. Otherwise, even the best of things remain odorless, colorless, shapeless, and bland. That which is most pleasing and effective bears the presentation mark of its chef, designer, or owner.

The text for today points toward the challenge to make the church over into the likeness of God through the moral character of its members. Form is certainly important. The author recognizes the fact that because Christ loved us, he gave himself for us not only as an offering and a sacrifice, but so we could be to God a

311

sweet-smelling fragrance. The image is one of Christians living together in such a way that they make an attractive presentation. This is pleasing to God. Since Christ loved us and gave himself for us, we Christians should live as Christ lived and love as Christ loved. Paul in Philippians also used the same expression, a "fragrant smell," to describe the self-giving love of Christians.

It is the thesis of Paul in his letters and in those epistles, like Ephesians, written by his followers, that the death of Jesus had a grand purpose. Jesus died to bring all the discordant elements of humanity into one, to wipe out the separation and reconcile each of us with the rest of us and with God. This sweetness, this shape, is God's grand presentation.

As such, belonging to God's church is not a mere walking down to become a member of an institution; not placing a signature on a commitment card.[1] It is becoming part of a special arrangement which bears the mark of its designer.

Like many today, the members of the early church had a genuine desire to be part of an institution that would help them be recognized by their neighbors as good people. Yet morals are difficult to learn and adopt. As Robin Lovin, Dean of Perkins School of Theology, has noted,[2] most Christians do not realize how serious are the obstacles to developing morality within an institution. Experience does not serve us like it does when we learn avoidance of danger lessons through having hurt ourselves physically. We do not retain habits of morality the same way we maintain the skills required to play golf or ride a bicycle. Some force in life keeps drawing us away from the best we know and making it difficult for us to act on our beliefs even after we have understood what they require. Turning from self to God is always a difficult task in any age. Living with others in a community called "church" makes it an *especially* difficult task. The letter to the Ephesians is written to those who live "face-to-face" with one another in a household church. We, too, find such face-to-face relationships fraught with anger, insensitivity, white lies, and gossip. Malice runs rampant in every age.

It is not easy to be forgiving and kind in our kind of world. We all need space, and it is becoming harder to find. Our grandparents had lots of room. Agriculture was the primary method by which people earned a living. They could do pretty well as they pleased on their property. They did not even have to lock the doors. When you got mad on the family farm, your mother just ran you outside to walk through the tobacco or corn fields until you cooled off. You didn't have to worry about being hit by a car or having someone try to kidnap you or sell drugs to you. Then, when you had cooled off, grandparents, parents, cousins, aunts and uncles, living in fairly close proximity, gave you a wide area over which to spread your feelings.

Our world is a lot more close-up. We live house to house, apartment to apartment, townhouse to townhouse, room to room, suite to suite. We drive fender to fender. We work elbow to elbow. We often get in each other's way. And when we try to spread out our feelings, we often find that the larger family is no longer there to absorb them. We have to focus our anger on fewer people. It naturally becomes more intense.

Living close-up has problems. We all love and hate the very people with whom we are the closest. The two feelings exist side-by-side.[3] Seventy percent of the people admitted to emergency rooms in hospitals on Saturday nights are victims of either domestic violence or violence among friends. All of us compete with one another for honors and recognition, and if we do not get them we become angry. We compete for power, and if we do not acquire it, more anger is generated. Fathers and sons compete with one another, and daughters and mothers compete with each other. We live in a competitive democracy.

We are living amid what one national newspaper has called "a new epidemic of anger." Shoppers get into fistfights over who should be first in a newly opened checkout line in a supermarket. A Massachusetts father has actually beaten to death another father in an argument at their sons' hockey practice. Bad tempers are on display everywhere. "Rage is the rage today," says C. Leslie Chambers in an article by Karen Peterson in *USA Today* (18 July 2000). The same article reports that 78 percent of Americans believe rude and selfish behavior has increased at highways and airports. High-tech devices like pagers, cellphones, and other devices fracture our days and fragment what little time we have to live life. We constantly have to "multi-task" and are overloaded with a sense of urgency.

Perhaps today's text comes at a good time in the life of our church. Ordinary Time can become the best and worst of times in the life of the church. The "image" days of Christmas and Easter are long gone. In these "ordinary" days when we wrestle with summer slump, people moving in and out of the fellowship, and heightened concern over the adequacy of church finances, being church can produce a rancid smell instead of a sweet fragrance.

A literary list such as the one in Ephesians was called by Martin Luther in his German Bible (*Deutsch Bibel*) a "domestic bulletin board."[4] It lists the Christian obligations and chores of members of the household. The concept is similar to the stick pads on the door of the family refrigerator or the message board by the telephone, on which parents post things for the children to accomplish during the day. Such biblical lists are meant to help us as we cope with the social ethical problems in the church. Certainly life in the church requires the "putting away" of certain forms of behavior:

> *Put away falsehood.*
> *Put away anger.*
> *Put away stealing.*
> *Put away unwholesome talk.*
> *Put away every form of malice.*

Such "putting away" of harmful aspects in social relationships reflects the mark of ownership of the Spirit of God. If we were lost in Adam but regained in Christ as the New Adam, we must represent the character of the New Adam. An old story illustrates the effect that anger can have on the way we present ourselves to the world around us. There once was a boy who had a bad temper. His father gave him a bag of nails and told him that every time he lost his temper, he must hammer a nail into the back of the fence in the yard. The first day the child had driven 37 nails into the fence. Over the next several weeks, the number of nails gradually dwindled down as he began to learn to control his temper. The day finally came when he didn't lose his temper at all. He had learned that it was easier to hold his temper than have to drive nails into the fence. He told his father about his success. The father suggested that the boy now pull out a nail for each day that he was able to hold his temper. The day finally came when he was able to tell his father that all the nails were gone.

The father led the boy out to the fence. He said, "You have done well. But look at the holes left in the fence. It will never be the same. When you do things in anger, they leave scars just like these. Regardless of how many times you say you are sorry, little wounds are still there."

Indeed, verbal wounds can be as bad as physical ones. We Christians cannot hold forth to the world images of noisy impertinence, elbowing self-conceit, bitterness, and anger. We must hold forth the graceful mood of God our creator and properly present that creator to those who labor with us, both within and without. The Biblical narrative clearly tries to close various loopholes that shackle Christians in every age. Whoever wrote this text to the Ephesians was not concerned with being nice. The writer was concerned to give us a clear focus on the call to Christian living. The *fragrance* that emanates from the lives of Christians as they live and work together in the church is as pleasing to God as are *fumes* which rise heavenward from the altar of worship.

Regardless of its physical beauty, a church "shows" better when it is furnished with Christians who are compassionate toward one another. The aura and smells of the church are important to its potential members. How we relate to one another is one of the ways we present God to the world. Sometimes *presentation* is everything.

---

1. K. David Cole develops the faith journey in an incisive sermon, "Through This Portal," in *Out of Mighty Waters: Sermons by African-American Disciples* (St. Louis: Chalice Press, 1994), pp. 173-177.

2. Robin Lovin, *Christian Ethics: An Essential Guide* (Nashville: Abingdon Press, 2000), especially pp. 74-75. This well-written work should be read by any preacher seeking to preach on the moral teachings of Christianity in general and the scriptures in particular. Lovin writes with a style that both edifies and inspires.

3. Leo Madow, *Anger: How to Recognize and Cope With It* (New York: Charles Scribner's Sons, 1972), p. 20.

4. Joseph A. Fitzmyer, S.J., *Paul and His Theology* (Englewood Cliffs, New Jersey: Prentice-Hall, 1989), p. 101.

Proper 15
Pentecost 13
Ordinary Time 20
Ephesians 5:15-20

Caution And Opportunity

A university president, as was his custom, attended the mid-week worship service in his institution's chapel. As he sat in the pew, he could not help but notice a reaction from two coeds seated directly in front of him. Midway through the chaplain's sermon, one of the young women wrote a message on the cover of her bulletin. She quickly passed it over to her fellow student. When she read the message, the reader turned to the sender and nodded vigorously. At the conclusion of the service the two students departed the chapel, leaving their bulletin on the pew. The curious president wandered over and picked it up. On the front of the bulletin were scrawled these words: "Why do they always have to talk about drinking and sex?"

Indeed, why do "they" always have to speak of such things as an expression of a central biblical principle for Christian living? In the context of a society in which the abuse of alcohol is such a serious problem, the New Testament epistles turn to the subject with frequent and consistent advice. In 1 Timothy among the characteristics listed for those who would be leaders in the church is that they be "not given to drunkenness" (3:3) or "not indulge in much wine" (3:8). In advice given to Titus, elders are to be examples who are "not given to drunkenness" (1:7) and the elder women in the church are to be taught not to be "addicted to much wine" (2:3). This central principle of Christian life surfaces again in today's text — "Do not get drunk on wine, which leads to debauchery."

Certainly a word of *caution* is here. We are urged to exercise discrimination concerning our own behavior. Christians are called

317

to be self-reflective. This is hardly fresh news to our listening ears. It certainly was not fresh news to the Ephesians. The Jewish wisdom literature had long since recognized the folly of drunkenness and Jesus himself had warned his disciples against drunkenness.

Aside from the fact that scriptural warnings have been issued as negative reflections on first and twenty-first century cultures themselves, perhaps there are deeper issues that we need to examine. This season of Ordinary Time is a good time to focus on some of the hard, practical realties of life. Separated a bit from the highly focused seasons of Christmas and Easter, these days are good days for focusing on caution, discernment, and meaningful worship.

Founders of democracy have often been as dismal about the human condition as have founders of religions. Thomas Paine, one of America's Founders, once stated: "Society is produced by our wants and government by our wickedness."[1] Certainly we can say that you and I populate churches out of our wants and needs. While churches may not always make us and our society more civil, they certainly expose the health of the societies in which they operate.

In sounding our word of caution we should also sound a word of *opportunity.* The church, even in this text for today, has never offered a mandate for Christians to withdraw from an evil society as though they were fanatics or ascetics. Whatever moral guidelines are laced throughout the Bible are constructed on the assumption that you and I can live a full Christian life in the context of "this world."[2]

Scripture always beckons us to look at the world through analytical lenses. Caution and opportunity go hand in hand. Both are necessary to protect us from a fragmented sense of reality that destroys the wonder of life.

Appropriately this scripture moves from a tone of caution about personal behavior to an emphasis on building up our lives through worship and personal reflection. This thrust is almost to say: "Here's a problem; here's the world; here's what you can do to make a difference to yourself, to others, and to that world."

When a writer or a teacher lays out a moral problem and contends that humans can be filled with a spirit and practice that can move their lives in other directions, that is good news. The good news is that love can be learned. With every *caution* there is an *opportunity* to do better.

In essence, that is much of what the Bible is about. People can learn. Abraham wasn't a spontaneous lover but he learned how to love. Jacob and Isaac and Moses were not instant lovers but they learned how to love. Peter and John and Paul and all the rest of the people Jesus affected were not spontaneous lovers but they learned how to love. *Love can be learned.* And we can learn how, too!

Fear is learned. War is learned. Prejudice is learned. Hate is learned. The Good News of the Bible is that love can be learned, too. That is the greatest hope in the world — even in the worst of circumstances. There is always the possibility that somewhere, at some time out there in the future, people can learn to love.

Sara Jewett tells the story of a woman who ascended the pathway leading to the home of a retired sea captain in the state of Maine. On the way, the woman sees a number of wooden stakes scattered about the property with no discernible order. Each stake is painted white and trimmed in yellow, like the captain's house. With great curiosity and no small bewilderment, she asks the captain what they mean. He explains. When he first plowed the ground, his plow snagged on many large rocks just below the surface. So he set out stakes where the rocks lay in order to avoid them in the future. *That way he did not have to relearn where every rock was every time he plowed.*[3]

The captain's caution gives him the opportunity to farm productively in what might otherwise be an inhospitable environment. So it is with our world, according to the scriptures. Evil is there, both within and without, for us. But that which is learned can be unlearned, or at least controlled. Christians are urged not only to be cautious as to their lifestyle but to put out stakes of opportunity: "Speak to one another with psalms, hymns, and spiritual songs. Sing and make music in your heart to the Lord, always giving thanks to God for everything, in the name of our Lord Jesus Christ."

Caution and opportunity serve us well in any endeavor. For sixteen years the North Carolina Museum of Art displayed one of its treasures, Cranach's *Madonna and Child.* The painting dated to the sixteenth century. Unaware of any problems with its provenance or history, the museum had displayed the painting in its European galleries since it was attributed to a major artist of the German Renaissance.

In the spring of 1999 the museum received a letter from an agency of the World Jewish Congress. The agency informed the museum that the painting had been illegally expropriated by the Nazis from an Austrian Jewish family.[4]

Obviously this was startling news. After a year of painstaking work, museum officials determined that the rightful owners were two sisters in Austria who were heirs of the Gomperz family estate. Deciding to proceed "with caution" concerning the moral dilemma, the museum returned the painting to the sisters.

In an equally startling development, the two sisters sold the painting back to the same museum at half its appraised value.

Now the devotional image of the Madonna and infant Jesus proudly resides in a state capitol museum, affording thousands the *opportunity* not only to view a masterpiece but to reflect on the outcome of an institution's ethical caution.

Christians in every age are confronted with inhospitable environments and histories. Over time the spirit which builds up and does what is right stands above the evil which assails it.

---

1. Thomas Paine as quoted by Robert D. Kaplain in his article and address, "Was Democracy Just a Moment?"

2. Ralph P. Martin, *Ephesians, Colossians, and Philemon: Interpretation: A Bible Commentary for Teaching and Preaching* (Atlanta: John Knox Press, 1991), pp. 62-63. Martin addresses the various methods the author of the text tries to recall readers to their Christian status and vocation.

3. Sara Orne Jewett's novel is *The Country of the Pointed Firs.*

4. "Museum Completes Research Into Painting's History," a press release by the North Carolina Museum of Art, Raleigh, North Carolina.

Security Concerns

Security has become big business in our world. Burglar and smoke alarms are wired directly from private homes to police and fire stations. Automobiles give forth major noises in the parking lots of shopping malls because some owner has inadvertently pushed the wrong button on a key pad. High school students walk through metal detectors to enter their school buildings. Even business phones and credit cards are "protected" by a user's password or "PIN" number. So pervasive is the concern for security that a whole new mentality animates parents who tour college campuses with their teenagers, seeking to make a choice among various institutions. No longer do such parents ask questions about the faculty, living accommodations, library, or dining hall. The questions have changed during the past decade:

> *"Will my child be safe here?"*
> *"Where are your call boxes located and how many do*
> *you have?"*
> *"How many cases of date rape do you have per year?"*
> *"Are your parking lots patrolled?"*
> *"Do you have a student volunteer escort service?"*

A concern with assaults from demonic powers seems to be an ever-present reality in our world. Parents want to make certain that their children have at their disposal all that is needed to help them resist an attack on their well being.

Ephesians chapter 6 has never been a favorite biblical text for many preachers. They do not like to mix strident military metaphors with talk about the Prince of Peace. They sometimes point out that all the armament listed by the author of the text is mainly defensive armor needed for survival rather than attack.

Yet we still must admit that for all our theological double-speak, the realities of our world throw us back often to possessing a kindred spirit with this text. While many of us live in "gated" communities and have key pads on our homes, there is much organized evil to be concerned about that we cannot avoid. We can't stay home forever. Even those children who have been "home schooled" or immersed in the trend toward "Christian" high schools, find their spiritual immaturity leaving them vulnerable and defenseless in a pluralistic world.

The tone of today's text contains an acceptance of real life in every age. The author intends to warn Christians that some frightening things are happening in the world. The Christian task is not to reflect these things but to answer them. This clarion call is a call that shivers its way to us. We seldom hear from "significant" pulpits these days talk about heaven, hell, the Kingdom of God, taking up the cross of Jesus, absolutely yielding one's existence to the Spirit of God or submitting to the rigorous demands of the Christian life.[1] It's like the more sophisticated we become, the more wealthy and polished and educated we become, the more God is pushed out.[2] We become totally trapped by our personal problems to the point there is a huge silence about public affairs. It's like the God of Israel has become a free therapist for our individual problems. People come away from church with the feeling they have been to a civic club to hear an encouraging talk about personal adjustment instead of having been challenged to reframe their ways of approaching life. We wrestle with personal problems. We hear sermons like "How to Cope with a Sense of Inadequacy," "How to Conquer Anxiety," and "How to Have Self-esteem." Sin has been reduced to a personal psychological problem. In an unbrave world, in which people have much to lose, we preach that people can enjoy the happiness of God if they just accept themselves and have some self-esteem. All they have to do is take a plunge into Jesus.

It's almost like Jesus can save our inner selves, but he's not much use for the world in which we live. To be blunt, it's as if Jesus Christ is a half-savior. He can bring relief to the burdened heart, but he is obviously helpless when it comes to the powers that be — we have to look elsewhere to capitalism or conservative or liberal politicians or the government for that.[3]

Yet look at the Bible. Amos, Jeremiah, Moses, Jesus, and Paul rather dramatically insist that we not only wrestle with personal problems but also "against the principalities, against the powers, against darkness," against systems and hallowed patterns of life which trap us. The letter to the Ephesians is clear: "For our struggle is not against flesh and blood, but against the rulers, against the authorities, against the powers of this dark world and against the spiritual forces of evil in the heavenly realms" (Ephesians 6:12).

Like the Ephesians, you and I have to fight principalities and powers that have us in sway. Our advertised lusts, which are bolstered by a high standard of living, trap many of us into a kind of dark bondage. To find security we must turn to the available resources from God. The text points to a defense that must watch the forces it is up against. Consider the Christian countermeasures against the dark world: "truth, faith, the gospel of peace, and all kinds of prayers and requests." Indeed, *the greater the forces of darkness, the greater the moral demands.* The author clearly states that the *whole armor of God* is needed, for there are huge powers that threaten us. A bow and arrow conscience cannot match the moral demands of our increasingly complex world. As our powerful world has progressed in its secular capacity for evil, our moral armament must stay in step.

Early humans learned how to use a club in self-defense. As humanity developed its destructive capacity, warfare extended from the club through the bow and arrow, gun powder, and the gasoline engine up to and beyond the jet-propelled plane and the atomic bomb. With each new development, we Christians have had to adjust our minds and spirits to each new power. Howard Thurman perceptively noted that with each new power we have been forced to find a scheme of life that would keep us from destroying ourselves. Difficult as this adjustment has been for our minds, it has been infinitely more difficult for our spirits.[4] The security concerns raised by the writer to the Ephesians, encouraging Christians to "put on the full armor of God," offer relevant advice for our own age. We must match the amazing power created by our mastery over nature with an equally amazing spiritual and moral maturity.

In the face of immense security concerns, we are not encouraged to withdraw from the world. To the contrary, we are called to reflect God and live. We need armor to challenge the forces in our world because the Church was never meant to hibernate its way into the future. The writer of Ephesians assumes that the social teachings of Jesus will not be watered down to encourage passivity and meekness. Certainly the writer could have never conceived of a Church that would withdraw from vigorous social action and turn its attention to physical improvement and institutional expansion.

The hard hitting narrative, that the armor of God can protect us as we engage with the social and spiritual powers of the world, applies to every onslaught that threatens to hold the Church of Jesus Christ hostage. Consider even the applicability of this passage to the pervasive habits of membership and leadership roles that threaten the Church. Women labor under what is often called the "cult of domesticity," outnumbering the men in the pews, in the church schools, and behind the scenes. Yet the ecclesiastical climate is often chilly toward them when it comes to the role of being a clergy person. Surely the armor of God is sufficient to enable a heightened role for capable women in professional positions within Christ's Church.

New Testament scholar Helmut Koester decades ago served as guest preacher in a Congregational Church in East Walpole, Massachusetts. Preceding the sermon, the ordinance of baptism was observed. As the young family of the infant being baptized stood around the font, one member of the family became frightened. Five-year-old Benjie, brother of the candidate for baptism, crawled up under the altar table with the cross on top. Benjie would not come out. The plaintive cries of his parents, the church's pastor, and a few choir members could not convince Benjie to move. Such only caused him to withdraw deeper under the table in full view of the congregation. As the congregants snickered and laughed at the bizarre scene, the pastor finally turned to the audience, shrugged his shoulders, and motioned for the service to continue.

Slowly and deliberately Koester mounted the pulpit. He turned around and in a clear voice spoke to the table under which the lad had found his security: "That's all right, Benjie, for centuries humans have taken refuge under the cross. You are not the first. You will not be the last."[5]

There is no greater security than that which enables us to walk the earth in the midst of our fellow humans with simple reverence and grace. When the day of evil comes, the armor of God proves sufficient. That knowledge should greatly strengthen our moral conscience.

---

1. John Killinger, "Mainline Preaching's Changed Pulpit," *The Christian Ministry* (September — October, 1987), pp. 7-9.

2. Thomas H. Conley, "A Mandate: Take Time Out!" Northside Baptist Church, Atlanta, Georgia, October 9, 1988.

3. This insight is found in David Buttrick, "Preaching In An Unbrave New World," *The Spire*, Vanderbilt University Divinity School and Oberlin Graduate School of Theology, Vol. 13, no. 1, Summer/Fall, 1988.

4. Howard Thurman, *For the Inward Journey: the Writings of Howard Thurman*, selected by Anne Spencer Thurman (Richmond, Indiana: Friends United Meeting, 1984), pp. 4-5. Thurman's essay is titled, "The Conscientious Demand."

5. The service took place in Union Congregational Church where I was assistant minister. Helmut Koester was speaking at my invitation.

Preface To The Sermons From James

While the epistle of James has never been an immensely popular book of the Bible, it is one of the more useful books for the contemporary preacher. James's work is referred to as *ethical exhortation*. It is designed for practical application within the Christian church. Instead of trying to evangelize church members, the author is trying to provide instruction concerning how one ought to live. As such, the work is an "in-house" document for use within the church fellowship.[1] While James is, perhaps, the most Jewish of the New Testament writings, quoting the Old Testament as authoritative and lifting up Old Testament heroes and heroines, the letter is also thoroughly Christian. This "in-house" document is addressed to people who have already heard the gospel of Jesus Christ.

At the time of its writing, this general exhortation was speaking to audiences within an institution that was struggling to help its members establish a consistent code of ethics. While the work does not give any instruction relative to the Resurrection or Spirit of Christ, many commentators have noted that James is well acquainted with the traditions of Jesus' teachings.[2] Rather strangely, and excitingly for a preacher, this strikingly Jewish epistle is a writing permeated by the thoughts and sayings of Jesus. Given the parallels between James and the Sermon on the Mount, the author apparently had access to circulated compendiums of Jesus' teaching long before the Gospels were written down. This might account for the work beginning in its initial chapter with a loose assemblage of originally independent sayings.

In many respects the modern preacher is very much in a similar situation as James. Both certainly presuppose the resurrection of Jesus. Both know Paul's letters to the Romans and to the Galatians and wrestle with the proper relationship between faith and works.

Both have to call readers and hearers beyond sheer listening to religious talk (whether from ancient Stoic moral philosophers and Jewish moral exhorters in the case of James or from televangelists in the case of modern society). True listening must generate an active life of faith in any age. As we preach, so should we teach.

Preachers should not hesitate to preach teaching sermons. As James Earl Massey notes: "Most of the New Testament writings reflect the fact that the spirit of teaching was strong in the churches during the first century." Indeed, many who heard Jesus called him "Rabbi" because of the substance of his work. Having viewed Jesus as "a teacher who has come from God," the church leaders continuing the ministry of Jesus knew that sound teaching eventuated in sound hearing. Their view of a "great teacher" was not someone who mixed well with people and handled administrative responsibilities with dispatch. They were mindful of the need to *develop* leaders instead of being viewed as one.[3] And the way to develop leaders is to teach others the ethical principles that undergird a Christian lifestyle.

The balance between preaching and teaching is not easy to strike. Yet, unless we have some ethical exhortation that enables us to test what the framework of Christian codes of conduct will allow, we probably will not have much of a moral life. Here James speaks to us and we can use his epistle to speak to others. In a time when Christians turn to advice columns in their newspapers, buy self-help books at their bookstores, and settle down to read their lifestyle magazines, preachers must not shy away from ethical exhortation in their pulpits. The dangers of double-mindedness, pride, times of trial, inequality between the rich and the poor, confusion over hearing and doing, and loose talk, are not time-conditioned. These practical concerns are timeless. So then, should our preaching be timeless in this or any other season.

---

1. Frances Taylor Gench, *Hebrews and James* (Louisville: Westminster John Knox Press, 1996), pp. 79-82.

2. Note in particular, William Barclay, *The Letters of James and Peter* (Louisville: Westminster John Knox Press, revised 1976), pp. 21-25; Earl S. Johnson, Jr., *James, Peter, John, and Jude, Basic Bible Commentary* (Nashville: Abingdon Press, 1998), pp. 7-10. Barclay attributes to James no less than 23 apparent quotations from the Sermon on the Mount. Johnson maintains there are more than 35 indirect references to the teaching of Jesus in the epistle, 25 of which come from the Sermon on the Mount.

3. James Earl Massey, "The Preacher Who Would Be A Teacher," in *Preaching on the Brink: The Future of Homiletics*, ed. Martha J. Simmons (Nashville: Abingdon Press, 1996), pp. 93-102.

Proper 17
Pentecost 15
Ordinary Time 22
James 1:17-27

Don't Forget What You Look Like

A young college graduate embarked on what he hoped would be a promising career in sales. He was outgoing, witty, and enthusiastic. His company assigned him his territory. It was a rural area in the Midwest. His responsibility was to sell the latest in farm equipment to the farmers in the area. With great fervor he memorized the strategy sales pitch and left his office to spread his message of "better farming through better equipment."

His first two visits had not resulted in a sale. But he could sense that the two prospects had been listening as he had rattled off his litany of better yields, faster harvests, and more long-term profits due to updated equipment. He noted in his customer data base beside each name, "Initial cultivation promising, return for follow-up visit."

Then, he stopped in front of his third farm house. The elderly farmer sat on his front porch gently munching a cracker as he rocked in his rocker. With a flourish the young salesman bounced up the rickety steps to the porch.

"Howdy," he exclaimed.

"Howdy, yourself," came the response.

"Sir, can I show you a catalog of modern farm equipment?"

"Nope," said the old farmer.

"Well, sir, don't you want to know how to improve your farming methods?"

After a few minutes of uneasy silence, the thoughtful old farmer raised his head and looked the young salesman directly in the eyes.

He spoke firmly: "Son, I don't farm half as good now as I already know how to farm."

In a very real way, the book of James reminds us Christians of what we already know how to do but do not do.

When we look at the book of James we already know the things it tells us to do. That's its point. Knowing what to do is not as important as *doing* what we already know to do. What we profess and what we hear is never as important as what we do.

Many Christians come to worship to have a moment of calm in the midst of a tempestuous world. Nothing wrong with that. Other Christians come to worship to have their spirits lifted by hearing the music, listening to the prayers, and reflecting on the sermon. Nothing wrong with that, either. We all need shelters which provide respites from the elements and filling stations where we can get a dose of high octane preaching. We sometimes feel refreshed, if not enlightened, when the service is about to conclude and the choir launches into its threefold Amen after the benediction.

In fact, professors of preaching tell us that the opening of a service as well as a sermon should be an attention grabber. Then with everyone on board, we should slide together toward illumination, right thinking, and lofty praise until the noon hour chimes and the threefold Amen moves us contentedly into the parking lot.

Today's text assumes such a posture toward the Christian life. Consequently it singes our hair with a *threefold alert*: receive the word, do the word, and reflect genuine religion so you will recognize yourself as a Christian. The hearers who forget are contrasted with those who translate the words they hear into their lives. Hearing and doing are one.

All too often we Christians deceive ourselves. Profession and confession must be enacted in order to be real.

The early Christian church contained a powerful healing ingredient. As these small groups of people, often meeting in secret, worshiped together, their order of service was geared first of all toward self-disclosure and confession (exo-mologesis). This was often followed by pleas for forgiveness and *plans for making restitution*. A period of fellowship then concluded their gathering. The early church followed this worship formula until A.D. 325 when

Constantine assumed control of the church for all Roman citizens. With an eye toward making the church acceptable, Constantine replaced the requirement of open, personal disclosure with private confession to a priest. Finally, in the thirteenth century, the church made private confession to a priest at least once a year an obligation. Martin Luther, of course, dispensed with closed confession.[1]

Verbal acknowledgment of one's failures and short-comings, whether to God in prayer or to one's brother and sister in Christ, is vital to emotional stability. We in the church are coming to a realization of this fact. Through the centuries confession became frowned upon by psychiatrists and clergy because it went to a pathological extreme and became a symptom of disease. Yet confession, in its proper context, remains one of our most effective methods of obtaining relief from guilt. In this respect we have much to learn from the early church.

But notice this important fact: *the early church did not end the process of guilt resolution with confession.* The early Christian church did more than pray and confess. Its members made plans for restitution so their lives could mirror their beliefs.

Reparation, the process by which one makes amends for wrongs or injuries done to others, has been a part of the Christian tradition since the inception of the church.[2]

The epistle of James and other verses throughout the New Testament illustrate that one's relationship with other human beings provides an accurate measuring stick for the status of one's relationship with God.

Reparation is a clear-cut, constructive method for guilt resolution. Sometimes a change in behavior can do more for our stability than all the platitudes we can utter, prayers we can pray, or beliefs to which we can subscribe.

James gives us the wonderful image of a mirror held before us which enables us to see who we are in the light of God's love. Then, he cautions, after looking at ourselves in that mirror we should not go out into the world and forget what we, as Christians, are supposed to look like. We are to be engaged with the world, but we are supposed to reflect our true Christian selves instead of the world's *persona*. We must so live that our Christian reflection is commensurate with what we reflect to the world.

The *persona* was the mask which actors in Greek drama wore during plays. One character could play many roles. By changing the *persona*, the mask, a character changed personality. One could easily slip into another role and be a different self. James is arguing for a self in which beliefs and behavior within the church are consistent with one's actions and attitudes beyond the doors of the church. Appearances are important.

Given the Jewish background of the epistle of James, there is much similarity with an ancient rabbinic story about two families, the family of Garmu and the family of Abtinos.

The Garmu family were the experts in baking the showbread for the Temple. Twelve special loaves were placed on the golden table of the Sanctuary and exchanged for new ones each week. The Abtinos family were the experts in making the incense used in the Temple ritual by the priests.

The elders of the Garmu family decided not to teach their skills to anyone outside the family, and the same decision was made by the Abtinos elders. The result was that the special methods of baking the showbread for the Temple and of making the holy incense were closely guarded secrets which no one outside those two families could ever learn.

The rabbis were not happy with the policy of the families and were afraid that the Temple service would be endangered if they allowed such a monopoly to continue. So they called in other specialist bakers and perfumery experts from Alexandria in Egypt to replace the two families. But things did not go at all well. The new bakers were unable to make the Temple loaves stay fresh all week, like the showbread of Garmu; and the incense of the Alexandrians did not send its smoke up in a perfectly straight line like the Abtinos incense.

So the Temple heads called in the heads of the two old families, but they refused to come. Finally, after their fee was doubled, they came before the Temple administrators who asked them why they did not instruct others in their skills. The Garmu and Abtinos patriarchs gave the same answer. The two families were concerned that outsiders might use the skills to their financial advantage and make the showbread and incense for purposes of idolatry.

In addition to their passionate concern that items used in the holy Temple would not be misused for idolatrous or secular purposes, the families of Garmu and Abtinos were highly praised for their moral concern that no one in their families should be suspected of using Temple material for their own purposes. That is why members of the Garmu family never ate pure bread loaves in case anyone would suspect them of eating Temple loaves or using the baking material for their own use. Similarly the women members of the Abtinos family never wore perfume so that there would never be any suspicion that they were taking some Temple incense ingredients for their private use. Indeed, they were so firm in this matter that before one of their men married a lady from another family, they stipulated to the bride that perfume was not to be used by their womenfolk, in order to rise above suspicion (*Yoma* 38a).

The historical story about the two families contains a powerful ethical lesson as noted by the late Rabbi Chaim Pearl, a noted authority on Judaism. The ethic is known in Hebrew as "For the sake of appearances." A situation should not only be correct, but it should appear to others that it is correct. In that way, outsiders can derive a good example from witnessing what is right. A great judge once declared: "It is not only necessary that justice be done; it is important that justice be seen to be done."[3]

The wider implications of the ethic run throughout Judaism and Christianity. *After the children of Israel had completed the construction of the tabernacle in the wilderness, the Bible records that Moses made a complete record of how every item had been used. The gold and the silver, the brass and every precious item were accounted for, to the very last piece. Why did he do this?*[4]

Moses did this for the sake of appearances so the image of himself that he saw in the mirror of God would match the image of himself that he held forth to others. He could not allow himself to forget what he looked like. *It was not only necessary for Moses to be honest in the sight of God; it was also important for Moses to be honest in the eyes of the people. He had glimpsed a high image of himself and he would not allow himself to look at himself otherwise.*

335

Christian history affords us examples of saints in every age that gave their lives over to an image of themselves far beyond any they had ever known. And from that day forward, they never forgot what they looked like in the eyes of God.

Saint Ignatius of Loyola did not begin his life as a religious person. To the contrary, he was caught up in images of medieval chivalry. His fantasies were those of gallantry and kingly romance. He became a professional soldier, good at gambling, fighting, and having affairs with women. While defending a fortress in 1521, an artillery shot crashed between his legs, shattering his right leg and wounding his left.

As he lay ill and deformed in his family's castle, Ignatius was told by village surgeons that the skewed bones of his right leg would have to be broken and reset — without anesthetic. Thirty years later he would still describe that agony as "butchery." While lying about and suffering further painful treatments that failed to help his brutalized leg, he sought books of medieval chivalry to read. But he could find no such books in the house. The only books available there were a four-volume *Life of Jesus Christ* (*Vita Jesu Christi*) and a kind of dictionary of saints. To combat his boredom he read those books. He possessed no thoughts then of either piety or religion.

In his later autobiography Ignatius wrote that as he read the books over many times, he became rather fond of what he found there.[5] He began to acquire a vision of himself far beyond what he had previously held. He began to see himself as capable of living a life similar to Saint Francis and Saint Dominic. This new view of himself, having come from looking into the mirror of God, goaded his mediocrity and highlighted a going forward into a completely different way of living.

Ignatius never forgot what he looked like from that day forward. He advanced from good to better and founded the Society of Jesus. At age fifty he was elected the first superior general of the Society, thus becoming the true father of the Jesuits who have given so much to our Christian heritage. Certainly his view of himself at age fifty was far different from the man he had fantasized he'd be when he was a royal page or a competent military commander at a younger age. He had seen a higher image of himself.

As you and I leave this service today, we go forth having glimpsed a high image of ourselves. We have prayed, sung together, confessed our sins, reaffirmed our beliefs, and listened to this sermon. When we encounter our world, may our actions and words show others that we have not forgotten the image of ourselves that we saw in this place. Don't forget what you look like!

------

1. Karl Menninger, *Whatever Became of Sin?* (New York: Hawthorn Books, 1973), p. 25 ff.

2. For a fuller treatment of the subject see "Confession and Reparation," in Harold C. Warlick, Jr., *Liberation From Guilt* (Nashville: Broadman Press, 1976), pp. 108-113.

3. Chaim Pearl, *Theology in Rabbinic Stories* (Peabody, Massachusetts: Hendrickson Publishers, 1997), pp. 101-103.

4. *Ibid.*

5. Ignatius referred to himself in the third person when reflecting on this experience. See Luis Goncalves da Camara, S.J., *The Autobiography of St. Ignatius Loyola*, trans. by Joseph F. O'Callaghan, S. J. (New York: Harper & Row, 1974), p. 23. Ron Hansen has a clear treatment of the stated events in his chapter, "The Pilgrim," in *A Tremor of Bliss: Contemporary Writers on the Saints*, ed. Paul Elie (New York: Harcourt Brace and Company, 1994), pp. 111-146.

Proper 18
Pentecost 16
Ordinary Time 23
James 2:1-10 (11-13), 14-17

People See Through Us

A lasting contribution to American life was made by a simple business woman who turned a small bakery on Long Island into America's best-known and largest baked goods company. In 1925, then nineteen-year-old Martha Schneider married her boss, William Entenmann. The two expanded their bread and rolls shop into a thriving home delivery business. When William died in 1951, Martha assumed management of the office and kept the company's books. At the time, quality baked goods came in white paper boxes tied up with red strings. Customers had to poke a small hole in the package to get a preview of what was inside. Martha Entenmann invented the see-through cake box. Suddenly all manner of baked goods from pies to doughnuts began to arrive in see-through boxes with a proud blue Entenmann banner stamped on them. This caused those Entenmann baked goods to fill the shelves from New York to Miami.[1]

As soon as the Christian church was organized as an institution, the letters and epistles of Paul and the epistle of James began to hammer home a message people did not want to hear. God in Christ is the Martha Entenmann of the church. People see through us. They really do! There is a see-through box top that covers every congregation. I wish James would just leave us alone and not call attention to what has been the ever-present problem, favoritism, within our church families. Most of us would like to reside in secure churches wrapped in white paper boxes tied up with red ribbons. Heck, the Lutherans even have red doors on all their churches. But no! James has got to remind us once again that we cannot have it the way we want it to be. The scene in the book of James makes a single point: Christians should not show favoritism. James sees through us. All three texts from today's epistolatory lection reflect this common theme.

The text opens with a memorable scene in which a rich man receives deferential treatment in finding a seat in the synagogue, whereas a poor man is politely seated on the floor or given standing room only. The author has little use for the rich who, in his opinion, oppress the poor, take them to account, and blaspheme the name of Christ. People see through us! What we have here is a direct, hard-hitting teaching about the seriousness of discrimination and neglect of the poor. If the Lukan beatitude, "Blessed are the poor; woe to the rich" (Luke 6:20), and Paul's condemnation of the Corinthians for their distinctions within the fellowship based on socioeconomic status were not enough, we now have to encounter James. The scriptures cannot leave us alone on this issue because people see through us.

You and I worship a Lord who in his inauguaral sermon said that he had come to preach good news to the poor and set the oppressed free. We are heirs of an Old Testament tradition that focused on special provisions in the Jewish law to make certain that those who were economically at the bottom of the ladder — slaves, strangers, widows, orphans, and the poor — would be protected as part of God's command to us. People see through us!

Daniel Maquire in his seminal work, *The Moral Core of Judaism and Christianity*, argues that the original Jewish and Christian teachings, like today's texts, produced real cultural and moral revolutions. These teachings pioneered subversive modes of community. They built communities on the basis of shared ideas and commitments and not on accidents of ethnic origin, financial wealth, or formal education. They bonded the nation of the *sacred* to morality. They marked off favoritism between male and female, Hebrew and Greek, slave and free person, and rich and poor as a prime target for sociomoral reformation. They broke with the surrounding cultures in not linking the sacred to military strength. They parted with the dominant views that the gods are with the mighty. In fact, they went in a completely opposite direction: God is most present when the needs of the poor and the weak are addressed. They pointed toward a world that had never been, but could be.[2]

You and I have to reclaim that revolution. People can see through us.

In the late 1990s my friend and colleague, Peter Gomes, authored a best-selling work, *The Good Book.* In his own unique way, Peter laid out before scholars and laity alike a comprehendible, theologically sound, and masterful treatise on the importance of the Bible as sacred scripture. His excellent work called needed attention to the usefulness of the Bible as a "centering" resource for daily living and for wrestling with dilemmas that have vexed us humans since antiquity as we have sought to apply belief in the God of our scriptures to the human condition. One day in a major bookstore I came across a man who was perusing through the books in the "Religion" section of the store. He read the dust jacket of the Gomes book and turned to me. "Isn't this refreshing?" he questioned. "The minister to Harvard University acknowledges what I have known all along: the Bible has been and always will be the Good Book."

Actually he was wrong (the man, not Peter Gomes). "The Good Book" is not a completely good book. It contains a lot of trivia, moral meanness, and human nonsense. It is not the classical work of a lone genius. It is, indeed, a classical vision of the unachieved possibilities of humankind. One must look for its central liberating personality, its central themes as it unfolds in diverse cultures, times, and communities. On this, I believe, Gomes would heartedly agree. Had the reader examined the subtitle, "Reading the Bible With Heart and Mind," and actually read the work, he, perhaps, would have grasped the point. The Bible becomes "The Good Book" only when its readers reclaim the social revolution which is its central theme. When we take into our hearts and minds its message of addressing the social discriminations and abuses of the poor that shackle our world, then it truly becomes "The Good Book" for everyone in our bifurcated, desperate, and codified world. At that point the words about God's love not only fall upon our ears but we actually hear them. At that point, the Bible's images of God's presence not only fall upon our eyes but we see them. At that point all the words of faith that have entered our brain become a part of our work for the kingdom of God. These sensory signals from the ancient text that come to us from every age and culture get through to our spiritual center where they can be translated from words and visions into the deeds of a living faith. We can begin to hear the words of Jesus not just as a voice to help us have peace when we feel lost and alone but also as a challenge to energize us to carry all other humans along with us. At that point Jesus heals us not only inwardly but outwardly as well. The Bible then becomes "The Good Book" for our whole culture. Scripture then enables us to become truly intimate with all God's children. Instead of a select *therapeutic* community, we can help our church become a *just* community. We cease looking for a narrow band of intimate encounters among like-minded and like-living social friends and embrace a wide-range of relations among strangers. We put aside favoritism for a larger vision.

This is the image of the church the world needs to see. Otherwise we present to the world nothing but a well-packaged institution that houses ancient words and images that are incapable of being translated by its members into the works and deeds of faith.

Parker J. Palmer's book, *The Courage to Teach*, offers insight into the human capacity to teach and learn. He contends that "connectedness with the strange and the stranger is at the heart of being educated."[3] You and I are both teachers of the word of God and learners from the word of God. Since antiquity teachers and learners like us have wrestled with the question, "What does God want from us?" We know full well what we want from God. Our fervent prayers, whether in times of crisis or joy, are full of our awareness of what *we* want from God. But what does God want from us? Certainly the text from the book of James offers a clear response: "Connect with strangers and don't play favorites when you do."

After all, *people can see through us*!

---

1. "She Saw Through Us," obituary of Martha Schneider Entenmann, *The New York Times Magazine*, December 29, 1996. The entire obituary may be found in Marvin Siegel, ed., *The Last Word: New York Times Book of Obituaries and Farewells* (New York: William Morrow and Company, 1997), pp. 326-327.

2. Daniel C. Maquire, *The Moral Code of Judaism and Christianity* (Minneapolis: Augsburg Fortress, 1993), p. 48.

3. Parker J. Palmer, *The Courage to Teach: Exploring the Inner Landscape of A Teacher's Life* (San Francisco: Jossey-Bass Publishers, 1998), p. 91.

Lethal Weapon

A popular series of movies has been the *Lethal Weapon* series. You might remember that in the series Mel Gibson plays a semi-unbalanced police officer named Riggs. Riggs is a capable detective but occasionally he goes berserk and mentally flips out. He's called a lethal weapon because you never know when he's going to go off.

Each of us has the potential to become a "lethal weapon." We possess within ourselves a weapon against which there is little insurance others can take out. This weapon enables us to engage in moral hit-and-run tactics. With this weapon we can engage in the sabotage of helpless victims. Anyone we touch with this weapon is in great danger. It can kill spiritually, socially, and even physically. This weapon acts with deadly destructiveness. No age group is untouched, no character immune, and no life safe from it. *This weapon is gossip.*

The little sing-song ditty is sometimes glibly mouthed: "Sticks and stones may break my bones but words can never hurt me."

Let's not believe that for a minute. Words can be lethal weapons. Words *can* hurt us! The Bible, rather correctly, has much to say about gossip. James talks about how difficult it is to tame the tongue and calls it "*a restless evil, full of deadly poison.*"

Jesus himself talked about gossip: "Why do you see the tiny little speck that is in your brother's eye and not see the huge beam that is in your own eye. You hypocrite!" Time and time again Jesus stated, "You have heard it said ... but I say to you ..." and "Blessed are you when people falsely say all kinds of evil against you because of me."

Apparently gossip has always been a lethal weapon. Margaret Johnstone[1] once told of an individual she knew who had actually been killed by gossip. A ten-year-old child had as cause of death: general peritonitis, ruptured appendix, and malicious gossip.

Some tests on the child revealed peritonitis. The doctor said the appendicitis was bound to recur. He advised an appendectomy and scheduled a date for the operation.

Two days before the child was to enter the hospital, his mother went to a dinner party. She returned visibly upset. "What's wrong, Helen?" her husband asked.

She responded: "John, we simply cannot have Doc do that surgery."

"Not have Doc? Are you out of your mind? Why, he's been our doctor for years."

"I know, but wait until I tell you what Marsha told me, and she ought to know. Her mother keeps house for Doc. Well, since Doc's wife died, he's not been himself. Marsha's mother says that even though he puts up a good front to his patients, he's having a nervous breakdown. Not that I'm surprised, John, after all Doc's been through. But our baby, John! Can we let anybody who might go out of his mind operate on our child?"

The next morning John canceled the surgery. The child seemed better. No use hurting Doc's feelings by consulting another physician. So months passed. One night the child started screaming. He was rushed to the hospital. There was no time to waste. Doc tried to save him but it was too late. The child died two days later.

At the funeral, Marsha was among the mourners. After it was over Helen went up to her and said: "I don't care what your mother says about Doc. John and I think he's a wonderful physician. No person could have done more for little Jackie."

"Why, whatever makes you say that?" exclaimed Marsha. "I've always said Doc was tops. Oh," she added as the recollection appeared, "do you mean that business about a year ago? I meant to tell you. There was nothing to it." Then, she dealt the final blow: "After all, Helen, you know Mother and her tongue."

Why do people let loose this lethal weapon? Lest we blunder into a misconception, let me tell you that the most vicious gossip tends to be spread by men, not women. Why do we humans tend to manufacture and spread unfounded gossip?

Let me suggest four motivations[2] why people victimize themselves and others. All of us have a *desire for excitement*. Most of us are rather bored with life. It takes more and more to get us excited. In fact, the church viewed boredom as one of the Seven Deadly sins. To be bored is "to cast a jaundiced eye at life in general" and most of all, your own life. *You feel nothing is worth getting excited about since you yourself are not worth getting excited about.* The number one complaint of students at Manhattan College is: "Boredom — there's nothing to do." As Fred Buechner says, "You can be bored by virtually anything if you put your mind to it."[3] *Gossip stirs things up.*

Secondly, *we all have a desire for attention.* Those who gossip are attention seekers. The concern for self-interest as you and I gossip outweighs our concern for the plight of the people about whom we gossip. We don't have the slightest intention of helping the person about whom we gossip. It's merely an attention-grabbing device for ourselves.

Thirdly, there is a *desire for prestige*. Most gossipers have a tremendous inferiority complex. "I know something you don't know." It bolsters our self-importance.

Finally, consider the *desire for security*. We think by ripping to shreds someone else we can make ourselves secure. This happens frequently in the world of politics. The past decade has spawned a new term, "disinformation." What it means is that lacking security a person leaks out to the media the version of truth he or she wants known, and suddenly that other person, that idea, and that institution are utterly destroyed. The gossip defeats them at a distance. We've elevated gossip to politically acceptable behavior. *Disinformation?*

So what do we do? There are three phases to gossip: the telling, the hearing, and the retelling. You and I can do little to stop the telling of gossip. There are too many bored, inferior-feeling, attention-seeking, insecure people in the world.

Gossip will continue to be told. And there's little we can do to stop hearing it. People will gather together and talk. But we don't have to retell what we hear. We can stop its spread. And to do that, the scriptures can help us.

A Christian person should never be bored with life. To be given the gift of life is the image of God. We have a purpose in life — to finish off God's creation. We have a memory, an imagination, and an ability to love, care, and sacrifice. We are on this earth as a privilege. One out of five million sperm swam its size equivalent from North Carolina to Oregon, upstream, to fertilize an egg and one egg only or you and I wouldn't even be here, someone else would. We should thank our creator each day for the sheer excitement of being here.

We certainly don't have to be interested only in ourselves to grab attention. When we hear of another's misfortune, true or not, we should pray for them, not talk about them. Jesus is right — in the long run, there can be no real joy for anybody until finally there is joy for us all.

You and I should never have an inferiority complex. Through Christ we have become sons and daughters of God. Is there anything more important a person could hope to be? The Son of God laid down his life for us. We can have a personal relationship with God. *Is there any greater security than eternal life?*

We have a high calling. Return good for evil, humility for boasting, and silence for falsehood. *It could be the start of a whole new life for us.*

As one reads the scriptures, it is sometimes difficult to separate those issues which are timeless from those that are time-conditioned. Such is not the case with this text from James. Control of the tongue is, perhaps, a bigger problem in today's society than it was in the society in which the early church existed.

Our society's images and language are devoured by references to male and female anatomy, human excrement, the biological urges of someone with references to their mother, a four-letter word for copulation, or the insistence that God's last name is "damn." And yet we are the people who think we are going to portray the typically happy American family at some point in the future with children who have their lives all together. We'll be parents who are strong and wise, noble in our words and actions, we think.

348

Yet our values are expressed in terms of images and language. These things, not the material constructs of life, provide human solidarity. Our children will look up to and learn the language our culture transmits to them.

James concludes his treatise on the tongue by referring to images drawn from the Old Testament stories of creation. The author moves from the taming of the animals, birds, reptiles, and creatures of the sea to the cursing of fellow humans who have been created in God's likeness. The image presented contains a profound theological statement.

One of the amazing claims of the Bible's account of creation is that humans as well as all of life were created by God's *word*. God spoke and things were created. God's word stirred life into being. The Bible also maintains that we are to be co-creators of our history with God, having dominion over our time on this earth. Our words, then, help create our lives. Our words have *us* in them. They tell people who we are. Words are incarnate. They flesh out who we are and how we live, our attitude toward others and even ourselves. As John said, "In the beginning was the Word and it became flesh and dwelt among us full of grace and truth." Words do have a tendency to become flesh and dwell among us. When our language is full of virtue and nobility, those words move us closer to the gentleness of spirit by which we become fully human. Our words become flesh. When our language is full of profanity, and four-letter references to sexual copulation or human waste, then those words, too, become *flesh*.

The tongue can become a lethal weapon that can destroy us.

---

1. Margaret Blair Johnstone, *Create Your Own Tomorrow* (Garden City, New Jersey: Doubleday, 1950), pp. 163-165. I transposed some of the story. The illustration is hers.

2. *Ibid.*, pp. 167-168.

3. Frederick Buechner, *Listening to Your Life* (San Francisco: HarperCollins, 1992), p. 142.

Proper 20
Pentecost 18
Ordinary Time 25
James 3:13—4:3, 7-8a

The Battle Of The Wisdoms

In the 1960s a favorite weekend night of entertainment for many was to attend events titled "The Battle of the Bands." One entered an auditorium packed to the gills with other raucous teenagers. One by one, equally loud and excited teenage bands would be paraded across the stage to display their wares. This meant that each band had an opportunity to play and sing three or four songs to the accompaniment of the screaming crowd. The cacophony of sound would permeate a three-block area. The band judged by the "panel of experts" to be the best of the dozen or so that performed would be given a trophy and cash award. This band could proclaim itself the winner in that city's "Battle of the Bands" contest. Such proved to be an advertising advantage when the band sought to earn a few dollars through securing a gig in another town.

Quite often the teenagers in the audience differed vehemently with the decision of the judges. No sooner would the "winner" in the Battle of the Bands contest be announced than all manner of "boos," "hisses," and beverage cups would start flying toward the stage. Audiences would dislike the fact that the "Battle of the Bands" would degenerate from, in their eyes, true competition to the personal preferences of the judges.

In most worldviews, life itself is just another instance of personal preference, rather than a meaningful judgment about the actual merit of things. Some see the world as just being what it is. It contains things and experiences that some people do not prefer and other people do. This type of thinking has nothing to say about the way things *ought* to be.

351

According to its proponents, from philosophers William James to Richard Rorty, modern pragmatism insists that there are no absolute standards against which to measure choices of "right" and "wrong" or even "better" or "worse."[1] There are only *our* responses to these choices based on *our* perceptions of what is best, eventuating in only a difference to *us* in ways that *we* can measure and appreciate.

The book of James attempts to refute the claims of personal preference. The author distinguishes between two types of wisdom: that which *is* "from above" and that which *does not* come down "from above." Here is a clarion call for a battle between two wisdoms, Godly and human. James seeks to stress the importance of some guidelines for proper conduct which make a person "wise." At the same time he disavows certain conduct that sabotages true wisdom and undermines human living. James ticks off a veritable catalog of objective qualifications for the wise person in a litany of *do*'s and *don't*s. The author is not standing with a smile on his face and stating that "good" and "evil" are matters of individual tastes. To the contrary, he is walking across the stage of Holy Scripture, grabbing a code of conduct, raising its hand high in the air and screaming, "This is the winner in the Battle of the Wisdoms and this is the loser."

James' ancient rhetoric meets our modern mind and often we are tempted to boo, hiss, and throw whatever is within our grasp at someone who would dare try to squeeze us with a "do-and-don't" list.

Elizabeth Achtemeier has noted, "Above all else these days we Christians want to be loving. We want to forgive. We want to accept people as they are."[2] Indeed, she posits, we have come to the point in our society where we will forgive almost any wrong and accept almost any lifestyle in the name of Christian love. Forgetting Christ's purposes, we, in similar fashion, expect to be forgiven and accepted no matter how *we* live.

According to James, not all wisdom is true wisdom come from above, and we do ourselves and those around us no great favor when we pretend that it is. James recognizes the battle of the wisdoms. While we humans do have responsibility and genuine options concerning the character of our lives, James does not minimize our difficulties.

There must be no waffling back and forth. Spiritual death is a genuine possibility. Our cravings for the material things of the world can take over our lives and win the battle over our love for the God to whom we have promised our devotion. James suggests that submission to God produces more than good behavior. It produces true wisdom.

For both Jews and Christians in the time of James, the concept of wisdom was a central theme. Wisdom was an important part of the Christian life. Consequently, certain passages of scripture describe wisdom as if "she" were a living person or an extension of God.[3]

James focuses on the constant companionship of God, or wisdom, to help all of us in our efforts to avoid the dreadful attrition rate that besets Christians. Early Christians knew their wisdom literature tradition quite well. From the Old Testament (Proverbs, Job, and Ecclesiastes) and the Apocrypha, to the circulated letters of Paul, wisdom as a gift of God's spirit was held before them. In like manner, they were familiar with the teachings of Aristotle. The initial readers of James' words were familiar with the law of logic called the Law of the Excluded Middle. Aristotle had invented it and students of logic had memorized it for centuries *before* James took up his pen. It said, "*A* cannot be both *A* and *B* at the same time." The early Christians knew that something could not be right and wrong at the same time. The *do*'s and *don't*s list and the battle between two wisdoms, heavenly and earthly, was *not* something James had to convert his readers into believing. That was not his purpose. The early Christians already were well versed (some, perhaps, better) in what he was stating. Why repeat the obvious? The danger of attrition lay before the Church. These Christians were settled into their world. The institutional church was way down the road from its initial contact with the faith espoused by the saints. It needed a reminder of its code of ethics.

Here, then, is the value of the passage for you and me. Attrition is our danger as well. Not long ago a pastor took his teenage son to visit some universities that were out of their resident state. One of those institutions was Clemson University. Since the teenager was good in math, they were given an appointment with the Associate Dean of the School of Engineering.

After a period of question and answer exchange between the Dean and the student, the parent finally asked a question. "What is the largest major in this university?"

With perfect candor, the Dean replied, "In the fall we have the highest number of majors — engineering. In the spring, business undecided has the highest number of majors."

He explained that new, eager, and bright students enter the School of Engineering in the fall with commitment, excitement, and promise. Their initial academic work goes well. Then, in the spring term, they are required to take a certain physics course. It is a back-breaker. Only the strong survive. Attrition begins to occur as more and more start to transfer away from engineering. The rubber hits the road, so to speak, and by the end of that term, when freshmen are no longer freshmen, the engineering major is no longer the largest on campus.

Unlike Paul who was writing to fall semester freshmen churches, James was writing to Christians who were no longer freshmen in the faith. His letter was a general or "catholic" epistle for us all.

Eugene Peterson has written a book for us that James would enjoy. It is called *A Long Obedience in the Same Direction*. The book speaks honestly about the Christian journey. Millions of people all over the world begin it. But as soon as discipleship gets arduous or prayers are not answered the way we wish for them to be, people start to drop out. The attrition rate is dreadful. Few of us have enthusiasm for what Peterson calls "the patient acquisition of Christian virtue."[4] The Christian journey, which starts like a sprint, winds up as a lonely, silent marathon. What starts out so beautifully is never finished. So it is with wisdom. We can start beautifully but often it's the middle of the race that breaks us. We *transfer* from heavenly wisdom to earthly wisdom. We often die with our greatest wisdom, that which comes from above, still within us, unused, unspent, unrecognized. Yet the world looks at us and calls us "wise in the ways of the world," "a great preacher," "a shrewd business-woman," or "a beloved philanthropist."

James wants us to avoid such endings. He wants us to be declared the winner in the Battle of the Wisdoms, by the only judge whose decision ultimately matters.

1. See the examination of pragmatism given in John G. Stackhouse, Jr., *Can God Be Trusted? Faith and the Challenge of Evil* (New York: Oxford University Press, 1998), p. 25.

2. Elizabeth Achtemeier, *Preaching As Theology and Art* (Nashville: Abingdon Press, 1984), p. 28.

3. Earl S. Johnson, Jr., *James, Peter, John, and Jude: Basic Bible Commentary* (Nashville: Abingdon Press, 1988), p. 35. At this point a warning is in order for the preacher. As Marion Soards, Thomas Dozeman, and Kendall McCabe have pointed out in *Preaching the Revised Common Lectionary: Year B, After Pentecost 2*, (Nashville: Abingdon Press, 1993), the picture James paints is not meant to be a scare tactic. The preacher can "lapse into mere moralism or pious drivel" (p. 53).

   Indeed, every ethical maxim of Christianity was expressed by the philosopher Seneca, called "the noble pagan" by many. Seneca once said that religion was regarded by the common people as true, by the philosophers as false, and by the rulers as useful. Such, I fear, could be the case with excessive moralizing in a sermon on this text. Harold Warlick

4. As quoted by Dr. Thomas K. Tewell in "Running the Last Lap," a sermon preached Sunday, June 28, 1998, The Fifth Avenue Presbyterian Church, New York, New York.

Proper 21
Pentecost 19
Ordinary Time 26
James 5:13-20

The Achilles' Heel Of The Church

Have you ever noticed how prevalent is the number 3 in religious history? The children of Israel wander without water for three days under their leader Moses upon their freedom from bondage to the Egyptians. The nation later interprets the event to mean one should go no more than three days without reading the Torah.

One Gospel writer depicts a rooster crowing three times, once for every denial of Christ by Peter. And we all know the Christian assertion that Christ rose on the third day. Symbols of three abound. Jewish rabbis usually had an inner circle of three, so Jesus, in like manner, had Peter, James, and John.

Small wonder, then, that major Christian concepts also seem to be bunched in threes. "Faith, hope, and love, these three abide," uttered Paul. And what would Christianity be without the doctrine of the Trinity — Parent, Child, and Holy Spirit?

The text for today lifts before its readers the conviction of James that the early church had three significant characteristics: *healing*, *praying*, and *rescuing*. The first two characteristics can be rather easily understood. The early church was a *healing* church. When a Jew was physically ill, it was to the rabbi that he or she went. The early Church in like manner used anointing as a means of healing the sick. An early church code even required that each congregation had to appoint at least one widow to take care of women who were sick.[1] The early church was well acquainted with physical sickness. It did not view sickness as a punishment for sin, but an ever-present part of life. The corporate life of the Christian community was concerned with every aspect of living. Small wonder,

357

then, that later Christians took the lead in establishing hospitals to meet emergent human needs in the name of Christ. Today there is hardly a major American city that does not have a hospital with a Christian or denominational name in its title. While some local congregations participate more than others in various efforts to effect *healing* (physical, ritual, or symbolic), every Christian hospital is an extension of the Church's *healing* ministry.

The second ingredient of the big three, *praying*, is also rather easily understood by contemporary Christians. We, like the text, recognize that praying and singing go together. Sometimes the circumstances are desperate and at other times the circumstances for prayer may be quite normal, if not buoyant. There really is no great tension between James' teaching and our own faith in modern medicine and psychiatry. The psychological effects of sin are well known. It has been clearly established that a sense of being forgiven for real or imagined sins is closely related to a sense of health.

The final ingredient in the big three bears examination. It often becomes the Achilles' heel of the Church: *Turn around people who have wandered from the truth, thus covering over a multitude of sins.* This is the most potentially volatile of the big three. Healing and praying haven't laid down the potential land mines of excess as has the last characteristic. Save for a few devout Christian Scientists and members of fringe cult groups, we have gotten the medical, psychological, physical, and spiritual aspects of life in manageable shape. We have peace between the churches and the hospitals. We have not only peace but a wholesome alliance between the best of our Christian traditions and the spiritual claims of Eastern religions. Meditation and yoga are now practiced in church gymnasia by brown-bagging business people during lunch hours. From preachers who view the scriptures as "Gospel Medicine,"[2] to the readers of Zen Master, Thich Nhat Hanh, whose *Living Buddha, Living Christ*[3] outsells most other religious works, especially among Christians, we had made our peace with healing and spirituality.

The issue of wanderers from the truth and what to do about them has always been the Achilles' heel of the Church. From the

Spanish Inquisition to the literal destruction of the Southern Baptist Convention in the previous generation, proponents of a litmus test of beliefs have sabotaged genuine Christians everywhere. The words of James are powerful words. They are also dangerous words.

Rather boldly, James asserts that Christian truth is something from which a person can *wander*. Truth in all its dimensions, intellectual, philosophical, abstract, and moral, is not a given within the Christian community. It is something from which the community can *wander*.

This in itself is a major statement. In his quest for discipline in the church, James acknowledges that humans are not by nature compassionate and truthful. Backsliding is a problem. Those who have confessed faith in Jesus Christ and wish to be compassionate people do not necessarily live their lives in accordance with what they have said they believe. Consequently, someone has to go after them and bring them back from the error of their ways. If not someone in the church, then who?

Many Christians even today are actively involved with care of the physically sick and in prayer for those in need. Who will go beyond those important characteristics of the faith and become active in efforts to bring back those who wander from the truth?

James is not encouraging Christians to condemn others. Nor is he asking didactic, autocratic smart alecs to become watchdogs over other people's beliefs. Singling out people who believe differently and categorizing and labeling them does harm. Efforts to pronounce others as wanderers from the truth can become mean, ugly, and vengeful.

James is on to something here. Living in a church community is more than honoring the freedom and independence of others. Living in a church community is more than going after funds for the budget and rescuing the property from decay and neglect. Living in a church community is also going after those who have *wandered* from the truth.

The late Reverend C. L. Franklin, former pastor of Detroit's New Bethel Baptist Church and father of singer Aretha Franklin, stated a profound truth about the Parable of the Prodigal Son. In a direct way the parable is an indictment of the father in the story.

359

The Parable of the Prodigal Son is the last of three parables Jesus tells about things that were lost. First he tells of lost sheep. Secondly he tells of lost money. Thirdly he tells of a lost child.[4]

In the story of the lost sheep, a shepherd went back over his steps and searched in every valley until he had regained the lost sheep. In the story of the lost coin, a woman swept under every bed and behind every door and in every corner until she had found her lost coin. But in the story of the lost son, no one went out to look for him.

The meaning is obvious. People will consult every lawyer they can find and retrace every step in the process to recover lost property (sheep). People will turn the house upside down or work two shifts in order to try and regain lost money. But few people will lift a finger to try to regain wandering children, or husbands, or wives, or even lost Christian friends. When people err, we tend to leave them alone.

When people think they know it all, err from the truth, and try to impose their will and their way on us, we don't call them on the telephone anymore. When people wander away from the truth, we tend to wait on them to "come to themselves" before making a move toward them. If they never "come to their senses," we just leave them alone in the name of "tolerance." Then, if they come around on their own, we run down the road like some silly clown, with our robes flying in the breeze, ready to throw them a party and serve prime rib like the father in the parable of the Prodigal.

Now, we should never practice a kind of "in your face" Christianity that disturbs the love ethic so poignantly evidenced in the life of Jesus the Christ. On the other hand, the Church can be victimized by its vacillations and compromised by its compromises. The work of reclaiming human beings who err must be part and parcel of the priorities of our churches.

Bringing back individuals who seem to be wandering from the truth is not an easy task in today's world. Yet those who live under the Lordship of God have a responsibility to be concerned about the beliefs and lifestyles of their fellow human beings. Participation in a covenant community requires a personal commitment to others who are part of that same covenant. This is not to say that

Christians form a "one-size fits all" type of fellowship. Interpretation is always a prime factor in any recognition of truth. Yet life in a covenant community calls on Christians to learn what is central to its relationships and the understandings of life that make the covenant people who they are. Robin Lovin, I think, is correct: "Unless we have ... some sense of mission in our institution ... we probably will not have much of a moral life, even though we may not be guilty of many moral mistakes."[5] Healing and praying come naturally with our territory. Turning around people who have wandered from the truth has been our Achilles' heel. Thank you, James, for reminding us.

---

1. William Barclay, *The Letters of James and Peter* (Louisville: Westminster John Knox Press, 1976), pp. 129-130.

2. *Gospel Medicine* is the exact title of the work by Barbara Brown Taylor (Boston: Cowley Publications, 1995), one of our most published and gifted preachers. She rightly summons Old and New Testament stories as ways to mend spirits and strengthen human weaknesses.

3. The two best-selling works of Thich Nhat Hanh are *Peace Is Every Step* (New York: Bantam Books, 1991), and *Living Buddha, Living Christ* (New York: Riverhead Books, 1995). Nhat Hanh adapts ancient Buddhist teachings to modern problems and seeks to make connections with Jesus in a manner I would call soft universalism.

4. C. L. Franklin, *Give Me This Mountain*, ed. by Jeff Todd Titon (Urbana, Illinois: University of Illinois Press, 1989), pp. 55-57.

5. Robin Lovin, *Christian Ethics: An Essential Guide* (Nashville: Abingdon Press, 2000), p. 60.

Proper 22
Pentecost 20
Ordinary Time 27
Hebrews 1:1-4; 2:5-12

Calling A Halt To The Angel Craze

Some stout claims are made in today's lesson. God becomes one of us so we can become one of God's own. Hebrews says that Jesus stepped into our corrupt world to enable and empower you and me to do the extraordinary work of God on this earth. Rather than look for and tap into angelic resources, you and I are to recognize our own power to do something about this world as a response to our presence in the same family of God as is this Jesus, whom we call Lord.

The scripture is clear: Jesus was no angel! In fact, the lesson goes on to contrast the majestic and everlasting nature of Jesus with the subordinate and fleeting nature of angels. This is a message we need to hear. This scripture is not a letter or a lecture. It is a sermon for weary Christians. One can imagine the preacher spreading out a host of sermon notes on a pulpit[1] and looking the congregation in the eyes before speaking. The preacher begins to evoke what God did *not* say about angels in the Hebrew Scriptures. The entire message is explicitly directed against angel worship. Obviously, the congregation being addressed sees no contradiction between the worship of God and the worship of angels. The crafty preacher to the Hebrews thinks it's time to call a halt to the angel craze. So he should! And so should you and I do the same.

As Fleming Rutledge has noted,[2] this passage to the Hebrews could well "have been written this morning." Many of our congregations have much in common with the Hebrew congregation and its society. The congregation is in a state of arrested development as Christians. These Christians have grown weary in the Christian journey and are in danger of abandoning their Christian vocation. From such malaise and lack of commitment, angel worship is always an easy way out. Lawrence Cunningham of Notre Dame is correct: "To move angels center stage is to trivialize Christianity."[3] Instead of expressing concern for the problems of the world, we can worship angels who are supposed to watch out for us. As Bob Ferguson contends, "We love angels because we can manipulate them to mean just about anything we desire — which is what we have done with just about everything religious in this age."[4]

To posit that American society is in the throes of angel worship would be an understatement. From angel pens to angel dolls, from guardian angels to the self-help bestsellers which urge us to get in touch with our "inner angel," we are infatuated with the current mythology. It's like we have made angels household pets at best or magical talismans to help us avoid diseases at worst. In our biblically illiterate age, few realize that the biblical references to angels don't depict beings fluttering around carrying harps and songbooks. Halt! The Bible offers stern warnings against cults of angels.

Like the good preacher to the Hebrews, we have to assert what angels are *not*. Angels are basically of no interest in themselves. In scripture they have no separate existence apart from the presence of God. God is always present in any use of the word "angel." When angels appear, the divine world has broken through into this one. Such a breakthrough is never "cute." God's breakthroughs have always been concerned with feeding the poor, clothing the naked, caring for the sick, standing up for widows and the poor, and visiting the prisoners.

The great psychoanalyst Sigmund Freud handpicked a man named Carl Jung to succeed him in the psychoanalytic movement. Jung used to argue repeatedly that men and women have always needed demons and cannot live without gods. Indeed, we have made angels our own little personal "gods."

Jesus of Nazareth had a difficult time convincing people that God could work through the human process. Many people wanted Jesus to run for God. One day he actually had to get in a boat and cross a lake to escape a wild mob who tried to push the title of God on him. Yes, Jesus was very skeptical of those who needed great displays in order to function as sound individuals.

Jesus was so turned off by people's ambition for him that one day when he happened by a fig tree that had huge leaves on it, he cursed the tree, and it withered away. As an explanation he offered words similar to these: "It is not the season for figs." He knew that when the leaves of such a tree put on a grand display, fruit should be present. But on close inspection he found no fruit, only a great deal of foliage. The tree was cursed for its pretentiousness. It's as if Jesus just reached out and screamed, "Halt!"

Jesus pointed to his humanity as the place where God was working. He sought realization on the part of the people that there is something wonderful in being human and being loved by other humans. If we can accept the one God's working through fallible people, then we have no need of preserving pretentious little gods and no need to find demons to destroy.

John A. T. Robinson wrote a marvelous book titled *The Human Face of God.*[5] In this work he viewed the man Jesus as the one who gave us God in human form and the tremendous implications that event has for *us*. Put simply, it means that salvation comes through the human process instead of through angels, gods, and demons.

Jesus' vocation, as he interpreted it, was to represent God and call on all who believed in this representative relationship to take on the task of also representing God.

This human aspect of the incarnation is extremely important for us.

Alfred North Whitehead said, "Moral education is impossible apart from the habitual vision of greatness." In other words, if you can't see yourself as a wonderful and incarnated part of God, it's virtually impossible to be moral no matter how many courses you take in values or ethics or religion or philosophy or whatever. If you can't see *yourself* as wonderful and good, how can you treat *strangers* as wonderful and good? We tend to grow like that to which we give our admiration. That essentially is what worship is about — little people looking up; you and I looking up and seeing something great and good and wonderful in whose image we were created and redeemed through Christ.

The divine likeness is something all humans share. Reverence for God is shown in our reverence for other human beings. To be arrogant toward another man or woman is to be blasphemous toward God. To take sexual or physical advantage of another human being is to violate the wonder and goodness of God. And to violate the wonder and goodness of God is to violate the wonder and goodness of you. Jesus is right on both counts: "You will love your neighbor as you love yourself," and "The person who says he loves God but hates his brother and sister is a liar."

Jesus came to earth and taught people to see their wonder and goodness. No one had ever done that before. All other religious personalities had just focused on sins, on how far humans fall short. Jesus came to Matthew and he said, "Matthew, you're not just a tax collector. You are wonderful and you are good." Jesus focused on Mary Magdalene and said, "Mary, you're not an ordinary woman; you are wonderful and you are good." Jesus spoke to Peter: "You're not just a temperamental, volatile, redneck fisherman. You are wonderful and you are good." To the abuser Saul, Jesus through the Holy Spirit said, "You're not just an educated, conservative thug. You are wonderful and you are good."

To all of us Jesus said, "You are so wonderful and so good, that God has sent me to remind you of that and lay down my life for the forgiveness of anything in your past that might cause anyone to think otherwise."

It is only when we view ourselves as wonderful and good that we are truly free to affirm the wonder and goodness of similarly created children of God — regardless of their beliefs, intellectual capacities, sexual orientation, or race.

The sermon to the Hebrews is clear: "Both the one who makes humans holy and those who are made holy are of the same family" (2:11). Jesus is not ashamed to call us brothers and sisters. We, dear friends, are called to be the guardian angels of the poor and the needy. Without our response to that call, we will subjectivize every religious experience. We may, in such malaise, have decorative angels throughout our homes. We may be full of light and energy to the degree that we can know what Zen masters mean by "the sound of one hand clapping."

But, in such times, one hopes some preacher like the one to the Hebrews will shout, "Halt!" Only then can we rearticulate the significance of Jesus Christ and stretch our limited response to his expansive call to us to get involved in our world.

1. Thanks to Thomas E. Long, *Hebrews: Interpretation, A Bible Commentary for Teaching and Preaching* (Louisville: John Knox Press, 1997), p. 4, for the image of the writer as a preacher spreading out notes.

2. Fleming Rugledge, *The Bible and The New York Times* (Grand Rapids, Michigan: William B. Eerdmans Publishing Company, 1998), p. 8. For an analysis of the congregation for which Hebrews was written, see Frances Taylor Gench, *Hebrews and James* (Louisville: Westminster John Knox Press, 1996), pp. 1-10.

3. As quoted by William H. Willimon, *Pulpit Resource*, Vol. 24, No. 4, p. 48.

4. Bob Ferguson, "Have You Seen An Angel Lately?" preached in Trinity Baptist Church, Seneca, South Carolina.

5. John A. T. Robinson, *The Human Face of God* (Philadelphia: The Westminster Press, 1973). See especially pp. 212ff.

Sermons On The Second Readings

For Sundays
After Pentecost
(Last Third)

Harold C. Warlick, Jr.

*These sermons are dedicated to the
two women in my life:
Diane Norman Warlick
Charlotte Anne Warlick*

Introduction

Preaching from lectionary texts is not always an easy task. Not only does it take discipline, but it also pushes us to parts of the Bible, like the epistle to the Hebrews, that we would not normally consider. Since the lectionary still gives a preacher great latitude in choosing among four sets of possibilities, those who consider the sermons that follow have already, perhaps, waded through several frustrations in looking for material elsewhere.

The sermons before you are not warmed-over sermons dragged from my archival repository. For better or worse, they are new creations. I hope they present an adequate mixture of interesting stories with sound reason. I realize that "reason" in the best Greek sense of the term is not a popular term in today's church. We live in a world of emotion, hype, and multi-media imagery. Span of attention is generally limited for all and motivation for listening to sermons is sometimes lacking for many.

Phillips Brooks' definition of preaching as "truth communicated through personality" seems to remain valid. That being the case, the task falls upon us, as we make bold to preach, of trying to make our personalities intelligible to our audience. I hope we can affirm together, author and reader, that there is still a place in contemporary worship for the exercise of intelligence. God still wants our heads as well as our hearts. For all the quickening of emotions and aesthetic senses available to us each week, our minds should also be kindled in worship. Christianity owes a great debt to the unknown author of the Epistle to the Hebrews. That author never made a virtue of ignorance. The mind is honored throughout the epistle as a fine instrument that appreciates and understands truth.

If there is a theme that runs throughout the lectionary texts considered in this book, it is that no one should be asked to make a fetish of old-fashioned religion. While each reader will have to

371

find her or his own "voice" in which to preach the themes herein suggested, this can be easily done. Our calling is to help one another find a way to talk about the moments when God has sent some insight to us. While much of this is personal stuff, I hope the sermons shared in this volume will activate dormant insights among many colleagues. It takes but a small spark to get God to flare up in a preacher's mind. God is always trying to get through to us. In the texts considered in this volume, the authors or scribes of those scriptures tried to put their understanding of Jesus Christ into a context that would show his strength, vitality, and permanence.

I have every confidence that as you work with this material, you will do the same.

Harold C. Warlick, Jr.
High Point, North Carolina

Laid Bare, Laid Out, And Laid Back

Today's sermon to the Hebrews hits close to home for us in contemporary America. The word of God is a complex phenomenon when it is let loose. It exposes. It clarifies. It comforts. To miss any part of it is, perhaps, to miss it all. Fred Craddock, Professor of Preaching at Emory University, contends that the fault of preaching today is that it is preached as if nothing were at stake. Such is not the case with this message to the Hebrews. Everything is at stake. Uncomfortable and unwelcomed imagery floods those who are exposed to the vitality of God's word. The word is "living and alive." It pierces. It penetrates. It divides with sharpness. Sharper than a two-edged sword, God's word lays bare the rawness of soul and spirit. Nothing in all of creation is hidden from God's sight. It is clearly laid out in this passage that those who hear the word must give an account to God. And, finally, the passage offers the comfort of a great high priest through whose mercy and grace its hearers can lay back in certain assurance and peace. Laid bare. Laid out. Laid back.

No one can hide from God. The word of God "unveils" every human life. In the words of Thomas Long, it turns "wandering human beings into principle actors in the magnificent story of divine redemption."[1] Indeed, realized or not, we wandering beings are clearly told that because of who Jesus is, a "divine claim"[2] is laid on our lives.

The role that scripture as the "word" of God plays in our understanding of the gospel is as pivotal for contemporary Christians as it was for the early Christians. Israel always understands the

373

divine word as a living active reality. Once spoken, it takes on a life of its own, bringing together past, present, and future.[3] The word of God is depicted in raw, judgmental language. *It culminates in a comforting notion of thanksgiving and praise, but its uncomfortable indictment of human life is unmistaken.*

That God's word can pierce and divide when it runs upon and over human reality is without question. When we are laid bare, our offensive resistance to the divine reality can rip us apart. Soul and spirit and joints and marrow are divided. The thoughts and attitudes of the heart are, indeed, judged (4:13).

So penetrating is the reality of Christ that it can rip human understanding apart. Indeed, the image and words about Christ can become a downright threat to our cherished images.

A simple sculpture of a crucifix laid bare the Old First Reformed Church in Philadelphia. Larry Moog, a member of the Bird and Dirt Collaborative, was the artist. He fashioned a Christ figure out of trash he discovered in the doorways and alleys of buildings near the church. The figure, meant to represent all of humanity, was designed to transcend gender, race, and age. It possessed aluminum beads as hair, coconut shells for breasts, and sumac branches for arms. The 1,000 one-inch nails that held together the vinyl body were placed in ancient Christian patterns — the fish and the Greek Chi-Rho. The crown of thorns on the head of the figure was composed of cast-off spark plugs. The horizontal beam of the cross bore the words: "He died to make us holy."

The huge crucifix-sculpture caused quite a stir. Geneva Butz wrote that the effect the artist wanted was for the figure to interact with the natural environment. "But the figure's interaction with the human environment was even more noteworthy."[4]

Many people thought the sculpture was a mockery of religion. Others found its grotesqueness to be inspiring. Words like "horrible," "hideous," and "horrendous" were used to describe the piece by those who considered it to be offensive. After only three weeks outside the church, the piece was ripped from the cross and stolen. When the sculpture was finally found, the artist reconfigured it. It was promptly stolen again.

The words of God, the images of God, the calls of God — who would have guessed that they could lay us bare in such profound ways? The author of Hebrews was afraid that his readers were coming close to falling away from the living God. Would they remain faithful in the face of one before whom each creature's innermost thoughts and intentions are naked and laid bare?

In his best seller, *The Good Book*,[5] Peter Gomes gives a striking example of the problems of anti-Semitism in Christian Scriptures and music. The Harvard University Choir, called by Gomes, "arguably one of the great choral groups in America," often sings the great works of Bach on Sunday mornings in the Memorial Church. One year after the choir had performed a Bach piece a female singer was in tears. They were not joyful tears. She was Jewish. She knew German. She had witnessed the pleasure the experience had given her and many others. Yet part of herself, while acknowledging the genius of Bach, knew also that the text represented everything horrid and hateful that had happened to Jews at the hands of Christians. The beauty of Bach's music was grounded in the realities of anti-Semitism.

Gomes asked the choirmaster why the Bach piece was not sung in English, since an English translation had been provided to the congregation. Why was it sung in German? The choirmaster responded: "In German it is less harsh; we can have much of the beauty without most of the pain." The "pain" referred to was the pain imposed on the Jews.[6]

Laid bare and laid out — the word of God can, indeed, *"pierce"* with discernment as in the case of Old First Reformed Church. It can also *"separate"* the soul and the spirit as in Harvard's Memorial Church. Both illustrations vividly portray the inevitability of judgment. We all must render an account to God. God's discerning judgment can be quite terrifying. Laid bare and laid out! Enter the high priest and his sympathy and comfort.

Trying to follow Jesus in the way of love is as hard for us as it was for the Christians who first heard the mini-sermon presented in Hebrews. Yet the scripture lays it out: "... the word of God is living and active." *If judgment is active and alive, then so is grace.* Jesus is not just a prophet. Jesus is also a priest in the fullest sense of the term. Everything is in motion and everything undergoes change. Even the heavens are not static but violent beyond our imagining. Science has, thankfully, shown us that stars are born, live and die, and both wreak havoc and display beauty.

In a very real way, the same is in play in spiritual matters. We believe in an incarnate God, one who has been revealed in physical form by choice. Jesus comes not only to judge but also to reconcile us to God and one another through showing us what true love means. That is our hope. Jesus lives through the physical world so that we can discover the grace in our own lives. We can lay back and trust the high priest to lead us to the place where "we may receive mercy and find grace to help us in our time of need" (Hebrews 4:16). What gives meaning to our travel through life is the constant recognition that we have a security net below us that guarantees safe passage. Consequently, while we live with a measure of prudence and caution, we are also living laid back in love with certain confident assurances ever in hand. This is called living by *faith*. An author of Hebrews poignantly calls the merger of action and faith "the assurance of things hoped for, the conviction of things not seen."

Laid bare, laid out, and laid back — all three postures must be taken very seriously. Some of us recovering prophets need a priest. We have laid it bare and laid it out so long until it is hard to tell where our insolence and cynicism drown out the Good News of God's salvation. *Laid bare in truth; laid out in judgment; but not laid back in love*. And some of us recovering priests need a prophet. We have been highly diverted from the importance of uttering uncomfortable warnings. All living things need nourishment and pabulum and syrup cannot feed a hungry soul in a world composed of the harassed and helpless and the mangled and miserable. Tailoring a church's menu to what it perceives to be the tastes of the masses will not cut it. The church is not an institutional cafeteria to cater to impulses and transient desires. The Good News of God's salvation is not just a cuddly child in a manger but a stark figure on barren Calvary.

Laid bare, laid out, and laid back. So be it!

1. Thomas G. Long, *Hebrews: Interpretation: A Bible Commentary for Teaching and Preaching* (Louisville: John Knox Press, 1997), p. 61.

2. The term is taken from Marion Soards, Thomas Dozeman, Kendall McCabe, *Preaching the Revised Common Lectionary: Year B, After Pentecost 2* (Nashville: Abingdon Press, 1993), p. 86.

3. See Harold C. Warlick, Jr., *How To Be A Minister and A Human Being* (Valley Forge, Pennsylvania: Judson Press, 1982), p. 75. This prophetic interpenetration of past, present, and future is called the "future perfect" by scholars.

4. Geneva M. Butz, *Christmas in All Seasons* (Cleveland: United Church Press, 1995), pp. 73-75. The account by Butz is a first-person account of the experience.

5. Peter J. Gomes, *The Good Book: Reading the Bible With Mind and Heart* (New York: William Morrow and Company, Inc., 1996), see especially, Chapter Six, "The Bible and Anti-Semitism: Christianity's Original Sin." Author's note: the six times I preached in Memorial Church, the anthem was sung in German three times, all Bach pieces.

6. *Ibid.*

Proper 24
Pentecost 22
Ordinary Time 29
Hebrews 5:1-10

Finding God In A Seller's Market

An elementary principle in the business world is the law of supply and demand. When supplies outrace the demand for a product, prices are low. We call that a "buyer's market." On the other hand, when there are more buyers demanding a product than there are supplies of the product, prices are high. We call that situation a "seller's market."

When we look at the early church, such as those who heard and read the words in the epistle to the Hebrews, we must remember that it was a seller's market for religions of all kinds. The Romans and Greeks were connoisseurs of religion. Cults were everywhere. Even Gentile converts to Christianity had had more than a passing acquaintance with Judaism.[1] Eastern philosophers offered exotic rituals and promises of individual salvation. Religious affiliation among the masses took precedence over virtually all other human ties and obligations.

There were more people looking to "buy" into a religion than there were religions being offered. Most of the converts to the Christian church were well acquainted with the traditional "roles" of religious leaders. From the staid, legalistic Christians in Jerusalem to the raucous congregation of Christians in Corinth, variety was the order of the day and time.

In a very direct way, conditions were not greatly removed from conditions today. In a seller's market it is always difficult to form genuine communities of faith among listeners who have gathered at the church only as consumers. How does one shape a community toward a common understanding? How can a leader be viewed

379

as one who exercises human authority or guidance while at the same time proclaiming the central confession of the church that Jesus is the Savior of the world?

The writer of Hebrews, like the person preaching to you at present, knows full well that you are in a world that values religious leaders. Oh, this is called the post-modern and post-Christian era, to be certain. Yet from self-help to inspirational focus to spirituality to new age music, it's still a seller's market. People are vitally interested in themselves and making a connection with a higher power.

In such a market, the epistle to the Hebrews speaks to us. When the demand is great, religious sellers have to compare their God to other Gods. Otherwise one is not superior to the others. The question for the Hebrews is the same for us: "If Jesus is the high priest of our soul, what kind of high priest is he?"

What makes this Jesus such a great high priest that he can carry our deepest sorrows and most embarrassing sins to the very throne of God? Why not try yoga? All of us, ancient Christians and modern, affirm that Jesus died on the cross. His temptations and sufferings were real. The sacrificial death seems rather primitive and barbaric to modern ears. We are quite far removed from the religious sacrificial system of first century Jews. When we read of the "loud cries and tears" offered by Jesus to the one who is able to save him from death, we certainly see the humanity of Jesus affirmed. There are, indeed, parallels between Jesus and other high priests. Both are placed in charge of things pertaining to God on behalf of other humans. Both suffer and can sympathize with us. Neither Jesus nor contemporary religious priests presumed to that office of priesthood. It was bestowed upon them by God.

But there is one significant difference between Jesus and every other high priest. A human high priest is every bit as sinful as his or her flock. Jesus is different. I agree with Fred R. Anderson: "Jesus experienced what you and I experience, save one thing — separation from his father. In that regard he was flawless — without sin."[2] Jesus knew suffering but he did not know separation. He came to remove the distance we had put between ourselves and God. He still comes to do just that for us humans in every generation.

380

The concept of Jesus as the only perfect high priest should be quite liberating. It should free ordained ministers from perfectionist expectations and it should free the church to carry out its mission in a seller's market.

Jesus is, indeed, the only religious priest who approaches the throne of God without having to carry his own sins in his hand. Consequently, no ordained minister should operate with a sense of failure whatever the circumstances. Like the priests of ancient Israel, you and I are as sinful and separated as the rest of the flock. We all feel guilty about our human impulses and actions at times. We all need forgiveness. We all march to some fairly lofty expectations but the truth is that the greatest of all the great human high priests are in need of heaven's mercy and heaven's grace. Sunday morning and Monday morning are two different worlds for even the best of us. Even the priest holds dual citizenship in two kingdoms — churchly and secular. Christians, professional and lay alike, live with a wide separation between Sunday visions and Monday realities. At the very least, a realization that even the holiest human is different from Jesus should help us realize that in Halford Luccock's words, "God helps those who *cannot* help themselves!"[3]

Rabbi Joseph Telushkin is the author of a book called *Jewish Humor*.[4] He tells a rather significant story. A man gives some fine material to a tailor and asks that the tailor make him a pair of pants. Finally, after six weeks, the tailor notifies the man that his pants are ready. The man tries them on, and to his delight, they fit perfectly. When it comes time to pay for the pants, he tells the tailor, "It took God just six days to fashion the world. But it took you six weeks to make just a single pair of pants." "Yes," says the tailor, "but look at the perfection in the pants, and just look at the world!"[5]

Indeed, the evening news reminds us that people do not fit nicely into our world. Ours is a horribly imperfect world. It needs a high priest unlike any human priest. So messed up is our world that novelist Stephen White in *Harm's Way* places an intriguing monologue on the lips of a character named Peter. This thoughtful personality contends that if there is a single God ruling the world that God must be an adolescent. "It's got to be a kid-God who's trying to take care of this planet." Indeed, there appear to be just too many screw-ups for this to be a mature adult God with four hundred million years of experience. Peter muses, "What kind of God could lose the dinosaurs except a God who was not paying much attention to what was going on?" In conclusion, Peter decides that our planet is really being run on the side by some kid-God who is more interested in starting a rock and roll band.[6]

Aside from the humor in this illustration, it points to a profound subject. Only one who has never been separated from God can bring together people whose separation has become their greatest flaw.

At the same time, this realization should give the church the courage to recapture its ancient vision. *The church itself was created to be a priestly people laboring in partnership with an adult God.* We misread this scripture if we do not realize its corporate audience. The epistle to the Hebrews is a letter to a *church*. We were never intended to view clergy as self-employed entrepreneurs for God and lay people as consumers looking for the best product at the cheapest price. Nor was Christianity intended to be a mere collection of needy individuals. It was intended to bind us together and challenge us in ways we would never expect.

The stories we tell and the way they bind us together in courage and deed can profoundly affect human lives. Church should be a place that constructs meaning and builds community. In the aftermath of the horrible massacres that occurred in Rwanda in the early 1990s, one of the many refugee camps of Rwandans in Tanzania called in a female psychologist. The women of that camp were not sleeping. These women had witnessed the murder of friends and family. The women had been told not to speak of these atrocities in the camp. Consequently, they were haunted by the memories of the carnage and could not sleep.[7]

In response to the situation the psychologist set up a story tree: a safe place where the women could speak of their experiences. She went out every morning to the edge of the camp and waited patiently under a huge shade tree. No one came to see her the first day. One woman appeared on the second day, conveyed her story, and left. Within the span of several days, scores of women were gathering under the tree to share their stories and listen to others.

Following weeks of listening and talking the women in the camp began sleeping at night.

After all, it is a seller's market.

---

1. A. Daniel Frankforter, *Stones for Bread: A Critique of Contemporary Worship* (Louisville: Westminster John Knox Press, 2001), p. 92.

2. Fred R. Anderson, "What Did He Do?" preached October 19, 1997, in The Madison Avenue Presbyterian Church, New York, New York. Printed in The Madison Avenue Pulpit, Sermon Archives.

3. Halford Luccock, as quoted by Wayne Brouwer in *Humming Till The Music Returns* (Lima, Ohio: CSS Publishing Company, 1999), p. 43.

4. Joseph Telushkin, *Jewish Humor: What the Best Jewish Jokes Say About the Jews* (New York: William Morrow and Company, 1992).

5. Dayle Casey, Chaplain of the Chapel of Our Savior, Colorado Springs, Colorado, uses this story in his sermon, "Fishers and Failed Poets," *Preaching Through the Year of Luke*, ed. by Roger Alling and David J. Schlafer (Harrisburg, Pennsylvania: Morehouse Publishing, 2000), pp. 15-16.

6. Stephen White, *Harm's Way* (New York: Penguin Books, 1997), p. 22.

7. The account is reported in Herbert Anderson and Edward Foley, *Mighty Stories, Dangerous Rituals* (San Francisco: Jossey-Bass Publishers, 2001), p. 3.

The Crawl Of The Ages

The young mother sat nervously in the office of the Christian counselor. "I have a question I would like to ask you," she uttered, "a serious, religious question."

"Why, certainly," replied the counselor. "Ask away. What has you so upset?"

"I would like to know," she said, "if when you and your family die and go to heaven, those family roles continue. Will I know my children and husband in heaven and will they know me?"

"What makes you ask a question like that, Alice?"

With complete candor, Alice answered, "Because I think I can make it to death. Beyond that I am not sure!"

There are some aspects of permanence whose prospects are downright frightening to some people. Today's scripture seems to render an earthly verdict on priests. Death certainly prevents them "continuing in office."

As we wrestle with God's word to the Hebrews, it is apparent that we humans go off on what Gerald May calls "a multitude of side trips" as we seek to express our primary longing for union with God.[1] One of these side trips concerns time. What lasts? For how long? The early church certainly expected Jesus to return to the earth in a matter of weeks. Time was short and flying toward extinction if not annihilation. Nothing needed to be viewed as permanent. Heritage counted for little.

Then the crawl of the ages started to set in. The Hebrew Christians — people of Jewish heritage who became Christians — began to face difficulties. As time relentlessly marched onward, they

385

seemed to recall their heritage with nostalgia. Maybe there was value in the institution and offices of Judaism after all. Maybe this Jesus Christ was not so unique and supreme after all. Maybe they should rethink the old order of the Jewish priesthood of Aaron. Indeed, why not go back to the old routines?

The crawl of history causes humans to reconsider abandonment of old routines. This happens frequently. It happened to the Jews themselves in Egypt. Before people were willing to follow Moses and his "new" God into the wilderness, it had to be shown that the old gods of Egypt no longer worked. Each and every plague visited on the Egyptians showed the weakness of a traditional nature god or goddess. One might have called the story of the plagues a chronicle of imperfect old Egyptian gods. The Nile River became a river of blood, which exposed imperfect old river god, *Hapi*, as the vital source of Egyptian life. The plague of frogs exposed old *Heqit*, goddess of fertility as imperfect and weak. So it went, plague after plague exposed the frailty of the Egyptian gods. *The message was clear: rivers, frogs, cattle, gold, economic systems, and the sun are imperfect gods and not permanent.*[2]

In short, if you are to get your daughter to embrace a new boyfriend, she must become aware of the imperfections of the old boyfriend. Like Israel of old, the Hebrew Christians were faced with a similar problem. The sacrificial system under Jewish priests had been the very routine of their religious system. Every human relationship with God had depended on keeping the system going. When old priests died, new priests had to be found. Sacrifices had to be offered by priests day by day.

How could the early church, short of a series of plagues on priests, address the issue? Herein is the key: they wrote an epistle to the Hebrews describing the imperfect nature of the old priesthood. If you are going to switch priesthood, you had better have good reasons. Otherwise the crawl of the ages will start people heading back toward what they once knew.

The epistle to the Hebrews rather clearly showed three things that were lacking in the old priesthood. *The former priests could not endure over time.* When they died, their influence went with them. The influence of the Christ, by contrast, persists and continues. Christ stands at the end of time as he did at the beginning. Should anyone doubt human endurance, just try to get someone to tell you the first and last names of all eight of their great-grandparents!

The former priests could not save humans for all time. Only Christ would always live to make the sacrifice for succeeding generations.

Finally, *the former priests could not make the perfect sacrifice.* Because the human priests were themselves imperfect, they had to make sacrifices for their own sins before they could take on the sins of other humans. This was not the case with Christ, who being perfect could make the perfect sacrifice.

While you and I live in a totally different religious climate, the issue is still the same. Where do we turn when time begins to crawl? How do we maintain our religious perspective when the crawl of the ages comes upon us? The more science summons its evidence from the stars, we learn that our universe is older than we had ever dreamed. This makes us as a species much younger than we had imagined. At least some Christians are beginning to realize that Jesus and the disciples, rather than the culmination of God's expression to us, may have been part of the first sentence of the first paragraph of the prologue.

The U.S. Department of Energy commissioned a study of how to create warnings that can survive and be understood as long as existing nuclear waste dumps remain toxic. This will be until at least the year 12,000. How, it was asked, can any message be transmitted to human beings of the 120th century? No one has ever tried to communicate written information over a 10,000-year span of time. The human story could well have another hundred centuries to go. Why do we expect God to act fast? God doesn't seem to have done that in the past, even for those who believed in the Judeo-Christian tradition. Some bright scientists suggest that the crawl of the ages might force us to ring our meaningful areas, from nuclear dumps to sacred sites, with modern Stonehenges into which huge cartoon narratives depicting what they are can be etched.[3]

Perhaps we, too, need to reflect on the once and for all nature of the Christ. We have a call to surrender to the permanence of

Christ every bit as much as the ancient Hebrews. Otherwise it will be tempting to stay put and cling to the corpse that every tradition ultimately becomes. We, too, must look up and out beyond every human imperfection. We will have to learn to like ourselves and feel important. Even on days when science makes us feel small, we have an appointed Savior who "has been made perfect forever."

We will also have to accept ourselves as being forgiven for all time. This is not as easy to do as it might at first seem. Many of us have grown up with the impression that God's love is something that has to be earned. For us, God loves only the behavior that justifies that love. From childhood days many form the image of God as a punitive parent.

Perhaps human parents warned us that God would punish us if we did not go to the store or carry out the trash. Perhaps a teacher reminded us that hell is the resting place for those who tell fibs; or the preacher may have remarked that eternal darkness is the result of breaking ethical codes concerning sex, dancing, smoking, or some other such item viewed as a sin of the flesh.

Recently a colleague asked a group of children to draw a picture of God as they saw him. One child drew a huge lightning bolt striking a cluster of stick men. "What's that?" he asked. "God killing all the bad people," was the reply.

Now we should not for a moment doubt that the teachers, ministers, and parents behind such situations are generally well meaning. They, as do all of us, consider it their duty to teach children to be God-fearing. On the other hand, they perhaps also find the fear of God very convenient as a tool for controlling behavior. Over the long run, though, since we are all fallible creatures, such fear does not succeed in controlling behavior. It succeeds only in the production of intense guilt.

To put it mildly, the life of Jesus the Christ created no psychological guilt in the lives of his followers. Jesus did not preach a tyrannical God of wrath and superstition. This is all the more amazing when we consider that he lived and preached in a place and at a time when mystery religions were making such claims. In like manner, the epistle to the Hebrews recognizes that a loving God is in the business of salvation over the long haul.

388

When we focus on the imperfect faces around us in an imperfect world, indulgence in self-pity need not be our common lot. We have an appointed Savior who has been made perfect forever.

When we are certain we are the least lovable creatures in the world, we can be surprised by God's grace. The crawl of the ages need not shackle us. We can move forward in the assurance that there is always a better covenant extended toward us.

---

1. Gerald A. May, *Will and Spirit: A Contemplative Psychology* (San Francisco: Harper and Row, 1982), p. 151.

2. Many sources can be used to back up this claim. Among the most readable are — Nahum Sarna, *Exodus: The Traditional Hebrew Text With the New JPS Translation Commentary* (Israel: Jewish Publication Society, 1991) and James K. Hoffmeier, *Israel in Egypt: The Evidence For the Authenticity of the Exodus Tradition* (New York: Oxford University Press, 1996).

3. See the ideas debated in Patrick Henry, *The Ironic Christian's Companion: Finding the Marks of God's Grace in the World* (New York: Riverhead Books, 1999), pp. 35-37.

Proper 26
Pentecost 24
Ordinary Time 31
Hebrews 9:11-14

Blood For Sale?

Sol Levin recognized the profitable market for safe and un-contaminated blood in America. Consequently, he quit his success-ful job as a stockbroker in Tampa, Florida, and founded Plasma International. The company soon found, however, that not every-one is willing to sell their own blood for money. Plasma International soon had to start buying blood from people addicted to wine. Several cases of hepatitis were reported in recipients, so the company had to start looking for new sources of blood. With help from qualified medical consultants, Plasma International did extensive testing worldwide.

Eventually they found that several West African tribes had blood profiles that made them ideal donors. Plasma International signed an agreement with several tribal chieftains and negotiated with the local government to purchase blood. Business was conducted smoothly until a Tampa newspaper broke a story that the company purchased blood for fifteen cents a pint and resold it to hospitals in America for $25 per pint. Obviously the newspaper story created quite a controversy.[1]

The existence of commercialized blood marketing systems in our country is well established and has a long history. About half the blood obtained in the United States is bought and sold like any other commodity. Hemophiliacs, in particular, have enormous bills for blood. The threat of AIDS from contaminated blood is so great that it causes even the most courageous of us to pause and examine the need for blood whenever surgery is on the horizon for us.

Obviously today's scripture about the "better blood" of Christ has some real-life relation to us in which we can interpret what the author says. Certainly all the sacrificial metaphors of ancient Judaism are no longer meaningful. Neither are the contrasts between the perfect heavenly realities and the imperfect earthly copies as meaningful to us as they were to the Greek world. The religious assumptions about a Levitical priesthood foreshadowing the priestly work of Jesus Christ and heavenly sanctuaries contrasted with earthly tents are not there for us.

But we understand blood! We well understand the difference between clean blood and unclean blood. As the outrage over the Tampa newspaper story evidences, we even understand the difference between cheap blood and expensive blood.

The message from the epistle to the Hebrews offers the good news that those who have been disconnected from our divine source can be reinstated. Just as Ancient Christians could re-enter the worship of God through the sacrifices of goats, bulls, and calves, so can we through one whose blood is much purer than even the best of animal bloods.

The purpose of the sacrifice is to enable people to have new permission to enter the worship of God. Jesus is like a permanent free pass or, in Monopoly terms, "get out of jail free" card for you and for me.

All universities have two committees whose operations greatly affect the future of young people. One is an admissions committee. These are the people who decide to admit, to place on a waiting list, or to reject those who apply for places in the entering class. The other committee is a "readmission" committee. This second committee is extremely important for students who have been placed on academic probation. Once a student is accepted by the admissions committee, they must make the grades required to stay in good standing. The readmission committee is the committee that examines the students who are "on the margins" and rules on their right to return to the campus.

Hebrews tells us that Christ entered once and for all into the Holy Place in heaven with his own blood and obtained an eternal readmittance for all of us. We have a new permission to worship

God. This single, unrepeatable offering of Christ's blood is a sacrifice that is good for all time.

The author of Hebrews is writing to people who were highly respectful of the traditions of Israel. The author realizes that there is a danger that these church members might abandon the name of Jesus Christ in favor of a worship of God that is more socially acceptable.

In this regard, worshipers need to grasp a bigger picture than that which is close at hand. We are part of a larger design than the social demands and rewards of the times in which we are living. The heavenly, once and for all nature of life needs to lift our little minds toward loftier awareness. A decade ago, a pop group named Kansas recorded a song called "Dust in the Wind."[2] The lyrics were sad:

> *I close my eyes, only for a moment and the moment's*
> *gone.*
> *All my dreams pass before my eyes in curiosity.*
> *Dust in the Wind, all we are is dust in the wind.*
> *Same old song, just a drop of water in the endless sea.*
> *All we do crumbles to the ground though we refuse to*
> *see.*
> *Dust in the Wind, all we are is dust in the wind.*

Certainly our lives are more than "dust in the wind." There is blood for sale and the price has been eternally paid for us. Our modern lives, like the lives of the early Christians, are touched by the realities of sin and grace. There are moments in our experience when we push the presence of God far away and other times when the presence of God is very strong. This is the every day challenge of life, the struggle between emptiness and discipleship.

The text for today teaches us to understand life as atonement, within a framework of human sin and divine grace. God has blood for sale. The cost is faithfulness. The scripture walks a careful road without proclaiming a punishing God or one who simply does not care, either. Who really knows what God meant by the cross? The Christian church has never been totally comfortable with the idea of the blood of Christ. Yet our blood is our life. Jesus did not seem too concerned about his blood being for sale. In him God's being-with-us included God's being in the flesh and blood with us.

In a strange way we have a reversal of the first recorded murder in our sacred scripture. When we read the story of Cain and Abel, we find worship to have created a problem. Jealousy over an offering in worship leads to the first murder. Genesis reports a well-known verse: "The voice of thy brother's blood crieth unto me from the ground" (Genesis 4:10). The verse can be compared to two gladiators fighting to the death in the arena. When one gladiator gets the better of the fight he looks up to the emperor who is watching the bloody contest. The world knows that if the emperor shows the "thumbs down" sign the victor has the royal permission to kill his victim. But if the "thumbs up" signal is given, the victim's life is spared. The Roman ruler has the fate of the unfortunate loser in his hands. More often than not, the "thumbs down" signal is the one given. The blood of martyrs always cries out from the ground to God, accusing those whose power could have spared their lives.

Every victim's blood cries unto God from the earthly realm. Only a great reversal can re-establish a relationship between victor and victim. This is precisely the message of Hebrews. The voice of Christ's blood cries unto humans from heaven. This blood can, indeed, cleanse our consciences from useless rituals, so we may serve the living God. We are readmitted to the circle of worship. There is blood for sale!

---

1. See the case, "Blood For Sale," in William H. Shaw and Vincent Barry, *Moral Issues in Business* (Belmont, California: Wadsworth Publishing Company, 1998), pp. 81-82. The case was prepared by T. W. Zimmerer and P. L. Preston for *Business and Society* (Cincinnati: South-Western, 1976), eds. R. D. Hay, E. R. Gray, and J. E. Gates.

2. For this reference I am grateful to the Very Reverend David M. O'Connell, C.M., President of the Catholic University of America, "Seize the Moment," a homily at The Basilica of the National Shrine of the Immaculate Conception, February 17, 1999.

Proper 27
Pentecost 25
Ordinary Time 32
Hebrews 9:24-28

The Real Thing

How do you know something is a genuine article, "The Real Thing"? Remember the great experiment that the Coca-Cola Company tried? They decided to replace their historical formula with a new product called Coke. People did not like the new Coke, so a cola civil war began with members of the public lining up behind the new Coke or behind the Coca-Cola Classic. Eventually the classic formula was much preferred and the inferior "copy," Coke, was sent to the scrapheap of cola history. Even the commercials began to trumpet, "It's the real thing!"

Some analysts insist that the Coca-Cola Company created the whole scenario to boost sales of its original Coca-Cola formula. Who knows? Certainly the public felt that it could taste and recognize the real thing.

Today's text is one we moderns can certainly understand. Did Jesus enter heaven once and for all as the real thing to take away our sin? Was once enough to cover everyone?

Wonder why this author had to keep writing about the sacrifice of Jesus being the real thing? The book of Hebrews sometimes reads like an integrity check on Jesus and his followers. One wonders if Christians had not been victimized by collaborative efforts to set traps to catch the hopeful.

As we reflect on this scripture which insists that Jesus was the real thing and only had to sacrifice *once*, we would do well to remember that heaven has a history. Human beings have thirsted for heaven and even killed for heaven. As Carol and Philip Zaleski have noted, "In every flourishing culture the image of heaven is perpetually renewed."[1] Countries change their names and borders. Humans are born, live, and die. But no picture of heaven ever becomes totally obsolete. From poets and painters to philosophers and theologians, heaven and how to get there have always been big business. Most societies have found earth to be hardly bearable without a vision of heaven.

We, like the audience of the author of Hebrews, want to know, "Is Jesus the Real Thing?" Are we destined to die *but once* and was the sacrifice of Jesus *but once* a sufficient occurrence to cover everyone?

In all matters of life and death, tragedy and comedy can be woven together. The serious people point out the literalistic formulas relating to scriptural texts about sacrifice and salvation. Jesus doesn't have to keep doing it over and over again. Once is enough for the real thing. Humans only die once. This was probably big news to some religious believers when Hebrews was first written. According to Graeco-Roman traditions, there were various astronomical spheres in heaven, up to as many as ten. A cosmic ladder supposedly joined the earth to heaven, keeping the high god very distant. In that culture, birth itself was seen as a downward journey, a fall, where the soul picked up from each sphere the qualities which marked its character. In like manner, the return journey to heaven at the end of life was viewed as a dangerous and complicated ordeal.[2] There were powerful figures at each sub-heaven or level of ascent to block the return. The notion of a human being destined to die but once was good news to those who read or heard the epistle to the Hebrews. Even better news was the message that Jesus covered everything in a once and for all sacrifice. Otherwise, Jesus would be bouncing around like a crazy pinball every time someone died and started moving upward. People took this once and for all sacrifice concept and the single death of humans quite seriously in the early church. Many still do.

On the other hand, perhaps we contemporary Christians do not see enough humor in sacred scripture. Just look at the answers being given and the questions that must lie behind them. The boring routines of the priests, forever entering the same place doing the same old thing, year after year, with blood that isn't even their own are vividly portrayed.

Maybe we are too much like Augustine when we read scripture. Saint Augustine, whose relationship with his mother, Monica, was a little unhealthy, got beatific when envisioning heaven. He described one such vision he and Monica shared. Mother and son leaned against a window at Ostia and looked over a garden. According to Augustine, their conversation grew so filled with love and longing that they began to ascend toward perfect wisdom and then for a brief instant to touch it before returning to the flesh. Is such comrades-in-rapture the communion of the saints to which the sacrifice of the real thing (Jesus) takes us?

Step back for a moment. May not the actual imagery of Hebrews be something more palatable to a humorist like Mark Twain? The images abound: man-made sanctuaries that are copies of the true one; the redundant high priests; blood that is stolen from someplace else; a Christ held hostage to endless sufferings back to the creation of the world; Christ appearing not to bear sin but to bring salvation to those who are waiting. These are the kinds of issues that Mark Twain relished when he wrote about human perceptions of heaven. How do you handle crowd control for billions of spirits assembled not only from earth but also from other worlds? How do you handle the middle-class hedonists who just want golf, sex, and great shopping?

Where do we come out in our thirst for the real thing? In a strange way you and I have become adept at looking at Jesus' sacrifice through other people's windows. The number of books on the shelves about angels are probably exceeded only by the accounts of how to ensure heaven for yourself as a kind of just reward for spirituality. This scripture from Hebrews invites us to cease being religious peeping Toms.

We are all lost. We have historically tried to make whatever culture we are lost in look as much like heaven as we can. In the West our longings have taken shape around the earthly cities of Athens, Jerusalem, Rome, and New York. On the other end of the spectrum have been those of us from more rural cultures. We, perhaps, can resonate with the dead Shoeless Joe Jackson in the movie

Field of Dreams. He asks, "Is this heaven?" The living farmer replies, "It's Iowa."

Heavenly literature has generally revolved around topography. Today's scripture does not do that. Frankly, it goes to great lengths to move us away from places and things, even holy places and things. It tries to get us to examine the magnitude of having a heavenly parent who loves you.

Having an earthly father or mother die is a traumatic experience. When both are dead it can be defeating. As long as a parent is alive you are, in Anne Lamott's words, "still the apple of someone's eye."[3]

When those parents are deceased, there is a certain desolation. No longer having the love of a mother or a father is sad. Regardless of how imperfect and complex these people were, we still call and thirst for those who never can come back.

Here, then, is where the scripture takes over our deepest longings. Jesus is the real thing. Jesus has already pre-cast a sacrifice that ushers us into a place where we are the apple of God's eye. We are the ones who wait. Christ comes to us at the end of our journey, not to sacrifice for our sins. Christ comes to us to bring salvation. That is the real thing. Our sins are not life's eternal realities. Our salvation is the real thing. Despair can be replaced by hope when we can be assured of something we cannot get by any earthly process.

---

1. Carol Zaleski and Philip Zaleski, eds., *The Book of Heaven: An Anthology of Writings from Ancient to Modern Times* (New York: Oxford University Press, 2000), p. 3.

2. *Ibid.*, p. 81.

3. Anne Lamott, *Traveling Mercies* (New York: Anchor Books, 1999), p. 225.

For The Person Who Is Everything

One of life's interesting experiences is learning how to respond to gifts. As a child matures toward adulthood, certain rituals help the child understand the importance of properly responding to those who provide a gift. On the occasion of graduation from high school, a student sends announcements to family and friends. Often a number of these recipients of announcements are people the student has never met. Then, the gifts begin to arrive. As the days since receiving the gift start to mount up, sometimes the student (especially a male student) must be "encouraged" to write a "thank you" note to the senders.

One hopes that by the time the child has reached the state of marriage, he or she is better experienced in understanding the importance of acknowledging and thanking individuals who send gifts.

These two rituals are important due to the fact that the ones receiving the gifts are themselves financially unable to pay back the senders. Acknowledging gifts that cannot be paid back is important. How does one acknowledge the sacrifice of Jesus Christ to bring us near to God? There is no thank you card worthy of being mailed. What words could possibly acknowledge a gift so large as the atoning death of Jesus? By his life, death, and resurrection, Jesus has made forgiveness the central reality in our life. Our sins are remembered by God no more. We are free to start over. All charges are dropped. All mistakes are forgiven. All failures are erased.

According to Hebrews, attendance at worship is the appropriate "thank you" card for acknowledging Christ's sacrifice. Why come to worship? Hebrews says because Christ died for us. The author encourages readers to bring out the best in his or her fellow Christians. And the best place to do this, the author says, is in the context of a worshiping community.

This whole issue seems self-serving when the preacher says it. Today's world is witnessing a number of desperate moves to try to increase worship attendance. In fact, much of what passes as contemporary worship is little more than a religious game of "bait and switch." You know how bait and switch works in advertising. A store will carry a few items that have been widely advertised at a low price. Then, when customers are attracted into the store looking for the product which has "sold out," the salesperson attempts to sell a higher-priced product. One attraction gets you there and you are blindsided into walking out with a pricey substitute.

In religious circles, sometimes the guitars, strobe lights, sports figures, food court, and the like get you into the "church" so you can be sold Jesus. Worship attendance has become that big of an issue. Marva J. Dawn's book, *Reaching Out Without Dumbing Down*, has tried to analyze the gap between meaningless, routine traditional worship practices and shallow, equally meaningless contemporary worship. In both instances, she notes that members of a congregation seldom hold each other as their primary community.[1] The kind of intimacy, encouragement, and persistence alluded to in Hebrews exists in either traditional or contemporary worship.

Let's face it, the clarion call not to forsake worship is difficult to hear in a world of self-interest. When we face diversity, the great temptation is, indeed, to "dumb down" instead of encourage the finest expectations that we can imagine. When one type of worship does not appeal to a contemporary Christian, the "church shopping" process begins. One way we deepen the problem is by holding to the unrealistic expectations of fellow church members. We torment ourselves with the image of perfect churches where people love each other and are each other's best friends, eager to admire one another's accomplishments. This is unrealistic and historically inaccurate. Why do you think people like Paul and the author(s) of Hebrews and other letters and epistles in the first century era wrote so many letters? The congregants were always bickering and arguing. The authors probably couldn't stand to visit them.

The church is a frail, human institution. But it is the one institution for which Christ died. God uses the church and its worship services to touch people's lives. The only way to learn about Jesus is to be with other people who know Jesus and share their lives with you. You must be around people who take great care to protect you from the influences that would corrupt you. You must be exposed to the stories and rituals that contain the heritage of Christianity so they can be passed from you to the next generation.

In a way, churches are like vegetables in a garden. They respond to different outside influences. Some spend more time in the sunlight. Others spend more time in dark, shady places. These will grow differently. Some, like vegetables, grow in crowded areas while others grow in open spaces. The crowded environment church may not be as full or developed as the rural environment church. But it most likely will be tastier!

The point is that all churches have one thing in common: worship is their proper response to the God who is everything to us. Corporate worship is not only the response God desires, but it is also our salvation. We like ourselves best when we like those around us who are also acknowledging Christ's death for us. Our efforts to encourage others come right back to us. As James Barrie said, "He who distributes the milk of human kindness cannot help but spill a little on himself."

This is not to be misunderstood as some kind of psychological triumphalism. To the contrary, worship is attachment to God in proper *response* to Christ's sacrifice and attachment to fellow Christians in common support. It is a social phenomenon. To be certain, it cuts against the grain of what Will Willimon has called the "Kantian fiction of the individual as the sole center of meaning"[2] for our society. As David Buttrick has noted, the Bible cannot be read as a mere collection of facts or as an exclusive message of personal psychological salvation. Such is to ignore its spiritual depth and its social message. The same can be said of participation in Christian worship. It seeks to form God's people in both faith and service. While worship deepens our knowledge of God through

Jesus Christ, it also encourages our obedience to God's will in Jesus Christ.[3]

This cuts through the false battle between the church growth people and the advocates of psychological and spiritual nurturing of individuals. Church is part of a new order in a New Kingdom that embraces the totality of all the citizens in the Kingdom. Worship is the cement that holds this Kingdom together. Consequently, the King who is everything considers worship to be the proper response to the great gift we have been given.

Worship is the primary heart of a church's life. We certainly need to thank God for the gift of Christ in our lives before we can spread that gift out to a world in need. We adults who are so insistent that our children learn to be gracious need to display our own gratitude to God for giving us the person who is everything. Before a jet airplane departs the runway, passengers hear a word of precaution from a flight attendant. It goes something like this: "Should we experience an unforeseen drop in cabin pressure, an oxygen mask will drop down in front of you. Take the mask and put it over your nose and mouth. Breath normally for a few seconds. If you are traveling with small children, put the mask on yourself first and then you will be able to help your child."

When we respond first to the person who is everything to us, we can then help those children who are traveling through life with us. One of life's important experiences is learning how to respond to gifts. How do we respond to the person who is everything to us? Read the epistle to the Hebrews.

1. Marva J. Dawn, *Reaching Out Without Dumbing Down* (Grand Rapids: William B. Eerdmans Publishing Company, 1995), pp. 26-28.

2. William H. Willimon, *Reading With Deeper Eyes: The Love of Literature and the Life of Faith* (Nashville: Upper Room Books, 1998), p. 23.

3. David Buttrick, *A Captive Voice: The Liberation of Preaching* (Louisville: Westminster John Knox Press, 2000), pp. 14-15.

Sweet Surrender

John Bradshaw tells a parable about a prisoner in a dark cave.[1] The man was sentenced to die. He was blindfolded and put in a pitch-dark cave 100 yards by 100 yards. He was told there was a way out of the cave. He was a free man if he could find it.

The cave was sealed and the prisoner took his blindfold off. He was to be fed for the first thirty days and then he would receive nothing. His food was lowered from a small hole in the roof of the eighteen-foot high ceiling. The prisoner could see the faint light above but no light came into the cave.

The cave contained some large rocks. The prisoner figured he could build a mound toward the light and crawl through the opening.

He spent his waking hours picking up rocks and digging up dirt. At the end of two weeks the mound was six feet in height. He figured he could duplicate that in the next two weeks and make it out before his food ran out. But he had used up most of the big rocks and had to dig harder and harder. After a month he could almost reach the opening if he jumped. But he was very weak. One day he thought he could reach the opening. But he fell off the high mound and was too weak to get up. Two days later he died.

His captors rolled away the rock that covered the entrance. The light illuminated an opening in the *wall* of the cave. It was the opening to a tunnel that led to the other side of the mountain. This was the passage to freedom. All the prisoner had to do was touch the walls around him and he would have found freedom. He was so completely focused on climbing up to the opening of light that it never occurred to him to look for freedom in the darkness. "The freedom was there all the time next to the mound he was building but it was in the darkness."

Certainly one of the major stumbling blocks in any life is the attitude of knowing that you are right. When we contend that we are absolutely right, we stop seeking new information.

This problem is at the forefront of today's passage from Paul's letter to the Romans. Paul, of course, was an educated Jew steeped in Jewish teachings. The theological issue at stake was the question of "works" and "the Law" versus "faith" and "grace." In writing to the Romans, Paul set forth, as positively and calmly as he could, his understanding of how the old law should not restrict the Gentiles. He understood that one is put in a right relation with God not through obedience to rules, however traditional, but only through faith in God through Christ.

Like the man in the parable of the dark cave, Jewish Christians were trying to escape their sins through leaping toward where they were certain the opening existed. So certain were they that the law held the way to freedom that they were in danger of ceasing to seek God's new information. In this passage Paul was not referring to the Torah but to the *observance* of Jewish ceremonial practices. He was referring to those special ordinances that separate Jews from Gentiles. Ceremonial observance of the law fixed a particular social identity for Jews. This apparently encouraged in Jewish Christians in Rome a sense of superiority over Gentile Christians who relied on their conversion experience and their abstinence from idolatry and immorality.[2] Certainly Paul advocated the Torah as a moral standard for Jews and Christians alike. He wanted to do more than that. He also wanted to advocate a new definition of community. Obviously this was as difficult to do then as it is now.

Spiritual narcissism is an ever-dangerous exercise. When we think we have mastered a religious process, that is when we can be most certain that we are fumbling around uselessly in a cave of darkness with true freedom obscured but close at hand. Pushing oneself too hard toward a spiritual path of good works and scriptural and legalistic obedience can create havoc within a Christian community. Paul called for a sweet surrender to God's grace and a total absence of boasting. Since all have fallen short and sinned, there is the inescapable demand of surrender. If the power to surrender to God's grace is lacking, then every effort must be put forth to find out what the hindrances are. In the case of the Romans, Paul focused on ceremonial observances of the law that created arrogance or boasting. This was their great hindrance. It may well be our greatest hindrance as well.

The yielding of the very nerve center of one's religious consent over to God's grace is a supremely personal act. Yet it has community ramifications. Surrendering one's inner consent to God is not contingent upon creed or ceremony. A person can do it directly and this is a consistency from Paul's time to ours.

To the proud Romans, confident in their boasting, Paul's words must have cut to the quick. A similar awareness may permeate the mindset of us proud Americans when we respond to those same words. The words of Saint John of the Cross sum up this sweet surrender to God's grace when he says, "In order to arrive at being everything, desire to be nothing. In order to arrive at knowing everything, desire to know nothing."[3] This is still one of the most important themes in Christendom. It is the notion that we cannot make it happen. We cannot achieve it. It is an awareness to which Christians must return in every age. Even our unifying experiences as communities of faith are gifts given by God through grace and not the total result of planning or right thinking on the part of any individuals.

The creation of the first community of The Way (later to become the Church) by Jesus when he called his disciples evidenced the gift of grace to make something happen that should by all human reason never have happened. The fact that Simon and Andrew and James and John followed Jesus was not the way things were usually done in the religious structure of their world. As Barbara Brown Taylor[4] has noted, rabbis did not go around seeking students in those days. To the contrary, students sought out rabbis. Teachers carefully interviewed the students who came to see them. They heavily weighed many factors before deciding to take on certain followers as their disciples. If you did not show an aptitude for religious thinking, you would not be selected. No rabbi would lower himself to recruiting his own students. Certainly the notion of selecting, as did Jesus, the first four you laid eyes on would have been completely bizarre. Yet Jesus set himself apart from the very beginning. God's grace, not human planning or ceremonial observance, began the Christian enterprise as much as it cemented it in the sacrificial death of Christ. *The sweet surrender to God's grace was ours from the beginning.*

Imagine the scene. Simon and Andrew were casting their nets from the shallows of the sea. James and John were a little richer, so they were fishing from their father's boat. Both sets of brothers walked away from families, friends, and businesses to follow a stranger who called them. Jesus called and they followed. They did not know this man, Jesus. They were not themselves religious types. Something just happened to them. They did not plan for it. They did not celebrate it. They did not agonize over it. They just surrendered to something that was beyond their control.

To make the best use of life, you and I must learn how to accept the new while we are retaining the best of our heritage. Jesus and his disciples worked within their inherited framework of Judaism. But they went beyond it. Paul, the great author of this text, was true to many aspects of his Jewish upbringing. But he went beyond the old even as he kept to the best that he had understood. The early Christians kept all the old truth and accepted all the new truth. James Freeman Clarke[5] is quite correct in stating that there are two kinds of people who can make no progress. One is the conservative who can never accept the new and the other is the radical who can only take a truth by dropping an old truth. One is illustrated by a person who refused to look through Galileo's telescope to look at the satellite moons of Jupiter. The man explained that there was no use in looking, for no moons would be there.

The radical is, perhaps, best illustrated by a little child whose hands are so small she must drop an apple she is holding to reach out and take another apple. The radical can only get to new ground by deserting the old ground. How complete is the surrender called forth in this scripture. Both heaven and earth are changing. The earthly realm is not an evil entity to be run from. Pie-in-the-sky escapism is not the surrender called for. Nor is an embracing of an obsolete tradition the kind of surrender that is visualized. God's grace is not that confined — to either the old or the new.

God can create the best out of the worst and feed our hungry souls. Once we get beyond the hindrance of our own ego, we can see just how right Paul was. What do you think, fellow Romans? Shall we listen and act? Or, is this stuff we have heard before?

1. John Bradshaw, *Healing the Shame That Binds You* (Deerfield Beach, Florida: Health Communications, 1988), p. 117.

2. See the excellent work by Alan F. Segal, *Paul the Convert: The Apostolate and Apostasy of Saul the Pharisee* (New Haven, Connecticut: Yale University Press, 1990), pp. 124-125.

3. Saint John of the Cross as quoted in Gerald G. May, *Will and Spirit: A Contemplative Psychology* (San Francisco: Harper and Row, 1982), p. 57.

4. Barbara Brown Taylor, *Home By Another Way* (Cambridge, Massachusetts: Cowley Publications, 1999), pp. 38-39.

5. James Freeman Clarke, "The Use of Time," *Half Hours Volume I*, pp. 227-228.

Promised Land

This day called All Saints' developed in a manner that every university fund-raiser can appreciate. The Early Christian Church wanted to honor each martyred saint with a designated day of his or her own. But in Rome and Antioch there were more known martyrs than there were days of the year. The Pope in 610 frantically moved as many bones as possible to a single building in Rome. On May 13, he renamed the building St. Mary and the Martyrs. Each year on May 13, the All Saints' Feast was held, honoring the entire group. A few hundred years later some of the descendants of "the martyrs" began to complain that the celebration's close proximity to Easter celebrations made All Saints' Day less prominent that it should have been. All Saints' was quickly moved to November 1. But after the Reformation an endowment issue raised its ugly head.

The Catholic Church had taken designated gifts, properties, and legacies from wealthy donors. Terms of these endowments required that the anniversaries of those donors had to be celebrated in buildings that the church no longer occupied. The Church didn't want to have to return the money. Many of these wealthy donors had been *anything* but saints, so November 1 was ruled out. Permission was given to celebrate three masses on November 2, under the guise of All Souls' day. Anybody could be a Soul, even a scoundrel. There they were separated but by a single day: the Saints and the wealthy Souls. Over the years, the Saints and the Souls came together in many of the liturgies, and the separate days even collapsed into one in some settings. Strange timing.

Given the rather mixed, confusing, and convoluted history of All Saints' Day, it is, perhaps, fitting that the lesson from scripture is from Revelation. The landscape of Revelation is full of bewildering and contrasting images. Saints and scoundrels are certainly the order of the day in John's theater-like writing.

Writing in approximately A.D. 90, the Apostle John was thrust into the future by the spirit of God and shown most vividly a city that is to come. He saw a new heaven and a new earth. He saw God himself wiping away every tear from the eyes of people. Death shall be no longer, nor mourning, nor crying, nor any further pain, because the former things have passed away. The idea, of course, is total liberation from all that terrifies us today. Death, crying, and pain are gone — no more pressures and struggles to succeed. John went on to envision no temple, no need of the sun or of the moon, and nothing unclean ever entering there.

John's vision, influenced by his love for a New Jerusalem, has fired both certainty and speculation for centuries. It is an historical fact that that is what John on the island of Patmos saw or dreamed or hallucinated about. He could have been a madman or a romantic, but he transcribed it and passed it on.

Most of us have a facility for viewing heaven or the Promised Land that way — as the life to come. We are hardly alone. Some religions have been quite specific about the nature and location of this future home. Geronimo, the great American Indian, wrote of a home in the American West that the god Usen had created for each Apache. The religion of Islam depicts heaven as a marvelous garden filled with wonderful food, drink, and companions. The heavenly home is so graphically described in the Quran and in other Muslim literature that many Muslims are quite eager to die in order to achieve this paradise. Life after death is one of the most ancient and persistent hopes of the human race, yet it is such an uncharted experience that some believe it may be a testimony to the power of wishful thinking.

Yet, Jesus Christ asserted that heaven doesn't all lie in the future. It is somehow interconnected with life now. Every time Jesus referred to the afterlife, he did so in terms of how people live, and the way this helps determine their happiness in the world beyond.

There is a sense in which we can experience a foretaste of what heaven will be like when we die. Jesus also maintained that heaven is a place for those who experience love. People are called out and esteemed because they clothed the naked, visited the sick, and welcomed strangers.

Herein lies the completeness of the vision. Both the earth and heaven are made new. All things, in fact, are being made new. Old Testament hopes are being fulfilled on earth as God dwells with God's people. At the same time, particular saints and all the faithful for whom the New Jerusalem is their ultimate destination need to be celebrated. That heavenly Jerusalem is our ultimate destiny as well. Our knowledge of its presence hastens and makes glad our earthly journey.

Alfred P. Sloan, Jr., built the General Motors Corporation. His wife, whom he idolized, died and Mr. Sloan was inconsolable. He sat like a granite cliff, strong and rugged. This man who had put together one of the giant industries in our country and possessed one of the most brilliant organizational and scientific minds in history called a minister friend to his Fifth Avenue apartment. He opened the conversation by saying, "I want to ask you a question. I want a straight answer. I don't want any equivocation. And I want the answer to be yes or no, based on facts. My wife has died. She meant everything to me. What I want you to tell me is this: Will I see her again?"

His friend looked at him and said, "The answer is yes."

I suppose all of us want some straight answers about the Promised Land. What's it like there? It's obviously a difficult question to answer without equivocation because none of us has ever been there. Apparently Abraham, Isaac, and Jacob didn't get straight answers. Yet for over 4,000 years people have had a glimpse of this Promised Land. We have had the Christ, his teachings, his assurances, and the visions of his followers.

What is the "Promised Land"? If we look at the Bible, God promised a special place to our spiritual father, Abraham. Throughout history God had promised a city to the Jews. Abraham was evidently the first to hear of it. We are told that he spent a good portion of his life in expectation of a city "whose architect and

411

builder is God." King David wrote of the city and told of his eagerness to move in and get settled. Isaiah wrote of this grand new place. And Jesus Christ said that we are co-recipients of these same promises and fellow heirs of this promised Kingdom of God.

Yet, the actual land God promised to give to these people is rather strange. It is not Hawaii or New Zealand or Norway, lands of clear blue water and abundant rainfall. You could think of better places to be a "Promised Land." Actually, the Promised Land was a tiny corridor of land placed right at the point where three continents meet: Asia, Africa, and Europe. It was a busy, dangerous, unsettling intersected land. On one side was the Great Sea where people believed huge monsters lived. The history of this land was like living between a tiger (the Assyrian and Babylonian empire) and a crocodile (the Egyptian empire). Abraham, Isaac, and Jacob were all hit by severe famine in the Promised Land and had to leave it to seek help.

What then did "Promised Land" mean? If we all ultimately go to the Promised Land, what is it? I think the term is and always has been a figurative one with deep meaning. First, Promised Land means intersected life. It is not an isolated place or an isolated life, but a life busily engaged in encounters. Second, the Promised Land is a place of tremendous vision. The whole of Palestine is no bigger than the state of Vermont. But it has wide vistas. The clean air and the lay of the land create incredible visibility. In Palestine it is not unusual to see forty miles and it is sometimes possible to see a hundred miles. In ordinary climates we can only see less than fifteen miles.

Right in the middle of this Promised Land is death. The wilderness of Judea is a mass of barren mountains bordering the Dead Sea. It is almost as dead as the sea against which it nestles. Yet if one travels along the ridges of that area of death, one can see the hills fall away and recede on either hand, opening up into encircled, fertile plains. The vistas are incredibly wide. Palestine is a bridge between different cultures, where people can see a long way. From ancient Bethel, the Mount of Olives at Jerusalem looks but a block away. Actually, it is twelve miles.

The Promised Land — a place at the intersection of life, with death in the middle, where you can see the fertile lands 100 miles away. That image of the Promised Land has great ramifications for our life on this planet and our life beyond death. John the revelatory seer summed it up for all the saints, past, present, and to come when he penned his beautiful vision of the new heaven and the new earth. Get ready to enjoy it.

Running Home In The Dark

Our liturgical calendar stands poised on the verge of a commercial feeding frenzy. Today is Christ the King Sunday. This is a day that is supposed to be a day of Doxology or praise. It is a time that we celebrate the Lordship of Jesus as the director of our lives. We are asked to reflect on our undivided loyalty to the reign of Christ in our lives. It is, admittedly, a rather strange time to do this. This is the last Sunday of the church year. Next Sunday begins Advent and the great season of expectation and hope. We are just ahead of all the baby Jesus talk and we are asked to affirm Christ as the King of kings and Lord of lords.

Jesus the king is an important and interesting title in our tradition about Jesus. Being a king really meant something in Jesus' day. When kings spoke, nations trembled. Kings were the most powerful human beings on earth. Time itself was marked on the basis of when a king began his reign. The most common Jewish messianic notion was that God would restore the anointed Davidic line to the throne of Israel. This process would restore the Israelite kingdom.

When we read the Gospels especially, we must admit that Jesus was a bit cagey on the subject of his kingship. Jesus certainly did not activate many of his royal prerogatives, did he? We struggle a bit when we try to name Jesus King, don't we? We are in some ways like Pilate of old when it comes to recognition of the kingship of Jesus. We name Jesus as King but for one reason or another we do not believe it. And if we believe it, do we really understand it?

415

Feminists reject Jesus as their King because they know that kings are only male and these male kings rule autocratically. Kings give orders rather than strive for consensus. Kings demand obedience instead of service.

Perhaps we take too seriously the world's notion of kingship and kingdom and do not consider Jesus' image and his words about the enterprise: "My kingdom is not from this world, if it were, my disciples would be fighting to prevent me from being handed over."

Let's just admit that we are in the dark and see where it takes us. Christ the King? There is oddness about a king who reigns from a cross instead of a throne. Jesus is an odd king and that must make us as his followers a bit odd as well. Every ruler has a vision for her or his kingdom. Jesus certainly had a vision or a dream for us. Although King Jesus never claimed for himself the title of King, even those who mocked him by placing a crown of thorns on his head recognized him as an odd king. Perhaps the clearest perception we can have of King Jesus is to say that kings make demands on their subjects and King Jesus makes demands on us. This King calls us to allow God to enter our lives. He invites us to walk by the light he has shed on the darkness of our world and run home in the dark with King Jesus.

For much of his life a minister lived with a chipped front tooth. When his children look through his old grammar school and high school annuals, he's easy to pick out. Their dad is the one with the big hole in his left front tooth.

The big disaster came one evening when four or five of the children in the minister's neighborhood were playing hide and seek. While the designated seeker was slowly counting to 100, this fellow searched for a place to hide. Normally he was not very adept at camouflage and was the first one caught. But that evening he was truly inspired. He put a ladder up to the roof of the house, climbed on the roof, and then hauled it up beside him. He lay there flat against the steeply pitched roof, breathing heavily, while the seeker looked everywhere for him. After some minutes, he realized that it had become pitch black dark. A thick cloud cover obscured even the moon. Now he didn't like the dark. So he kept inching his way closer to the edge of the roof to see if he could see a light on any-where. Over the side he fell and he came up off the picnic table where he landed missing the lower third of his left front tooth.

You and I know how difficult it is to lie still for long periods of time in the darkness. A number of us do not like to travel long distances in the dark. Some like to sleep with a light on.

I can remember some evenings when I had to walk home from church or school late at night. The only comfort was the distant presence of streetlights. When I was under the streetlight, I would casually walk along at a slow pace. Then I would run as fast as I could to the next streetlight. I would make my way home running from light to light, with darkness for the rest of the way. Now that I am an adult, I must confess that life is still pretty much like those experiences for even us adults. We have to travel long distances without much light and lie still for long periods of time without much light.

We have questions for which there are no immediate answers. We encounter confusion, and clarity seems to stay away from us. We get in these dark moods and the sunlight seems to vanish.

John Killinger has opened my perception to an amazing fact about the first wise men; they made most of their journey in the dark, without benefit of the star in the sky.[1] The wise men saw the star in the East and it guided them in the direction of the little nation of Israel. Then it seemed to desert them and leave them on their own in the darkness. In fact, all the star had done was shine in a general direction for a brief time. They had to cover vast distances in the dark. So they stopped off at the palace of King Herod. They thought that perhaps the astrologers of the royal court could help them in solving the puzzle of the star.

Like a group of wild-eyed freshmen descending on the science building, they sought out the professors. "It was so bright and clear but now it's disappeared. What's the answer? Where do we go to find it again?" They did not receive any kind of clear answer.

Then, when they had left the court, the mysterious star appeared again and led them, of all places, to a stable in Bethlehem.

That's reality, is it not? Life is running from one light to the next. And often we have to travel great distances in the dark and confusion. Life is up and down; answers and questions; confusion and clarity; wild-eyed fears and quiet assurances.

Life is a come-and-go affair, isn't it?

Perhaps the critical question is this: How do we find a faith to guide us in the great stretches of darkness and fear, when we must walk alone, with only the memories of past lights to guide us?

Actually, faith itself means "to trust," "to hope," that there is light beyond the shadows of our present darkness. The author of Hebrews said it best: "Now faith is the substance of things hoped for, the evidence of things not seen" (Hebrews 11:1).

The star does not shine all the time. Faith is indeed the evidence of things not seen. We run from streetlight to streetlight, trying to outpace the darkness. It happens in the choice of a mate. How do you know with absolute clarity that this is the man or woman for you? How do you know for certain that this is the right career or job for you? You don't know for certain *all* the time. How do you know you're doing the right thing with your friends or lifestyle? How do you deal with the death of a friend or loved one? Sometimes there isn't a clear spotlight and definite answers to walk under. Oh, we do see clearly in which direction to head. But then the star disappears for awhile. We move from streetlight to streetlight trying to find our way home. If faith has a role in life, it has to offer some hope as we walk in the darkness between the streetlights.[2]

What does King Jesus have to say about the time we spend in the darkness?

It's the age-old question. And we can only offer the age-old answer: At the end of the journey is the light of home. Behind the impetus of my headlong dashes from streetlight to streetlight was the underlying faith in the comfortable light of home at the end of the journey. I hoped not in myself but in the permanent existence of home. Hope in myself was not enough to calm my anxiety attacks in the darkness because there were things in the darkness that were much bigger, more powerful and more fearsome than I was. But the glow of home, that was different.

Such was the message of Saint John the Revelator as he wrote about his revelation of God. John was writing in code to a group of

418

people in what is now Turkey. He wrote of the demons in the dark, weird images of a hornet with a man's face, of a monster rising from the sea, of the moon the color of blood, of a huge beast with a poison tail, and of the end of the world.

It was a book for people in the darkness to remind them that there was light at the end of all the darkness. He was telling the people in a secret code that the darkness would not win, that the end of the journey would one day come — the good people would triumph. "Hope not in yourselves," John wrote. "Hope in God for he is the light at the end of the darkness." That is why he wrote, "Christ says, 'I am the Alpha and Omega, the beginning and the end, the first and the last.' " He was reminding the people that they were not alone in their persecutions, their heartaches, and their darkness. God was the first light and is the last, and the darkness in between is only temporary.

John was writing from a concentration camp to a group of people under Roman persecution. But his revelation has a meaning for all of us who run with King Jesus between the streetlights: Don't be buried in the darkness; hope not in yourselves; you are not alone in your journey. When you have lost the star, hold on; you will eventually make it beyond the darkness and there will be a light there that you cannot now believe. Knowing that, we can endure our times of darkness. We can journey forward in our pain and hardship. We can survive even loss and death. Knowing he is there, we can journey in faith between the streetlights in our existence.

The history of our race has proven John to be correct. We wonder if our world can persevere in its trials. Nation is pitted against nation. Drugs and evil, sexual promiscuity, and nuclear chaos thrust us into darkness. Yet history has proven the existence of a light at the end of the darkness, time and time again.

Emil Brunner, in his Zurich sermons,[3] told of a former Russian officer who related this event. During the dark days of Joseph Stalin, Christians were persecuted in Russia. The young officer's father was a Christian, but he was so persecuted by Communist authorities that his wife collapsed and died from sheer terror. One night this man, the officer's father, was taken away and disappeared in the mines of Siberia, never to be heard from again. The officer related to Brunner that on one occasion in the year 1940 he was present at an Easter service in the region of Odessa. The service took place in an isolated church, the only church in an area of several hundred miles. Over 40,000 Christians came to the Easter service. The Communists had organized a counterblast assembly and had erected huge loudspeakers around the church. They attempted to disrupt the service in every way possible. They compelled these 40,000 people, stretched over the land around the church, to listen to their godless Communist propaganda for four hours until darkness had fallen. Finally one of the Christians got up and announced his desire to speak through the amplification system. At first he was refused. But when he promised to say only one sentence, they allowed him to come to the platform. In unbroken tense silence he stood in the darkness and said: "Brothers and sisters, Christ is risen." And the 40,000 responded in unison with the Easter response: "He is risen indeed." For 23 years amid the bitter sorrows and darkness, for 23 years in the darkness of oppression and denial with no cultural and societal streetlight to stand under, those people had safeguarded and held fast to what they had. Their faith sustained them in the darkness. Now, of course, those people are able to see the star and stand under the streetlight again.

We do run from streetlight to streetlight at times. John is right; there are beasts and demons in the darkness. There are hornets with human faces and monsters rising from the ocean. We have sex for beginners, home pregnancy tests, genetic engineering, and advertisers spending over $600 million a year selling sex to children on television. We have a bomb the size of a basketball that can generate a heat explosion 1,100 times as hot as the face of the sun. We can watch MTV, as many of our children do, and see hornets with the heads of men. There are demons in the sea. Divorce has become a middle class status symbol. There is much darkness at times. We are saturated people. Today's high tech world has placed our very individual lives under siege. We live in a swirling sea of social relationships that move us from excitement to exhaustion in a short time. With e-mail we can now keep up with the illnesses of friends a continent away. Our lives, instead of finding time for withdrawal and relaxation, are often little more than parades of information and intrusions. The darkness can follow us wherever we travel.

But John is right — there is another force in the darkness. "I am Alpha and Omega, the first light and the last light," says the Christ. "I am the light at the end of the darkness." Christ the King in its spiritual meaning may be a concept that is needed now. As we reflect on the Alpha and Omega nature of God in Christ, maybe we can relax this time of the year. Too often at Advent the churches of America act like hospital trauma units preparing to receive mortally wounded patients instead of confident banquet halls preparing tables in the midst of enemies.

May Christ the King enter our consciousness and grant us some downtime in this upcoming season. Maybe King Jesus can help us reclaim the threads of our spiritual life. Come, King Jesus, and run home in the dark with us.

---

1. John Killinger, "Losing the Star," a sermon he preached January 8, 1984, in First Presbyterian Church, Lynchburg, Virginia.

2. See the introduction to Harold C. Warlick, Jr., *The Rarest of These Is Hope: A Resource for Christians Facing Difficult Times* (Lima, Ohio: CSS Publishing Company, 1985).

3. Emil Brunner, "Perseverance in Trial," *Zurich Sermons of Emil Brunner*, trans. Harold Knight (London: Cutterworth Press, 1955), pp. 74-75.

Thanks

A minister held an administrative position in a major university in a large city. Part of his responsibility was overseeing the program for minority students in that school. The counselor for minority students and the faculty members teaching and working with minority students were under his supervision. The program had not been well run, so prior to his arrival the school had terminated the entire staff. He had to employ a new part-time director for the program. Everyone from the president to the students told the minister that one of the most powerful and capable persons in the city was a black pastor who was serving his forty-third year as pastor of the same parish. This person called "Mac" was 73 years old at the time.

The administrator had some misgivings as to how effective a 73-year-old could be in working primarily with people almost fifty years younger than he was. He hired him anyway. The man was a perfect fit in the job. He was warm, gentle, caring, and experienced. The number of minority students in the school tripled within four years. Much of the increase was due to the presence of the silver-haired "Mac." "Mac" called everyone his "boy" or his "girl" and treated them like they were his own children.

Every Wednesday, Mac taught a course on the black church experience. But it enrolled almost as many non-black students and other minorities as blacks. After the end of that Wednesday class, Mac and the administrator always had lunch together at a small table in one of the University dining rooms. They did this every

Wednesday, without fail, for five years. Mac never changed his routine.

He would order two tuna fish sandwiches. He would slowly devour one, as if it were a gift from God. Mac would relish every single bite. Then, when they had finished their meal and conversation, Mac would reach into his coat pocket. He would whip out a plastic sandwich bag and drop the other sandwich in it. With great care he would smooth out the wrinkles and eliminate the air from the bag. Then he would be off to catch a subway home.

On a visit to Mac's home one day, the administrator learned that Mac's wife was an invalid. She had been confined to a wheel-chair for many years. Mac, of course, brought her a tuna fish sandwich for lunch every Wednesday.

But one thing began to puzzle him. Mac's wife would go into the hospital for treatments. Sometimes she would fly south in winter months and spend a whole month with a relative. The warmer climate was necessary for her health. Yet Mac never varied his routine. Always he took home the second sandwich. Finally, the administrator said, "Mac, what gives? Your wife's not home. Why do you take the second sandwich? What do you do with it?"

Mac replied: "Oh, I've got to get my second sandwich. You see, son, every Wednesday I've been getting a second sandwich. When I get one, I thank God I've had a woman who loves me. When I get one, it reminds me of the children and the breath of life God gave us. That sandwich calls out of my being a sense of gratitude and thanks to God that I'd hate to lose. In this hard, sometimes cruel, old world it would be easy to let that part of me die for awhile until she gets back. I'm afraid other urges would take over and I'd never get that part of me back. I've got to get that sandwich. Can't lose what it says to me. If my wife's out of town, I throw it away at the end of the day. Then I get another one the next Wednesday. Because she isn't there, I have to work harder at remembering."

Mac's right. It is a principle of life that we eventually lose those of our powers we do not use. More than we realize our lives are made up of hundreds of emotions and urges that we have developed or lost through the years. God and other people don't need our gratitude as much as *we* need to be the sort of people who know how to be grateful. When we read Paul's instructions to Timothy, we find this principle at work. Paul urges us Christians as we worship that Thanksgiving be made for everyone — for kings and all those in authority — that *we* may live peaceful lives. It's not that these other people will notice or even have their lives affected but that *we* will have peaceful lives. It's not even that these others will become good people but that *we* will become good people.

You and I are composed of various urges and emotions. Sometimes these urges express themselves in very direct ways — eating, making love, studying, playing sports, finishing a difficult project, fighting, singing, complaining. We are always summoning these urges, which we cannot even name, up into our lives from our minds and souls. Within each of our lives there is the urge to destroy. There is a dark, demonic side of life and it fights to control us. It can destroy our relationships; it can destroy our body; it can destroy our happiness.

The original Greek has Jesus telling a rich young man, who has lost his ability to be thankful and be generous to others, these words: "Fool, this very night *they* will demand your life." Who are *they?* They are these urges. They will destroy us. The things in our life — the money, the status, and the arrogance — they will destroy us.

The yearly season of Thanksgiving is upon us. Most of us have come home to joyous occasions. Some of us have returned, perhaps, to an environment that is sad and lonely for a number of reasons. But all of us are given the gift of salvation. And all of us have facets of our personality that radiate gratitude and love. We must draw on those positive urges in our being. We give thanks in order that *we* may live a peaceful life.

Rudyard Kipling was one of the popular writers of his time. Someone reported that Kipling received an average of ten shillings for every word he wrote. Well, you know how college students can be. They like to test everything and everyone. Consequently, some Oxford University students decided to put Kipling to the test. They sent Kipling a copy of the report and ten shillings with the request, "Send us one of your very best words." Kipling wrote back: "Thanks!"

"Thanks" is, indeed, one of everyone's best words. It can render as much service as any word we use. In fact, if we all gave thanks for the bounty we have, instead of worrying about wanting more, we might appreciate life itself a great deal more. A widely circulated true story hammers the point home for us. One day a financially wealthy father took his son on a trip to the country. The purpose of the trip was to show the boy how poor people live. They spent a couple of days and nights on the farm of what would be considered a very poor family. On their return to their affluent neighborhood, the father asked his son, "How did you like the trip?"

"It was great, Dad," the boy replied.

"Did you see how poor people live?" the father asked.

The son answered, "Oh, yeah."

Very pleased, the father inquired, "So what did you learn about poor people on the trip?"

The son answered, "I saw that we have one dog and they have four. We have a pool that reaches to the middle of our garden. They have a creek that has no end.

"We have imported lanterns in our garden and they have all these stars in the sky in their garden at night.

"Our patio reaches to the front yard and they have a vista that looks out over the whole horizon.

"We have a small piece of land to live on, and they have fields that go almost beyond our sight.

"We have many servants who serve us, but they get to serve everybody that they know.

"We buy our food off shelves in a store, but they grow theirs. We have walls around our property to protect us, but they have friends to protect them."

With this the boy's father was speechless. Then his son added, "Thanks, Dad, for showing me how poor we are."

Life is a matter of perspective. Imagine our lives without the perspective of the Holy Bible. Thanks, Heavenly Parent, for showing us at times how poor we are despite our trinkets and toys. Thanks.

Lectionary Preaching After Pentecost

The following index will aid the user of this book in matching the correct Sunday with the appropriate text during Pentecost. All texts in this book are from the series for the Second Readings, Revised Common Lectionary. (Note that the ELCA division of Lutheranism is now following the Revised Common Lectionary.) The Lutheran designations indicate days comparable to Sundays on which Revised Common Lectionary Propers or Ordinary Time designations are used.

(Fixed dates do not pertain to Lutheran Lectionary)

Fixed Date Lectionaries *Revised Common (including ELCA)* *and Roman Catholic*	**Lutheran Lectionary** *Lutheran*
The Day of Pentecost	The Day of Pentecost
The Holy Trinity	The Holy Trinity
May 29-June 4 — Proper 4, Ordinary Time 9	Pentecost 2
June 5-11 — Proper 5, Ordinary Time 10	Pentecost 3
June 12-18 — Proper 6, Ordinary Time 11	Pentecost 4
June 19-25 — Proper 7, Ordinary Time 12	Pentecost 5
June 26-July 2 — Proper 8, Ordinary Time 13	Pentecost 6
July 3-9 — Proper 9, Ordinary Time 14	Pentecost 7
July 10-16 — Proper 10, Ordinary Time 15	Pentecost 8
July 17-23 — Proper 11, Ordinary Time 16	Pentecost 9
July 24-30 — Proper 12, Ordinary Time 17	Pentecost 10
July 31-Aug. 6 — Proper 13, Ordinary Time 18	Pentecost 11
Aug. 7-13 — Proper 14, Ordinary Time 19	Pentecost 12
Aug. 14-20 — Proper 15, Ordinary Time 20	Pentecost 13
Aug. 21-27 — Proper 16, Ordinary Time 21	Pentecost 14
Aug. 28-Sept. 3 — Proper 17, Ordinary Time 22	Pentecost 15
Sept. 4-10 — Proper 18, Ordinary Time 23	Pentecost 16
Sept. 11-17 — Proper 19, Ordinary Time 24	Pentecost 17
Sept. 18-24 — Proper 20, Ordinary Time 25	Pentecost 18

Sept. 25-Oct. 1 — Proper 21, Ordinary Time 26	Pentecost 19
Oct. 2-8 — Proper 22, Ordinary Time 27	Pentecost 20
Oct. 9-15 — Proper 23, Ordinary Time 28	Pentecost 21
Oct. 16-22 — Proper 24, Ordinary Time 29	Pentecost 22
Oct. 23-29 — Proper 25, Ordinary Time 30	Pentecost 23
Oct. 30-Nov. 5 — Proper 26, Ordinary Time 31	Pentecost 24
Nov. 6-12 — Proper 27, Ordinary Time 32	Pentecost 25
Nov. 13-19 — Proper 28, Ordinary Time 33	Pentecost 26
	Pentecost 27
Nov. 20-26 — Christ The King	Christ The King

Reformation Day (or last Sunday in October) is October 31 (Revised Common, Lutheran)

All Saints' Day (or first Sunday in November) is November 1 (Revised Common, Lutheran, Roman Catholic)

U.S. / Canadian Lectionary Comparison

The following index shows the correlation between the Sundays and special days of the church year as they are titled or labeled in the Revised Common Lectionary published by the Consultation On Common Texts and used in the United States (the reference used for this book) and the Sundays and special days of the church year as they are titled or labeled in the Revised Common Lectionary used in Canada.

Revised Common Lectionary	Canadian Revised Common Lectionary
Advent 1	Advent 1
Advent 2	Advent 2
Advent 3	Advent 3
Advent 4	Advent 4
Christmas Eve	Christmas Eve
Nativity Of The Lord/Christmas Day	The Nativity Of Our Lord
Christmas 1	Christmas 1
January 1 / Holy Name of Jesus	January 1 / The Name Of Jesus
Christmas 2	Christmas 2
Epiphany Of The Lord	The Epiphany Of Our Lord
Baptism Of The Lord / Epiphany 1	The Baptism Of Our Lord / Proper 1
Epiphany 2 / Ordinary Time 2	Epiphany 2 / Proper 2
Epiphany 3 / Ordinary Time 3	Epiphany 3 / Proper 3
Epiphany 4 / Ordinary Time 4	Epiphany 4 / Proper 4
Epiphany 5 / Ordinary Time 5	Epiphany 5 / Proper 5
Epiphany 6 / Ordinary Time 6	Epiphany 6 / Proper 6
Epiphany 7 / Ordinary Time 7	Epiphany 7 / Proper 7
Epiphany 8 / Ordinary Time 8	Epiphany 8 / Proper 8
Transfiguration Of The Lord / Last Sunday After Epiphany	The Transfiguration Of Our Lord / Last Sunday After Epiphany
Ash Wednesday	Ash Wednesday
Lent 1	Lent 1
Lent 2	Lent 2
Lent 3	Lent 3
Lent 4	Lent 4
Lent 5	Lent 5
Passion/Palm Sunday (Lent 6)	Passion/Palm Sunday
Holy/Maundy Thursday	Holy/Maundy Thursday
Good Friday	Good Friday
Resurrection Of The Lord / Easter	The Resurrection Of Our Lord

Easter 2	Easter 2
Easter 3	Easter 3
Easter 4	Easter 4
Easter 5	Easter 5
Easter 6	Easter 6
Ascension Of The Lord	The Ascension Of Our Lord
Easter 7	Easter 7
Day Of Pentecost	The Day Of Pentecost
Trinity Sunday	The Holy Trinity
Proper 4 / Pentecost 2 / O T 9*	Proper 9
Proper 5 / Pent 3 / O T 10	Proper 10
Proper 6 / Pent 4 / O T 11	Proper 11
Proper 7 / Pent 5 / O T 12	Proper 12
Proper 8 / Pent 6 / O T 13	Proper 13
Proper 9 / Pent 7 / O T 14	Proper 14
Proper 10 / Pent 8 / O T 15	Proper 15
Proper 11 / Pent 9 / O T 16	Proper 16
Proper 12 / Pent 10 / O T 17	Proper 17
Proper 13 / Pent 11 / O T 18	Proper 18
Proper 14 / Pent 12 / O T 19	Proper 19
Proper 15 / Pent 13 / O T 20	Proper 20
Proper 16 / Pent 14 / O T 21	Proper 21
Proper 17 / Pent 15 / O T 22	Proper 22
Proper 18 / Pent 16 / O T 23	Proper 23
Proper 19 / Pent 17 / O T 24	Proper 24
Proper 20 / Pent 18 / O T 25	Proper 25
Proper 21 / Pent 19 / O T 26	Proper 26
Proper 22 / Pent 20 / O T 27	Proper 27
Proper 23 / Pent 21 / O T 28	Proper 28
Proper 24 / Pent 22 / O T 29	Proper 29
Proper 25 / Pent 23 / O T 30	Proper 30
Proper 26 / Pent 24 / O T 31	Proper 31
Proper 27 / Pent 25 / O T 32	Proper 32
Proper 28 / Pent 26 / O T 33	Proper 33
Christ The King (Proper 29 / O T 34)	Proper 34 / Christ The King/ Reign Of Christ
Reformation Day (October 31)	Reformation Day (October 31)
All Saints' Day (November 1 or 1st Sunday in November)	All Saints' Day (November 1)
Thanksgiving Day (4th Thursday of November)	Thanksgiving Day (2nd Monday of October)

*O T = Ordinary Time

About The Authors

Frederick R. Harm has served the Lutheran Church — Missouri Synod for over 35 years. In addition to his pastoral ministry, Harm taught at McHenry County College and Concordia University (Illinois) and was Associate Professor of Systematic Theology at Concordia Seminary in St. Louis, Missouri. Educated at Long Island University, Concordia Seminary, DePaul University, and Faith Lutheran Seminary, Harm has provided numerous articles for theological journals and has written or contributed to thirteen books, study manuals, and encyclopedias.

Paul E. Robinson is currently the pastor of Trinity United Methodist Church in Grand Island, New York, and has served congregations throughout the state of New York as well as Basel, Switzerland. He holds degrees from Lycoming College (B.A. in German) and Wesley Theological Seminary (M.Div.). Robinson is the author of *Hope Beneath The Surface* (CSS).

Glenn W. McDonald is the senior pastor of Zionsville Presbyterian Church in suburban Indianapolis, Indiana, a congregation he helped to organize in 1983. During that time, his church has grown from a few dozen to over 1,800 members, and is notable for its small groups, ministry teams, and highly decentralized style which prioritizes lay leadership. McDonald has been a consultant for several governing bodies and congregations in the Presbyterian Church (USA), and was part of the national teaching team for *Evangelism Connections '98*. A graduate of Purdue University and Trinity Evangelical Divinity School, McDonald is the co-author of *Imagining A Church In The Spirit*.

Harold C. Warlick, Jr., is Dean of the Chapel and Professor of Religion at High Point University, High Point, North Carolina. He is the author of fifteen books as well as over thirty articles and sermons in religious journals and publications. Dr. Warlick has served as Director of Ministerial Studies and Lecturer in Applied Theology at Harvard Divinity School, and has pastored churches in South Carolina, Texas, and North Carolina. He holds degrees from Furman University (B.A.), Harvard University (S.T.B.), and Vanderbilt University (D.Div.). Among Warlick's many CSS titles are *You Have Mail From God!* and *The Human Condition In Biblical Perspective.*